STUDIES IN SHAKESPEARE, MILTON AND DONNE

STUDIES IN SHAKESPEARE, MILTON AND DONNE

BY

MEMBERS OF THE ENGLISH DEPARTMENT OF
THE UNIVERSITY OF MICHIGAN

HASKELL HOUSE
Publishers of Scholarly Books
NEW YORK
1964

published by

HASKELL HOUSE

Publishers of Scholarly Books

30 East 10th Street • New York, N. Y. 10003

Library of Congress Catalog Card Number: 65-15881

PRINTED IN UNITED STATES OF AMERICA

CONTENTS

LOVE'S LABOUR'S LOST RE-STUDIED

LOVE'S LABOUR'S LOST RE-STUDIED

O. J. CAMPBELL

UNTIL very recently, *Love's Labour's Lost* has not received the critical attention to which its position in Shakespeare's dramatic work entitles it. It is probably his first comedy and often thought to be the first play that he wrote without collaboration. A thorough study of this drama might, therefore, be expected to reveal what Croce would call Shakespeare's "comic presuppositions." It might have discovered the bases of his entire comic technique. Such a genetic study might have simplified the history of Shakespeare's development as a writer of comedy and given it a coherence now lacking. It might even have thrown light upon his puzzling beginnings as a playwright.

No study of *Love's Labour's Lost* has cast such illumination upon Shakespeare's career. The comedy, rather, has been considered as a little apart from the straight course of his development, as a kind of experiment which yielded its author few permanent results either intellectual or technical. Moreover, a sort of unrecognized mystery has hung over this drama. No source for the plot has been discovered. To be sure, the scene is laid at the court of Henry of Navarre and the action is supposed to have been suggested by historical and social events in the life of that monarch, vaguely like those presented in the play. The style or dramatic manner of the play has been almost universally recognized as very like that of John Lyly. The dialogue has been thought to be in every way an approximation to that developed by Lyly, and the spirit and tone of the social life of the courtly ladies and gentlemen as depicted by both writers to be identical. One play of the earlier dramatist, in particular, *Endimion,* is believed to have furnished in Sir Tophas and his page, Epiton, models for Armado and Moth. One other derived character appears, Holofernes, the Latinizing pedagogue, who is a stock character in the sixteenth century comedy of France and Italy.

Except for these slight echoes of earlier comic practice, this drama, according to orthodox critical opinion, is Shakespeare's own invention, — his sustained travesty of contemporary court life, and of the fashions in speech and behavior that prevailed there. In this satire he adverts to incidents of current social and political life, and in it he directly satirizes figures well known in that world. In brief, *Love's Labour's Lost* has been regarded as Shakespeare's *Precieuses Ridicules.*[1]

Some of the elements of this rounded theory have been called into question. The sceptics, for example, have pointed out that it was extraordinary that a young man who had come, but meagrely educated, from the provinces a few years before, should show, at the outset of his career, enough familiarity with the uses and temper of a court to satirize them before an audience composed largely of courtiers. This was pointed, but negative criticism. Recently, newly discovered facts about this play have yielded positive results and have made a partial revision of the traditional estimate necessary. Indeed, they have rendered a complete reëxamination of the comedy highly desirable.

The most important of these new truths is the discovery that the central fable of the play reflects faithfully some definite historical events which took place at the court of Henry of Navarre, at Nérac in 1578. This important discovery is due to the researches of M. Abel Lefranc, published in *Sous le Masque de William Shakespeare.*[2] Inasmuch as the thesis of this book has prevented most American scholars from acquainting themselves with the sound historical investigations which it contains and which in no way depend upon the author's contention that the plays of Shakespeare were written by the sixth Earl of Derby, I shall review briefly his evidence on this question of historical fact.

[1] The facts are thus presented in Sir Sidney Lee's *William Shakespeare* (third revised edition, London, 1922), pp. 103 ff.

[2] *Sous le Masque de William Shakespeare* (Paris, 1919), II. 17 ff.

Vague correspondences between the play and events at the contemporary court of Navarre had been recognized since 1880. In that year Sir Sidney Lee suggested[3] that the plot of *Love's Labour's Lost* reflected events occurring at the court of Henri Quatre in the year 1586. At that time Catherine de Medici, the dowager queen of France, journeyed to Saint Bris, with the ladies of her court, in an attempt to settle the perennial disputes between Henry of Navarre and the King of France. General similarities between the meeting of Navarre and the princess in the play and the historical interview at Saint Bris undoubtedly exist. The social atmosphere of the two is identical, but the political objects are utterly different.

Queen Catherine's expedition was concerned principally with an attempt to persuade Navarre to divorce his dissolute wife, Marguerite of Valois, who had left her husband for fear of his resentment at her moral vagaries.[4] This accomplished, the dowager queen was to persuade Henry to marry Christine, a daughter of the Duke of Lorraine.[5] The expedition in Shakespeare's comedy is not concerned in the remotest degree with this project. Furthermore, the historical embassage was led by Catherine, then old and grievously afflicted with gout.[6] She is not a likely prototype of the lovely princess in *Love's Labour's Lost,* nor is her expedition a seed from which would grow naturally a comedy of amorous persiflage.

Now M. Lefranc shows that an expedition made to the court of Navarre in 1578 by Catherine and her daughter, Marguerite, is much more nearly like the fictitious one. The political object of this mission is identical with that in the play. It sought the settlement of the question of sovereignty in Aquitaine, which in the drama is accurately called "the dowry of a queen,"[7] and of a dispute over the payment of a hundred thousand

[3] *The Gentleman's Magazine,* October, 1880.

[4] There was also a declared intention to convert Henry from Protestantism, but that event can hardly have been expected.

[5] Davila, *Memoirs of Civil Wars in France* (trans. London, 1758), I. 505 ff.

[6] *Ibid.*

[7] *Love's Labour's Lost,* II. i. 8.

crowns to Navarre by the King of France.[8] Furthermore, contemporary accounts of this diplomatic mission show that its social atmosphere was very like that presented in the play. Marguerite of Valois in her *Mémoires* herself describes the occasion as follows: "faisant la pluspart de ce temps-là (quatre ou cinque ans que je fus en Gascogne) nostre séjour a Nérac, où nostre cour estoit si belle et si plaisante, que nous n'envions point celle de France, y ayant Madame la Princesse de Navarre sa soeur, qui depuis esté mariée à Monsieur le Duc de Bar mon nepveu, et moy avec bon nombre de dames et filles; et le Roy mon Mary estant suivy d'une belle trouppe de seigneurs et gentils-hommes, aussi honnestes gens que les plus galants que j'aye veu à la cour; et n'y avoit rien a regretter en eux, sinon qu'ils estoient huguenots." [9]

As one of the historians of the period remarks, the presence of the two queens transformed the town into a capital of the rank which it held in the reign of Henri d'Albert.[10] It is not strange, then, for Marguerite to confess that the court was so brilliant that she and her ladies did not envy the life at the greater court in Paris.[11] These descriptions invoke the essence of the social atmosphere of the diplomatic mission in *Love's Labour's Lost*. In the play, as doubtless at Nérac, the diplomatic questions are early referred to the experts and the social gaiety is all that meets the eye. The diplomats become courtiers and the political aims of the ladies are completely hidden by the social brilliance which attends them.

The dramatic figures, too, have some curious personal traits in common with the historical personages whom they represent. Ferdinand of *Love's Labour's Lost*, as he now appears in the comedy, is obviously not Henry of Navarre, yet he inherits one of the monarch's foibles as a courtly lover. The princess describes a *billet doux* which she receives from Ferdinand as follows:

[8] Cf. *Sous le Masque,* II. 67 ff.; also Batz-Trenquelleon, *Henri IV en Gascogne, 1553–1589* (Paris, 1885), pp. 75 and 122.

[9] *Mémoires et Lettres de Marguerite de Valois* (ed. par M. F. Guessard, Paris, 1842), p. 163. (Société de l'Histoire de France.)

[10] Batz-Trenquelleon, p. 129.

[11] *Mémoires,* p. 163.

> As much love in Rime
> As would be cram'd up in a sheet of paper,
> Writ on both sides the leafe, Margent and all
> That he was fain to seale on Cupid's name.[12]

M. Lefranc reports[13] that an authentic original of one of Navarre's poems, *Charmante Gabrielle,* which was sent in the form of a letter to Gabrille d'Estreés, presents these same characteristics. Strophes are written in the margin and the letter is sealed with the seal of which the word *Amor* forms the center.

Similarities of a like sort exist between the princess of the play and Marguerite of Valois. It is significant for this identification that the princess was obviously called "queen" in the early editions of the play. In the first quarto she is called "queen" a number of times;[14] and many of these designations are retained in the Folio edition. Moreover, there are clear references in the comedy to journeys that Marguerite had made with her ladies in the years just previous to this historical visit to Nérac.[15] They have no dramatic point in their context and can be regarded as introduced only for the sake of "local color." M. Lefranc finds other rather cryptic references in the plays made clear by regarding them as adversions to events in the history of the entourage of Marguerite which are narrated in her *Mémoires,* or to actual conditions of life in the little court at Nérac.[16]

[12] *Love's Labour's Lost,* V. ii. 6–9.

[13] *Sous le Masque,* II. 64.

[14] II. iv, once; IV. i, eighteen times; V. iii, once. All of the eighteen of IV. i are retained in the Folio.

[15] II. i. 60–65. There is a reference to a visit made upon her brother, the Duke of Alençon in 1578: cf. *Mémoires,* pp. 156–57. Berowne's "Did I not dance with you in Brabant once?" is a reference to a trip to Flanders made by Marguerite and her train in 1577: cf. *Mémoires,* pp. 88 ff., particularly the ball referred to on page 97.

[16] V. ii. 13 ff. contains a reference to the death of Katherine's sister from unrequited love which may be a recollection of the sad fate of Helène de Tournon referred to in the *Mémoires,* pp. 110–114. The taunt (V. ii. 574) hurled at the actor playing Alexander: "You will be scraped out of the painted cloth," may refer to certain tapestries decorated with images of *The Nine Worthies* which we know hung in the royal apartments, sometimes at Pau and sometimes at Nérac.

Taken in their entirety, these similarities between Shakespeare's comedy and historical conditions at the court of Nérac in 1578 during an embassy of Catherine, Queen Marguerite of Valois and their ladies-in-waiting are completely convincing. The author of the fable of *Love's Labour's Lost* was evidently well acquainted not only with the spirit, but with the details of the life there.

One aspect of the picture, however, seems inharmonious with the facts of history. How could an author familiar with this gay life and undoubtedly also with the notorious love intrigues of the youthful Henry of Navarre, present him and his court as tinged with asceticism and determined intellectuality? The device of the oath, as I shall show later, may have been an invention necessary to solve a distinctly theatrical problem of the dramatist. However, in the solution of a technical problem an author must not destroy more important sorts of verisimilitude. As a matter of fact, the court at Navarre had the reputation among Englishmen of the time of being an exceedingly decorous place, — a safe spot for the completion of the continental education of Protestant Englishmen. M. Lefranc calls attention to a letter written June 9, 1583, by Cobham, the English ambassador to the Court of France to Walsingham.[17] In this report he remarks that Navarre has furnished his court with distinguished gentlemen of his religion and reformed his house. He ends with this significant phrase: "There are divers special persons of quality of intention to resort to that Court, and others send their children, understanding the honorable order that is there observed."

To Cobham, at least, it would have seemed not improper to speak of Navarre's court as a "little achademe." To the gay and licentious Marguerite of Valois this atmosphere of study seemed less admirable. She writes contemptuously to her husband, "Si j'osais dire, si vous etiez honete homme vouz quitteriez l'agriculture et l'humeur de Timon pour venir vivre parmi les

[17] *Calendar of State Papers. Foreign Series of the Reign of Elizabeth, June–January 1583* (London, 1913), P. 394.

hommes."[18] Such a woman would obviously enjoy thrusting herself and her flying squadron into such a world, with the deliberate purpose of enticing the students from their sobrieties into a society devoted to courtly love with all its artificial gallantries and barren felicities. At every point the knowledge of the court of Navarre during this expedition of 1578 reflected in *Love's Labour's Lost* proves to be, in the highest degree, intimate and accurate.

This hitherto unsuspected fact can be made to throw light upon the youthful Shakespeare's methods of composition from two angles. In the first place, we are able to say now what was, in effect, the source of this play and so we are able to determine by familiar methods of genetic cricitism what parts of this comedy are the product of Shakespeare's dramatic invention. In the second place, M. Lefranc's discovery may aid in the solution of some of the ever puzzling questions of Shakespeare's early relations to persons of the very highest social station and of the part that they played in stimulating and directing his early literary activity. The second of these problems I shall discuss first, because it will be seen to have a bearing on determining what material the dramatist found ready to his hand when he began to write.

The first question that comes to mind is how could Shakespeare have possessed this accurate and detailed knowledge of life at Navarre's court.[19] We must dismiss at once the possibility of Shakespeare's having himself been at the court at Nérac. In none of the wide journeys from Elsinore to Venice, postulated

[18] It is interesting to remark that Berowne seems to refer to the King as Timon (IV. iii. 170 ff.):

> "O me, with what strict patience have I sat
> To see a king transformed to a Gnat,
> And Critticke Tymon laugh at idle toyes."

[19] Marlowe's knowledge of French history shown in *The Massacre at Paris;* Chapman's, shown in his five plays dealing with the same subject; or Dekker's and Drayton's, undoubtedly exhibited in their plays on *The Civil Wars in France,* recorded by Henslowe, is not analogous to that of Shakespeare shown in *Love's Labour's Lost.* Their knowledge is of public political fact; Shakespeare's is of intimate personal incident.

to explain fancied local color detected in his plays, has he been made to visit this little Protestant court. The chance of the poet's having had access to any printed account of such intimate details of social life at this court of Henry IV as *Love's Labour's Lost* reflects, seems equally remote. The remaining possibility [20] is that the information was given to him in some form by one of the many English gentlemen who in the age of Elizabeth made this court one of the principal places of sojourn on their *grands tours.*[21]

The peculiar nature of *Love's Labour's Lost* lends this theory plausibility. It was clearly not written for a popular audience. The form in which we now possess the drama is that which had been newly corrected for a court performance in the Christmas season of 1597–1598, but its original version was undoubtedly intended for a similar occasion. Professor Baker has presented effectively the reasons for believing that the essential character of the entire comedy was determined by a prospective courtly, — nay royal — audience. He says, "The general attitude toward women, the sonneteering, and, above all, the eulogy of women which Biron utters near the end of Act IV, suggests strongly that originally, as in 1598, it may have been performed before the queen and her court, or that, as first written, it was given before an audience mainly composed of women. Throughout, the characters so much play with love rather than become its subjects, that one wonders whether it was not composed as a whole with a definite view of pleasing the Virgin Queen, who was such an adept in coquetry and was so fond of putting off her admirers just as they seemed nearest to the attainment of their wishes." [22]

Furthermore there is reason to suppose that the comedy was originally composed not for one of the professional companies, but for the children. An unusually large number of parts has been provided for boy actors. Moth, the Princess, her three ladies in waiting, Jaquenetta, and possibly Don Adriana de

[20] Except, of course, the one sponsored by M. Lefranc that Shakespeare did not write the comedy.

[21] *Vid. sup.* 5.

[22] Baker, G. P., *The Development of Shakespeare as a Dramatist* (N. Y., 1907), pp. 107–108.

Armado, were rôles to be played by boys.[23] Surely six, and possibly seven, parts were written for child-actors. This number is nearly twice as large as that usually provided for boys in Shakespeare's comedies. None of these figures, furthermore, has been excluded by any critics who have sought to reconstruct the hypothetical original version. Their presence, therefore, suggests that the play, as originally conceived, was written for the children, and so not for Shakespeare's company and its London stage, but for a special occasion.

In such a fête as the one conjectured above a gentleman of the court would have a special interest. He might be concerned as the host to the Queen on the occasion for which the play was planned, or he might wish the drama to advert allegorically to facts or projects in which he had a personal interest. Guesses as to the identity of such a person have been made. Professor Austin K. Gray[24] seeks to prove that the drama was devised at the instigation of Southampton as part of his entertainment for the Queen when he received her at Tichfield Park in 1591. He furthermore attempts to show that part of it is the young Earl's plea under the guise of an allegory to have his proposed marriage with Lady Elizabeth de Vere, Burleigh's granddaughter, postponed for at least a year. Southampton later obtained release from this undesired engagement through the payment of a round sum. The correspondences between the dramatic situation and this real one are close and entertaining; but however ingenious this sort of study, such facts as it seeks to establish, are, I believe, now quite beyond proof. Such conjecture, however, serves to strengthen the plausibility of the view that the drama was composed under the eye of some gentleman of the court.

There is nothing intrinsically improbable in such a dramatic collaboration or coöperation between an actor-playwright and an Elizabethan gentleman, particularly in the construction of an occasional play. Hamlet's reception of the travelling players

[23] This fact is mentioned by Austin K. Gray in *The Secret of Love's Labour's Lost and the Earl of Southampton. Publ. of the Modern Language Association,* vol. XXXIX (Sept., 1924), No. 3, p. 602.

[24] *Op. cit.*

and, in particular, his discussion of dramatic composition with the first actor may be regarded as a realistic picture of an interesting phase of Elizabethan life.[25] Hamlet greets this player affectionately with " O my old friend " and discusses with him the play that was "caviare to the general " in such a way as to suggest that the actor was himself the author. Then he asks him to " study a speech of some dozen or sixteen lines " which he " could set down and insert " in one of their plays.[26]

In the frequent sojourns of travelling companies at the castles of nobility in Elizabethan times lay natural opportunities for the establishment of acquaintance and friendship between young literary nobles and talented actor-playwrights. At no time since have such occasions existed. The great concern of the Derby family for the drama, and particularly of the sixth Earl, whose interest as dramatist and patron M. Lefranc has abundantly established, is an example of an interest of which the scene in Hamlet is a dramatic picture. Shakespeare's later close friendship with Southampton is proof that he became the object of such an interest to one of the greatest nobles of his time. Such facts give us ample warrant for supposing that some travelled gentleman had established close enough relations with Shakespeare to induce the dramatist to use his personal reminiscences of the court of Navarre as a nucleus for his play.

From whatever source derived, this material would surely contain a description of the diplomatic mission, of its object, its methods, and its results. The Queen and her ladies would appear in the account with their atmosphere of graceful, half-sportive love-making and with their courtly badinage. The narrative, if true to history, would close not with marriages, nor with promised consummation of the half-playful wooing, but with the indicated success of the ladies' diplomatic mission and their regretful departure. The desire of the directing genius for an allegorical suggestion of some contemporary social situation may have determined other features of the play, such as the

[25] *Hamlet,* II. ii. 446 ff.

[26] In the play *Sir Thomas More,* Sir Thomas himself steps in and improvises a part for " Good Councell " until the fellow Luggins comes in to take the rôle.

grouping of the lovers and the abrupt termination of the projects of the lovers by the surprising death of the father of the visiting princess.

Let us suppose, then, that Shakespeare received such a story from a source which must remain unknown. Upon this he was to build a comedy. To what events within the range of his experience would he most naturally turn, in order to find details which could give his play verisimilitude to an Elizabethan audience? The one obvious source for this sort of dramatic material was the entertainment given to Queen Elizabeth when she visited the country houses of the great lords of her kingdom. Shakespeare and his audiences would agree that in these elaborate and diversified Progresses were to be discovered the approved methods of honoring and amusing a sovereign. Catherine de Medici or Margaret of Valois on the English stage would be expected to receive a similar form of entertainment from Henry of Navarre when they visited him at Nérac.[27]

The influence of these Progresses upon *Love's Labour's Lost* has been suggested before, but in an unfortunate manner. Efforts have been made to discover in the play reflections of one particular Progress. For example, Arthur Acheson in his recently published *Shakespeare's Lost Years in London,*[28] believes that *Love's Labour's Lost* reflects the events which took place at Cowdray House in August 1591[29] at the Honorable Entertainment given by Lord Montecuto (*sic*). The evidence which he presents in support of this theory is not convincing. His thesis proves to be mere interesting conjecture. Indeed attempts to discover reflections of any one particular Progress in *Love's Labour's Lost* seem doomed to failure. However, the constructive dramatic principle of this comedy proves to bear close resemblance to that of a Progress, regarded as a dramatic type.

[27] Shakespeare could readily have obtained knowledge of the nature of these Progresses either through personal experience or through a perusal of the accounts of these fêtes, which were often printed within a year of their occurrence. For a comparison of the dates of the Progresses with those of the printed accounts, see Nichols' *Progresses, passim.*

[28] *Shakespeare's Lost Years in London* (London, 1920), p. 186.

[29] Nichols, Vol. II.

The Progresses of the Queen comprised a series of highly diversified sorts of out-of-door amusement, lasting from four to ten days. Modern students think of these shows as consisting mainly of spectacular classical and allegorical pageants, like the sumptuous water-fête at the Earl of Hertford's entertainment in 1591. They may also remember that there were masque-like shows in which Daphne, or Pan appeared, or in which there was graceful dancing by Ceres and her nymphs before her Majesty. But in truth these features formed but a small part of the entire entertainment. Upon her arrival at the castle of her host the Queen is invariably greeted with some sort of oration; and verbal devices in prose and poetry pursue her wherever she walks. She hunts, in her youth riding to the hounds, in her more mature age shooting at the game from a covert. She is encountered by wild men.[30] She dines often in the walks of the garden, at tables sometimes as long as forty-eight yards. She is honored by the folk of the country-side, who present various forms of rustic and popular dramatic sport. She attends plays given by professional actors. All these forms of entertainment are presented out of doors, so that the Queen is constantly in some part of the park surrounding the castle of her host. When she is kept within doors by inclement weather, no pastime worth chronicling is offered to her. Just such a situation is presented in *Love's Labour's Lost*.

The first striking similarity of the play to the Progress lies in its setting. The scene of the entire play is the park of the King of Navarre. This, it will be noted, is not at all the pastoral wood which serves as the scene of *As You Like It;* nor is it the enchanted Arcadia of *The Tempest*. Furthermore the audience is constantly reminded by place notes[31] that the action is

[30] For the meaning and tradition of this "wild man," cf. Chambers, *Mediaeval Stage* I. 182; also note 2.

[31] Cf. Boyet's explanation of the King's reception of the ladies, II. i. 91–94:

> "He rather means to lodge you in the field,
> Like one that comes here to besiege his court
> Than seek a dispensation for his oath:
> To let you enter his unpeopled house."

continuously laid in the park. The critic is indeed almost justified in conjecturing that the ascetic vows of the gentlemen were introduced to enable the poet to use the story of the visit to the court of Navarre and yet to keep all the action out in the purlieus of the castle. In this way he could give the comedy the first essential of a Progress, — the setting and the atmosphere of an English park.

Another peculiarity of this comedy may be attributed to its Progress-like nature. Critics have often noted the disproportionate length of the last two acts. Henry David Gray speaks of it as "A disproportion as amazing as it is unique in Elizabethan drama."[32] Various explanations of this fact have been given. Sir Sidney Lee thinks it a fault of the original writing, — a youthful blemish. Professor Gray, on the other hand, believes that it is due to additions made to the play when Shakespeare revised it for presentation at court. These were largely made for the purpose of introducing the *Pageant of the Nine Worthies.*

A more satisfactory explanation for this apparent lack of proportion may be found in regarding the play as a drama intended to represent the events and the atmosphere of a royal Progress. Such dramatic disproportion as the critics have lamented would not have been noticed in this sort of comedy. It professed to be only a counterfeit presentment of a mere series of diverse entertainments. A division of such a sequence of scenes into acts was extrinsic to the nature of the play and clearly forced upon it when it was prepared for publication.

Furthermore, such a performance as that presented by the clownish figures was a conventional part of a prolonged Progress. I do not refer to the appearance of the people of the countryside in native costume in folk-dance and folk-song. Such

---

Also II. i. 181–183:

> "You may not come, fair Princess, in my gates,
> But here without you shall be so received.
> As you shall deem yourself lodged in my heart."

[32] Gray, Henry David, *The Original Version of "Love's Labour's Lost" with a conjecture as to "Love's Labour's Won," Leland Stanford Junior Publications,* 1918, p. 19.

picturesque entertainment was common.[33] But "countrie shows," either intentionally or inadvertently burlesques, were often presented. These inventions the courtly audience was supposed to receive, not with respect, but with raillery, like that rained upon Holofernes and his fellows. At least two shows of this sort are described by Laneham in his famous epistolary report of the Progress at Kenilworth. One was a mock nuptial celebration made a burlesque by the actors, who were louts or pretended to be. They presented their show with a portentous seriousness that aroused a gay spirit of ridicule in the audience, as the following extract from Laneham will show:

"Then followed the worshippful bride, led (after the countrie maner) between two auncient parishioners, honest toownsmen. But . . . ill-smelling was she: a thirtie-five yeer old, of colour broun-bay, not very beautiful indeed, but ugly, fooul, ill-favor'd: yet marveyloous faine of the offis, because shee hard say she woould dauns before the Queen, in which feat shee thought shee woold foot it az finely az the best."

It is exactly this combination of eagerness and ineptitude that makes Holofernes and his actors so amusing to the courtly audience in *Love's Labour's Lost.* Laneham's delight at this rustic fooling was fully as hearty as that of the ladies and gentlemen at the bombast of the *Nine Worthies.*

"By my Trooth," he exclaims, "twaz a lively pastime, I believe it would have moved sum man to a right merry mood, though had it be toold him hiz wife lay a dying."

The hock-tide play presented on the same occasion by the men of Coventry led by one Captain Cox was received by the Queen in the same spirit of ridicule.[34] The first time that the

[33] Cf. The Earl of Hertford's Entertainment, Nichols, Vol. II: "Three musicians under the window disguised in ancient country attire did greet her with a pleasant song of Coridon and Phyllida." In the Cowdray Entertainment (*ibid.*), we read the following: "On Thursday — in the evening the Countrie people presented themselves to her Majestie in a pleasant dance with taber and pipe."

[34] Chambers (*The Mediaeval Stage,* I. 155) points out the fact that the germ of this play is clearly a very old festival celebration, and, like Hock-tide customs, found in many places throughout England. Its folk significance, however, had been entirely lost at this time and it was merely sport for the people and humor for the gentry.

folk played this pageant she was able to see but little of it. She therefore commanded that it be repeated on the following Tuesday "to have it full oout. Accordingly it waz prezented; whereat her Majestie laught well."[35] *The Pageant of the Nine Worthies* has been related to dramatic forms slightly different from these. It is well known that on the Progresses of the Queen the village schoolmaster, or some equally self-important local functionary often prepared a show. Some of the crude plays of this origin have been thought to have suggested Shakespeare's burlesque in the pageants of Holofernes and Bottom.[36] But it is more probable that such burlesques as those presented at Kenilworth suggested to the playwright the dramatic propriety of making a similar form of comic entertainment an integral part of his stage version of a royal Progress.

The curious detachment from the rest of the play of the *Pageant of the Nine Worthies* and the men who enact it has been often unfavorably commented upon. Professor Baker remarks that an audience must take an entirely fresh start with the announcement of the play that Holofernes and his fellows are to present. He says, "The interests in the final act have been, so to speak, thrust in from the outside, rather than developed from elements of story started in earlier acts."[37] Henry David Gray cannot accept this patchwork construction as evidence of Shakespeare's limitations, even at the outset of his career. He believes that the first edition of the play was shorter than that represented by the quarto of 1598, and that the *Nine Worthies* and the men who presented it were not a part of the original version. Holofernes and Nathaniel are abruptly introduced in the fourth act, because they are needed for the play, which has been rather loosely appended to the original comedy. Professor Gray asserts that "they have not the faintest excuse for being in the play, except to take part in the 1597 version of the masque."[38] But if the dramatic mould of *Love's Labour's Lost*

[35] Laneham, p. 25, in Nichols, Vol. II.

[36] Thorndyke, Ashley, *The Pastoral Element in the English Drama before 1605. Modern Language Notes,* 1889, p. 230.

[37] *Op. cit.*, p. 112.

[38] *Op. cit.,* p. 15.

be the essentially loose and episodic Progress, the late introduction of Holofernes and Nathaniel is natural and proper. Like the country folk in the burlesques presented at Kenilworth, their presence would not have been expected or tolerated until the time for their performance approached. Obviously the fortunes of the visiting Queen could not be involved in any plot-like fashion with these clowns. They were actors expected to appear only to furnish certain moments of amusement for their sovereign and then to vanish.

Light may be cast upon still another original and puzzling aspect of the comedy by considering it a dramatic initiation of a Progress. No satisfactory reason has been given for the unique and indeterminate ending of the drama.[39] When the ladies, at the moment of their departure, are sought in marriage by their lovers, they put them off for an entire year. This is an heretical ending for a romantic comedy, which never before had deliberately postponed love's felicity. Biron remarks the unconventionality of this close:

> Our wooing doth not end like an old play
> Jack hath not Gill: these ladies courtesy
> Might well have made our sport a Comedy.[40]

But this ending is harmonious with the origin of the drama as here presented and to the type as here conceived. In the first place, the story of the visit of the two queens at Nérac offered just this sort of indeterminate ending. No marriages were arranged. Marguerite of Valois was already the King's wife. The expedition resulted in a treaty between Navarre and France; and the flying squadron of ladies, its diplomatic service rendered, departed. In *Love's Labour's Lost,* too, the Princess seems to have succeeded in her diplomatic mission. In her farewell to the King she says:

> Excuse me so comming so short of thankes
> For my great suite, so easily obtained.[41]

[39] The only explanations are (1) that Shakespeare at this time, like all youthful genius, aimed at novelty of form (cf. H. D. Gray, *op. cit.,* p. 14; also Grant White, quoted *ibid.*), or (2) that the play was written as a plea of Southampton to have his projected marriage postponed.

[40] V. ii. 950 ff.

[41] V. ii. 811–812.

In the second place the Progresses of the Queen ended in the same way. However alluring the coquetry of Elizabeth and her ladies, however ardent the gallantry of the gentlemen, the imperial vot'ress passed on in maiden meditation fancy free. Therefore if *Love's Labour's Lost* had closed with the marriages of a typical romantic comedy, it would have departed in an important feature from the dramatic form which Shakespeare had chosen for it.

What hypothesis of the genesis and growth of *Love's Labour's Lost* have our studies up to this point enabled us to form? It occurred, we may suppose, to some Elizabethan gentleman that life at the court of Navarre, reflected at a moment when it was stirred into brilliant and picturesque movement by a famous visit of Marguerite of Valois and Catherine de Medici, would form an admirable foundation for an English court play. Whether his attraction was purely aesthetic or whether he saw in the possibilities of the situation an opportunity to make some personal plea in his own private interest, cannot now be determined. This idea became the property of Shakespeare. He believed that this situation would find its most suitable dramatic investiture in a play modelled on the royal Progresses of Elizabeth. It would be a new and piquant experience for the Queen to behold, as a spectator, the drama of a typical Progress, in which so many times she had been the central figure. Consequently as many as possible of the characteristics of these royal entertainments were preserved in the play. The scene of all the action was set in such a spacious park as surrounded many of the castles at which the Queen had been received. The play itself was not given any closely knit structure, but was deliberately planned as a chronicle of entertainments such as were provided for Elizabeth on successive days. The royal guest was given her inevitable opportunity to shoot deer from a covert. The gentlemen presented a merry anti-mask; the clowns, a burlesque show intended to provoke raillery. Finally there was a lyrical debate between the owl and the cuckoo and innumerable social conflicts of wit and dainty devices of speech and repartee. No one of these bits of entertainment in the Progress bore any intrinsic relationship to any other. Consequently Shakespeare felt no obligation to bind his dramatic pictures of such episodes any more closely together. They remain, as it were, a number of acts of the highest sort of Elizabethan vaudeville. Finally the Progress, as a dramatic form, would impose upon the playwright a kind of obligation to give his comedy an indefinite ending. The revels are over and the guests depart: "You that way; we this way."

In the Progress, therefore, we seem to have discovered the structural principle of *Love's Labour's Lost.* Other features of the play remain to be explained. They come from various sources. After the Progresses Shakespeare's most natural source for suggestions for the dramatization of his French story would be the plays of John Lyly, particularly the following comedies of court life: *Sapho and Phao, Endimion, and Midas.* Shakespeare's debt to these dramas in *Love's Labour's Lost* has often been assumed to be all-embracing. Bond expresses this opinion in the enthusiastic form of a special pleader. "In comedy," he says, "Lyly is Shakespeare's only model — and Lyly's influence is of a far more permanent nature than any exercised on the great poet by other writers. It extends beyond the boundaries of mechanical style to the more important matters of structure and spirit." [42] Professor Baker regards *Love's Labour's Lost* as a play constructed on the model of Lyly's work. He believes that it follows the earlier dramatist's method as it appears in his court comedies.[43]

In the latter statement there is much justice, if the critic be referring primarily to Shakespeare's style in this early play. The younger playwright may be said to have learned from Lyly the following important lessons, all of which he incorporated into *Love's Labour's Lost:*

1. How to present the intercourse of refined people conducted with the ease and grace of people to whom verbal ingenuity in conversation has become the supreme form of social delight.

[42] Bond's *Lyly,* II. 243.

[43] Baker, *op. cit.,* p. 114.

2. How to write dialogue, most of it in prose, which is the proper conversation for such a group. It is always witty, brisk, and adorned with fancy and learning; it sometimes degenerates into a somewhat artificial wit combat.
3. How to make love the principal subject of this conversation, which is guided largely by the women who treat their lovers in a tantalizing, flippant manner.
4. How to lay so much emphasis upon dialogue that both plot and characterization become unimportant by comparison.
5. How to introduce many songs.

The influence of Lyly upon *Love's Labour's Lost* in all these respects is indisputable. The conversation of the ladies and gentlemen deals almost exclusively with love. Biron and Rosaline occasionally peer over their flying words to behold each other as man and woman. The others, however, are too completely engrossed in their verbal encounters for such human entanglements; they are blind mouths skilled only in the play of amorous words. This atmosphere of gay badinage is that of Lyly and the witty dialogue a mere echo of his.

The characters in this game of words are grouped somewhat as Lyly's are. The Princess is balanced by the King, and the three ladies, Rosaline, Maria and Catherine are wooed by the three gentlemen, Biron, Longaville and Dumain. In Lyly's plays the same sort of formalism often exists. In *Midas*, for example, there are three councillors, three pages, a group of ladies and a group of shepherds; in *Endimion* there are three pages, two councillors and two philosophers.

All of these elements appear in *Love's Labour's Lost* in greatly altered form. There they have been deepened until they form a somewhat definite comic view of life. Bond says, with warrant, that "there is however, a humanity behind the trifling, the jokes and the affectations to which Lyly in his ripest work never attains." [44] In *Love's Labour's Lost* true love stories emerge, fitfully at least, from what would have remained in Lyly mere verbal trifling. Some critics, as has been noted, have seen in

[44] Bond, II. 262.

Shakespeare's comedy an "obvious satire on the notion that polite society, its sayings, and its doings was life in any real sense at all." All these differences serve to emphasize the fact that none of the structural elements of *Love's Labour's Lost* were derived from Lyly. His comedies were little more than manuals to which the younger dramatist referred for authentic details of proper courtly behavior.

Certain writers have believed Lyly's influence much more extensive. They maintain that most of the comic characters in Shakespeare's drama are copies of similar figures in Lyly. "The comic figures," says Baker, "except Costard and Jaquenetta, owe much both in the content and the phrasing of their speech to John Lyly.[45] Elsewhere Baker says that Shakespeare "presents somewhat caricatured figures of the day, in place of Lyly's exaggerated classic comic figures."[46] Bond says, a little more specifically: "The pretentious Sir Tophas, the ridicule of him by the pages and his pairing with Bagoa, are the originals of the magnificent Armado, of his relation in the Moth and his declension upon the country wench Jaquenetta."[47]

Shakespeare's imitation of Lyly in these respects seems very much more doubtful. Indeed upon examination these comic characters in *Love's Labour's Lost* prove to resemble the corresponding ones in Lyly only in the most general features.

The generally noted resemblances between Sir Tophas in Lyly's *Endimion* and Don Armado are the following:

1. They are both braggarts.
2. They are both in love with ill-favored rustic wenches.
3. The adventures of both reflect in humorous fashion the action of the main plot.
4. Each has, as an attendant, a derisive page or boy.

These similarities exist, but they are characteristics held in common by all the descendants of the Plautine and Terentian braggart soldier. Within the limits of that wide-spread tradition the two figures will be seen to differ so strikingly that it can be clearly shown that one is in no sense a model for the other, but

[45] Baker, p. 113. [46] *Ibid.*, p. 114. [47] I. 297.

that they attach themselves to the hoary tradition at quite different points. Sir Tophas is a farced *miles gloriosus,* a descendant of such exaggerated figures as Thersites in the English interlude of that name, sometimes attributed to John Heywood. His boasts are extravagant to the point of folly. He threatens to do bloody execution upon the mildest of God's creatures. He will slay the monster *Ovis.* "I will draw their guts out of their bellies," he shouts, "and tear the flesh with my teeth, so mortal is my hate." [48] He beholds two pages who he insists are wrens. Epiton, his boy, tells him that the objects are two lads. But Tophas replies, "Byrdes or boyes, they are both but a pittance for my breakfast." [49]

Now in the drawing of Armado no stress whatever is placed upon his grandiose boasting or such display of his military process. In fact, if he were not called "braggart" throughout the play, we should hardly recognize him as belonging to the *miles gloriosus* type. He is introduced rather as a voluble traveller, nice in his speech to the point of affectation. He speaks of himself as "Armado, a soldier, a man of travel, that hath seen the world." [50] Biron says:

> Armado is a most illustrious wight
> A man of fire, new words, fashions owne Knight.[51]

Ferdinand just a moment before has referred to him as

> A refined traveler of Spain
> A man in all the world's new fashion planted
> That hath a mint of phrases in his brain

This figure is no swashbuckler and windy braggart, but a fop in manners and a virtuoso in speech.

This Armado in many of these important respects in which he differs from Sir Tophas and the *miles gloriosus* resembles the

[48] *Endimion,* I. 11.

[49] Thersites, when he catches sight of a snail, makes a similarly absurd remark:

> "But what a monster do I see now
> Come hitherward with an armed bow?
> What is it? Ah it is a sow."

[50] V. i. 103.

[51] I. i. 189–190.

braggart as he had become conventionalized in the Italian popular comedy or the *Commedia dell' Arte.*[52] There, too, he was usually a Spaniard.[53] This transformation of the Latin braggart into a Spanish swashbuckler was a natural result of political conditions in Italy during the sixteenth century, when the Spaniards held much of the country as conquered territory. Their rule in many places, in Naples, for example, was cruel and repressive and provoked many uprisings and revolutions. The unpopular Spanish soldier quartered upon the unwilling Italian inhabitants was satirized by means of the age-old stage figure. Hence the *miles gloriosus* became the *Matamoras.* He was made to affect Spanish stateliness, to talk Castilian, and to adopt a vocabulary of magnificent high-sounding phrases.[54]

In this process of change most of the roughness and noisy extravagance of the rôle disappeared to be replaced by the polished elegance of a gloved gentleman, who carries on his warfare with the utmost dignity and seriousness.[55] A contemporary pen-sketch of the character, reproduced by Rasi,[56] shows the figure to be in no sense grotesque in form or in his

[52] Winifred Smith has noticed this general resemblance. She says (*Italian and Elizabethan Comedy, Modern Philology,* V. 561), " Not less important is Shakespeare's Holofernes, whose name, manner of speech, and general imbecility place him far nearer to the Italian stage-type than to a possible village personage of Shakespeare's acquaintance."

[53] Luigi Riccoboni says that the character was introduced into Italian drama comedy from Spanish drama. — *Histoire du Théâtre Italien depuis la Décadence de la Comédie Latine* (Paris, 1730), I. 56. This statement, of course, ignores the obvious relation of this figure with its Latin prototype. Cf. also Scherillo, Michele, *La Commedia dell' Arte in Italia* (1884), p. 96, and Lee, Vernon, *Studies of the Eighteenth Century in Italy* (1880), p. 235.

[54] Contemporary Italian critics declared that the Spanish tongue was admirably suited to this verbal extravagance. Cecchini (*Frutti delle Moderne Commedie,* 1628) says, " Questa iperbolica parte par che suoni meglio nella spagnuola che nella Italiana lingua, come quella a cui vediamo esser più proprii a più domestici gl'impossibili."

[55] Rasi, L., *I Comici Italiani; biografia, bibliografia, iconografia* (Firenze, 1897), I. 63: " La maschera chiassona, urlona che atterrà un reggimento di soldati con un semplice Guarda voi, ha ceduto il campo al gentiluomo, inguantato, levigato, compassato, che offre a tutti e non da al alcuno, che spara bombe colassali colla maggior calma e serietà del mondo."

[56] Rasi, I. 513.

costume. His sword does not protrude behind at an absurd angle. His hat is embellished with two huge feathers, but he has no trace of the long pointed nose. On the whole he is a graceful gentleman overnicely clad.

Francesco Andreini, the most important impersonator of the *capitano* in the sixteenth century, was a captain of this sort, and became famous for the verbal virtuosity that he exhibited in his reading of the part. This Andreini was a contemporary of Shakespeare; he acted in the company of the Gelosi in 1571, 1574, 1576, 1599 and 1603–4 before the French court and in Paris at the Hotel de Bourgogne.[57] He was so famous as an actor and a writer that an English actor and playwright of any intellectual curiosity could hardly have failed to hear of him and his work.

This actor-dramatist was a highly intelligent man, a member of a Florentine academy, and interested primarily in the entertainment he could afford by twisting *concetti* and every sort of literary allusion into the speech of his captain,[58] whom he called Capitano Spavento of Hell-Valley. These speeches were so much admired that he collected and published them in two different collections.[59] Of this braggart, as of Armado, it could be truthfully said that he had " a mint of phrases in his brain." At least it need surprise no one that the influence of a *Commedia dell' Arte* figure upon a farcical character like the *miles gloriosus* has been to refine it in much the same fashion in which Armado has been refined.

Shakespeare's figure certainly shows more points of relationship with this Italian re-creation than with Sir Tophas. It is, of course, probable that Shakespeare, like all literary artists, drew upon his personal experience when fashioning a character. He may have had his eye on the fantastical *monarcho,* a Span-

[57] Baschet, A., *Les Comédiens italiens à la cour de France sous Charles IX, Henri III, Henri IV, et Louis XIII* (1882), pp. 67 ff.

[58] Rasi, II. 513.

[59] Belwacqua, Enrico, in *Giornale Storico,* XXIII. 87: " Egli cita spesso il Petrarca, l'Ariosto e il Tasso, cita il Marino, il Chiabrera, il Caporali, reporta in verso di Dante, sebbene per isbaglio dica che e del Petrarca, recorda molti scrittori greci e latini."

iard who for years hung about the court of Elizabeth, when drawing Armado. However, the more we know of Shakespeare's sources, the more we realize that he usually had dramatic warrant for his so-called innovations, — that his original conceptions were poured into dramatic moulds already cast. Such a rude mould existed in the Spanish braggart of the *Commedia dell' Arte.*[60]

Strong corroborative evidence of this origin can be found in the fact that each one of Don Armado's clownish associates in *Love's Labour's Lost* bears a close resemblance to a corresponding type-figure in the picturesque clown-group of Italian comedy. Such likenesses between characters as individuals, and as members of a conventionalized group, can hardly be fortuitous.

Before these points of similarity are indicated, a word should be said about the term "Italian comedy." This term is commonly applied to two types of drama: the *Commedia Erudita,* or "learned" comedy, of which Gascogne's *Supposes*[61] is the best known English example; and the *Commedia dell' Arte,* the professional or improvised comedy. The differences between the two in the essential qualities of plot and character were never very great. The same authors often wrote both sorts of comedy and brought the same literary conventions, the same notions of construction, and the same comic devices to both sorts of work.

The extent of the knowledge of *Commedia Erudita* in Elizabethan England can be fairly easily determined. That of the *Commedia dell' Arte* is obviously more difficult to fix. Yet the probabilities that this more popular form exercised an influence

[60] Indeed in Elizabethan drama the term "braggart" came to be applied to this Armado type rather than to the traditional "Miles." Braggardino in Chapman's *The Blind Beggar of Alexandria* is such a creature; and Osric in *Hamlet* once in the first quarto (V. ii) in a stage direction is called a "braggart gentleman." Shakespeare was probably not the first English dramatist to introduce this Spanish braggart to the Elizabethan stage. Basilisco in Kyd's *Soliman and Perseda* is a mixture of braggart and virtuoso in the use of inflated verbiage, as Bond has noted in his introduction to this play. Miss Smith (*Italian and Elizabethan Comedy. Modern Philology,* V. 562) calls this Basilisco "the forerunner of Shakespeare's Armado and Parolles."

[61] A free translation of Ariosto's *Gli Suppositi,* appearing in 1575.

upon Elizabethan dramatists in general, and upon Shakespeare in particular, are strong.

The evidence in the records, of various sorts, of the presence of Italian actors and Italian companies in England during the later half of the sixteenth century has been often presented.[62] Payments were made by the Privy Council to Italians both singers and actors from 1550 on,[63] and there are occasional references in the Revels Accounts to representations by the Italian Players.[64]

The first notice of the appearance of an Italian company in England concerns a reward "gevin to the Italyans for serteyne pastymes that they showed before Maister Mear and his brethen" [65] in September, 1573. This company apparently stayed on into the next year, because we find in the Revels Accounts various payments and furnishings and properties of some Italian actors who "followed the progresse and made pastyme first at Wynsor and afterwards at Reading." [66] The next Italian company apparently visited England early in the year 1578; at any rate the Treasurer of the Chamber paid "Alfroso Ferrabolle and the rest of the Italian Players" [67] for an entertainment presented at court on February 27, 1576. Finally, on January 13, 1578, The Privy Council ordered "The Lord Mayor of London to give orders that one Drousiano, the Italian, a commediante, and

[62] (a) Schücking, L. L., *Studien über die Stöfflichen Beziehungen der englischen Komödie zur italienischen bis Lilly,* Halle, 1901.

(b) Wolf, Max, *op. cit.*, pp. 1–20.

(c) Smith, Winifred, *The Commedia dell' Arte* (1912), pp. 172 ff.

(d) The latest and most complete account of Italian companies in England is to be found in E. K. Chambers, *The Elizabethan Stage* (1923), II. 261–265. This I follow rather closely.

[63] *Acts of the Privy Council,* II. 88.

[64] Edited by Feuillerat, A., *Documents relating to the Office of Revels in the Time of Queen Elizabeth . . .* (*London,* 1903), pp. 225 ff.

[65] Murray, J. T., *English Dramatic Companies 1558–1642,* II. 374.

[66] Chambers (*op. cit.*, p. 262) points out that "Queen Elizabeth was at Windsor on 11 and 12 July; on 15 July she removed to Reading and remained there to July 22."

[67] Chambers suggests that this is probably a clerical error for Alfonso Ferrabosco, the first of three generations of that name attached to the English Court. Cf. G. E. P. Arkwright, *Notes on the Ferrabosco Family* (*The Musical Antiquary*), III. 221; IV. 42.

his companye may play within the Cittie and the liberties of the same between this and the first weeks of Lent." [68] This Drousiano was first identified by Collier as Drusiano Martinelli; [69] and this identification has been accepted by practically all subsequent historians of Italian comedy. He was the brother of Tristano Martinelli,[70] the Arlecchino of the Gelosi. He was probably associated with this famous troupe himself, although there is no direct proof to establish this as a fact. However, this was the only company known to have been in France during the summer of 1577 and Italian players universally left some trace of their presence in France on their way to England. We can, therefore, say with assurance that Drusiano took certain members of this troupe across the Channel to perform before popular London audiences.[71] Later he took the leading rôles in the Duke of Mantua's company of comedians.[72] The nature of the repertory of this company can be inferred from the plays acted by the Gelosi in Paris and by Drusiano's company while it was in Mantua. Besides the *Commedie dell' Arte,* he almost surely presented some of the *Commedie Erudite* written by members of the bourgeois academies to which many of the actors belonged.[73]

This company and others of a similar nature which probably followed it [74] evidently made a profound impression upon Eng-

[68] *Acts etc.,* X. 144. Quoted by Smith, 175.

[69] *History of English Dramatic Poetry* (1826), III. 398, note.

[70] Cf. Rasi, *op. cit.,* under " Martinelli."

[71] Dr. Furness, referring to the visit of this company, remarks (*Much Ado About Nothing,* Variorum ed., Intro., p. xxvii) that it is evidence of " an intimate relationship at that early date between the English and the Italian stage, of which too little account is made by those who wish to explain Shakespeare's knowledge of Italian manners and names."

[72] D'Ancona, Alessandro, *Teatro Montovano nel Secolo XVI, Giornale Storico,* VI. 37.

[73] Winifred Smith, in *Italian and Elizabethan Comedy, Modern Philology,* V. 557, says that there is no particular reason why the Inganni of Alessandro Piccolomini, which many have compared to *Twelfth Night,* may not have been given in London by the Italian actors.

[74] Miss Smith (*ibid.*) says that Coryat in his *Crudities* (London, 1776, from ed. of 1611), II. 16, 17, must be alluding to such a company in his comment on a play he attended in Venice. " I saw women acte, a thing I never saw before, though I have heard it hath been sometimes used in

lish authors and audiences. Nash's famous attack upon "the players beyond the sea" as "a sort of squirting baudie comedians that have whores to play women's parts — forbeare no immodest speech or unchast action that may procure laughter"[75] is but one of a score of references,[76] complementary and, like this, condemnatory, made during the final quarter of the sixteenth century.

Indeed there is evidence to suggest that the comic dramaturgy of these years in England was permeated with the ideals of Italian comedy. Stephen Gosson in his *School of Abuse,*[77] and his *Plays Confuted in Five Actions,*[78] uses the terms "comedies" and "Italian devices," or variations of this latter phrase, practically synonymously. His own comedy, an indiscretion of his youth, of which he heartily repents in his obscurantist maturity, he calls "a cast of Italian devices" with the title *The Comedie of Capitaine Mario.*

Plays, he is certain, came from the Devil, who first corrupted Englishmen by giving them wanton Italian books to read,[79] but "not contented with the number he hath corrupted with reading Italian bawdry, because all cannot read, presented us comedies cut by the same pattern." This trash is called "new-learning" by those which "bear a sharper smack of Italian devices in their heads, than of English religion in their hearts." "Compare London to Rome," he cries in *The School of Abuse,* "and England to Italy. You shall find the theatres of one, the abuses of the other to be rife among us." Repetition of more of these familiar passages should be unnecessary. Gosson's description of the constituent elements of comedy as he understands it fits Italian comedy best. "The Grounde Work of

London." Visiting Italians were the only ones who in those days could have had women actors in their troupes.

[75] Nash, *Pierce Penilesse* (1592, ed. Grosart), p. 92.

[76] Cf. Smith, *Commedia dell' Arte,* p. 177; also Schucking, pp. 58 ff.

[77] For the text, see *The Shakespeare Society Publications,* No. 2, 1841.

[78] For the text, see Hazlitt, *The English Drama and Stage under the Tudor and Stuart Princes: 1543–1664* (Roxburgh Library, 1859), pp. 157 ff.

[79] It is well known that the age of Shakespeare's youth was, as Schelling says (*Foreign Influences in Elizabethan Plays,* p. 49), "literally soaked in Italian literature and fiction."

Comedies," he says, " is love cosenedge, flatterie, bawderie, slye conveyhance of whoredom; the persons cookes, queans, knaves, baudes, parasites, courtezannes, lecherous olde men, amorous young men." Allowing for the zealot's exaggeration, this passage might refer to either sort of Italian comedy, or even to that of Plautus or Terence; but taken in connection with the passage to be cited, it seems clearly intended as a description of the popular comedy.

The Devil, continues the implacable Gosson, seduces man by way of comedies, particularly through the eye, because he sendeth in " gearish apparell, maskes, vauting, tumbling, dancing of gigges, galiandes, morisces, hobbi-horses, showing of iudgeling castes."

The properties and devices here mentioned are of the very essence of the *Commedia dell' Arte.* The passage is primarily a description of the *lazzi* of the clowns with which the improvised comedy was replete. Moreover, it is highly probable that the word " maskes " in this context refers to the actual masks that the typical figures in this comedy wore. It obviously does not refer to the highly refined court show of the same name.[80] " Gearish apparell " obviously refers to costume and describes nothing so accurately as the fantastic parti-coloured garments of the popular Italian comedy. " Maskes," Gosson opines, are equally designed to seduce the eyes of the vulgar. They must be, therefore, something related to " gearish apparell " and so probably the word refers to the grotesque half-faces which the clowns like Harlequin and Pulchinella habitually wore.

These passages tend to confirm our *a priori* judgment in this matter. Of the two sorts of Italian comedy one would expect the *Commedia dell' Arte* to have the more definite influence upon English drama.[81] Only those few literary comedies which were translated into English could have exerted any pervasive influ-

[80] The word was frequently used to mean a disguise or mumming. In the *Documents relating to the Office of Revels 1559–60*, one may read such entries as " A Maske of Patriarkes " and " A Maske of Italyen Women."

[81] The almost universal knowledge of Italian among Elizabethan courtiers and gentlemen of distinction (cf. Schelling, *Foreign Influences in Elizabethan Plays,* p. 41) did not extend to the popular playwrights.

ence. The appeal of the *Commedia dell' Arte,* on the other hand, was largely independent of language. It flourished in nearly every capital and important city of the continent during the latter half of the sixteenth century. English travelling comedians are known to have played at the same places with Italian companies for prolonged periods. Before 1580, London had at least once submitted itself to the charm of the *Commedia dell' Arte.* Its appeal was striking, picturesque, unique. Such plays, once seen, would be held securely in memory and all their comic devices cherished.

The historical facts adduced and such utterances as these of Gosson show that English dramatic life during the seventies and eighties of the sixteenth century was permeated by the form and spirit of Italian comedy,—largely of the popular sort. What reason is there to suppose that Shakespeare during the latter part of this period fell under the wide-spread influence of this striking comedy?

At the end of his career, Shakespeare knew well a certain type of Italian comic scenario. It has recently been shown that the story of *The Tempest* and many of its distinctive theatrical features are undoubtedly derived from a romantic type of *Commedia dell' Arte.*[82] A group of five scenarios, written down first in 1622, but representing much older traditions of the masked players, contains practically all of the constructive and distinctive histrionic features of *The Tempest,* in a combination which makes the evidence for their influence upon Shakespeare absolutely convincing. These newly discovered facts justify our assuming that by 1610 he had direct and specific knowledge of the *Commedia dell' Arte.* His general or traditional knowledge seems to have been much older. Specific allusions to the various Italian "masks" can be found throughout his work.[83] Even in

[82] See Neri, Ferdinando, *Scenari delle Maschere in Arcadia* (Città di Castello, 1913). Number I of *Documenti di Storia Letteraria Italiana,* edited by Pietro Mattiacci, for the text. Cf. also Gray, Henry David, *The Sources of The Tempest, Modern Language Notes,* XXXV (1920), 321.

[83] He refers to Pantalone as "the old Pantaloon" in *The Taming of the Shrew,* III. i. 37; as "the lean and slippered Pantaloon" in *As You Like It,* II. vii. 158; as "the old Magnifico" in *Othello,* I. ii. 12. Cf.

the comedy under discussion Biron speaks of " some carry-tale, some pleseman, some slight zany." [84] These facts simply confirm what is an almost inevitable inference, — that a young writer like Shakespeare, who throughout his career showed himself to be closely in touch with all the dramatic tendencies of his time, could hardly have failed, especially in the opening years of his career, to be aware of the spectacular action and striking stage-figures of the *Commedia dell' Arte.* Its influence, perhaps next to that of Lyly, would be the most natural one to draw Shakespeare within its sphere. His clowns, indeed, would almost inevitably be related to that comedy of clowns. That the character of Armado should resemble the Spanish braggart of Italian comedy, then, and not the Latinate Sir Tophas of Lyly, need astonish no critic familiar with the European dramatic situation in the years when Shakespeare began to write for the stage.

All the points of likeness usually asserted as existing between Sir Tophas and Armado can now be recognized as traditions of the *capitano.* For example, Sir Tophas is said to be the prototype of Armado because he is forced to marry an ugly wench Bagoa, just as Armado pairs with the country lout Jaquenetta. But this is one of the conventional ways of disposing of the *capitano.* Thus are his amorous conceit and amorous ambition broadly satirized. He is regularly either utterly humiliated and driven off in disgrace at the end of the play or he is married to some clownish and ill-favored female. Francisco Andreini, for example, in one of the discourses which he composed for this part of the *capitano* [85] presents the plight of the *capitano* who is married to the terrible fury Megara.[86] A less extravagant situation of this sort is that of Captain Crackstone in *The Two*

Smith, *op. cit.,* pp. 178 ff., where references of a similar sort by other Elizabethan dramatists are also collected.

[84] *Love's Labour's Lost,* V. ii. 463.

[85] *Le Bravure del Capitano Spavento . . . di Francesco Andreini da Pistoria Comico Geloso* (*Venetia,* 1607), Ragiomento ventesimo, 134–141.

[86] Cf. 138: " Quella notte tremo più volte l'Inferno, mentre ch'io rompeva lancie con la mia bella sposa, e per quando io mi sapessi fare non hebbi gratia di renderla gravida di me, peresser ella troppo furiosa negli amorosi conflitte et per haver la matrice arsa, e bruciata."

Italian Gentlemen, an English adaptation of an Italian comedy.[87] This braggart woos the vulgar maid Attilia and apparently wins her. "How saist those Alice tittle tattle," he cries in the last lines of the play "art thou content by love to be bound?" Sir Tophas and Armado decline upon sorry wenches, then, because that amorous disaster is in the typical *capitano's* part.

A relationship between Lyly's and Shakespeare's figure has been assumed because each is accompanied by a page, who ridicules the self-importance and the extravagant assumptions of his braggart master, particularly his rôle of lover. But here again Sir Tophas and Armado have merely both inherited a common appendage of the *capitano.* He was invariably accompanied by such a servant. In the *Commedia dell' Arte* this fellow was one of the clowns, often Arlecchino, and his relation to his master was that of the page to Sir Tophas or to Armado. This figure, the zany, was originally the clown or mountebank, whose first requisite was the physical agility demanded for the performance of his *lazzi* or bits of horse-play. His brains in time came to be as swift as his muscles, because his function in the plot became more and more that of managing events in the interest of the *amorosa.* His quick wit was also shown more and more in puns, in word-play of all sorts, and in satiric repartee. He assumed so many forms and inherited so many characteristics of the "servus" of Latin comedy and resembled so closely the clown in native English drama that it is impossible to prove that a figure like Moth is a direct descendant of the zany attached to the *capitano.* However, the two belong to the same family, and it is reasonable to suppose that the servant would come from the same source as the master. If Armado came into English comedy as an Italian type, Moth probably had a similar origin.

A strong confirmation of this theory may be found in the fact that all the members of the subsidiary comic group have prototypes in the figures of the *Commedia dell' Arte:* Costard, the slow-witted rustic, in Pagliaccio, a similar heavy lout; Holofernes, in a figure with various names, charlatan, pedagogue, and pedant, with his speech habitually crammed with macaronic

[87] *Il Fedele,* written by Luigi Pasqualigo.

Latin and Bolognese riddles; Nathaniel, in the Parasite or *affamato,* who only in the *Commedia dell' Arte* is attached to the Pedant. Even Dull, English to the core in his particular form of conscientious stupidity, has a prototype in Italian comedy.

Costard's ancestor, a stupid rustic, appears in the earliest scenario that we possess.[88] There he evokes laughter only by his ridiculous clothing and rustic behavior,[89] and bears no relation whatever to the plot. The proper " business " for an actor presenting this character is explained in a dialogue about scenic performances composed between 1567 and 1590 by an actor-manager, Leone di Sommi.[90] His advice to the actor on this point is " If he plays a fool, besides answering off the point (which the poet will teach him by his words) he must be able to act the imbecile, catch flies, kill fleas, and do like foolish actions."

This rustic or fool first became an integral part of the bourgeois group who form the vehicle of the love plot, in the company of the Gelosi. He there usually bears the name of Pedrolino,[91] and is the servant of Pantalone. He is generally outwitted by the other servants, stupidly falls asleep at his post, or gets drunk with the *capitano* and his servant. In particular, he made himself ridiculous when encountering the principal zany and becoming involved in the toils of his wit. By the time of Barbieri's *Il Supplica,* written in 1634, the dramatic contrast between the two servants had become a thoroughly established dramatic convention and treated as such in this book of dramaturgy. Barbieri says, " The first servant provokes laughter by most subtle tricks and ready replies, the second by foolishness."

[88] In a description, written by Massuno Trojano, of an improvised comedy which he, as court choir-master, wrote for presentation at the Duke of Bavaria's wedding in 1568. Cf. Smith, *op. cit.,* p. 70.

[89] He is introduced " alla Cavajola." That is, he impersonated the peasant as he appeared in the " farse caviole," which represented the life of the folk in the southern Italian town of Cava. Cf. Torraca, F., *Il teatro italiano nei secoli XIII, XIV, XV* (Firenze, 1885), pp. 431 ff.

[90] Cf. Smith, *op. cit.,* p. 70.

[91] He inherits certain traits of a Pagliaccio of an earlier company and of a character called Bertoldino. Cf. the present author's *The Comedies of Holberg,* pp. 175 and 350.

The dramatic contrast between these two servants Shakespeare did not develop strongly until he wrote *The Two Gentlemen of Verona.* However, the possibilities of humor in such a contrast are suggested in *Love's Labour's Lost.* Costard, at any rate, is a very close equivalent of this Italian fool. Like his prototype described by Leone di Sommi, his humor is rustic behavior and the vice of mistaking the word or of answering off the point. Every time that he appears, he contributes bits of verbal misunderstanding like the following:

> *Armado.* Sirra, Costard. I will infranchise thee.
> *Clown.* O, marrie me to one Francis, I smell some Lenvoy, some goose in this.[92]

The following dialogue illustrates the same point:

> *Ber.* O my good Knave Costard, exceedingly well met.
> *Clown.* Pray you sir, How much Carnation Ribbon may a man buy for a remuneration?
> *Ber.* What is a remuneration?
> *Cost.* Marrie, sir, halfe pennie farthing.[93]

Shakespeare naturally gave this Costard traits of English rustics, but the character is very clearly cast in the dramatic mould of the Italian figure.

Holofernes, another permanent member of the group of clowns, is also modelled on the very popular Italian figure of the pedant. Many critics, following the lead of Warburton, have attempted to see in this character Shakespeare's satire of some individual whom he knew and scorned. Warburton asserted without any apparent warrant that Holofernes was intended to represent John Florio.[94] Karl Elze makes the unsupported assertion that Shakespeare's pedant is a satirical picture of Thomas Hunt, the poet's teacher from 1572 to 1577.[95] Abel Lefranc, finding a manuscript play on the *Nine Worthies* by Richard Lloyd, the

[92] Act III, Scene ii.
[93] *Ibid.*
[94] Variorum of 1821, p. 479: " By Holofernes is designed a particular character, a pedant and schoolmaster of our author's time, one John Florio . . ."
[95] *William Shakespeare* (translated by L. Dora Schmitz, 1888), p. 37: " There is, probably, little doubt that the poet has immortalized Thos. Hunt as Holofernes.

tutor of the Sixth Earl of Derby, concludes that Holofernes is comic portrait of this schoolmaster. Arthur Acheson believes that Holofernes represents Chapman and that " In the pedantry and verbosity of Holofernes he (Shakespeare) caricatures Chapman's style, and in the person of Holofernes excoriates Chapman himself." [96]

These theories, by no means all of the sort that have been advanced, besides being impossible of proof, ignore the existence of one of the most wide-spread and popular of the Italian stage conventions of the time, — that of the pedant. The model from which this character was drawn was an international figure, the product of Renaissance culture. With the coming of the new learning the intellectual methods of the scholastics or medieval school-philosophers naturally became the objects of ridicule. This sort of scholar came to appear as an absurd combination of the rigid logician and formal rhetorician. In drama he was made to argue according to all forms of the syllogism, — to concede the major and deny the minor. He fatuously came forward on all occasions with some general rule which he considered applicable to the particular case in hand.

Later the exaggerations of the humanist himself were made the object of satire, — his confident and superior wisdom, which yet rendered him helpless in any difficult situation, and his motley tongue, half Italian and half Latin. He is particularly prone to use his learning in colloquies with people of the lower class, among whom he produces misunderstandings which fill him with rage. He usually falls in love, in which state his insatiable quotation of Latin maxims and classical precedents render him particularly ridiculous. He is always cozened and misled, but he seeks to make his learning yield him comfort. He thinks of the great men of the past who have been pursued by misfortune and hopes that thought will bring him equanimity. Occasionally he is made a philosopher in words and a licentious hyprocrite in fact. As such he is exposed and driven off the stage with scorn.

In Italian comedy, also, the pedant is usually the school

[96] Acheson, *Shakespeare and the Rival Poet* (1903), p. 83.

teacher or tutor. In *Gl'Ingannati*[97] (1526), for example, one of the principal characters is Piero, the tutor of Fabrizio. In *The Two Italian Gentlemen,* Pedante, the tutor of Fidele, enters "attired in a gown and cap like a schoolmaster." Both of these teachers fill their discourse with Latin and are particularly eloquent in that tongue before dolts who cannot understand them.

In *The Two Italian Gentlemen*[98] Attilia, the loutish maid, is the object of the pedant's attentions and is forced to listen to much incomprehensible Latin.

Attilia:
I pray Sir, what was it you sayde of love?
Pedante:
Est Deus in nobis agitante calescimus illo.

I dare not tell you the meaning, lest I make your cheeks glow. This pedant, too, inserts Italian into his discourse with a freedom only once or twice attempted by Holofernes:

Andante allegramente, you are right under her window now

or

Oche cricca di vacche? What cattell have we heare?

To be sure these Italian schoolmasters are in love and show their Latinate folly most completely in this situation.

Holofernes clearly belongs to this type.[99] He is a schoolmaster who "teaches boys the Horne-book." He apostrophizes good old Mantuan, whose Eclogues were a favorite text for study in the schools. Nathaniel, his parasite, praises his work as follows: "Sir, I praise God for you, and so may my parish-

[97] This play has been considered to be a possible source of *Twelfth Night.* Dr. Furness goes so far as to suggest that this might be one of the dramas brought to England by Drousiano in 1577–78 (*New Variorum Twelfth Night*, p. xxi). This play was also translated into Latin under the title of *Laelia* and presented at Queens College, Cambridge, in 1590 and again in 1598. Cf. Churchill and Keller, *Shakespeare Jahrbuch,* XXIV (1898), 286, 291.

[98] The characteristics of this pedant are important for our purpose, because he is one of a very few representatives of the Italian type who appeared in extant plays written before Shakespeare began to compose.

[99] See note 52.

ioners, for their Sonnes are well tutor'd by you, and their Daughters profit very greatly under you; you are a good member of the Common-wealth." [100] Later in this same scene Holofernes says, " I do dine today at the fathers of a certaine Pupill of mine."

He crams his discourse with Latin and is outraged at the ignorance of the clowns who cannot understand him.

> *Nath.* . . . but sir, I assure ye, it was a Bucke of the first head.
> *Hol.* Sir Nathaniel, haud credo.
> *Dul.* 'Twas not a haud credo, 'twas a Pricket.
> *Hol.* Most barbarous intimation: yet a kind of insinuation, as it were in via, in way of explication *facere,* as it were replication, or rather *ostentare,* to show as it were his inclination after his undressed, unpolished, uneducated, unpruned, untrained, or rather unlettered, or ratherest unconfirmed fashion, to insert againe my haud *credo* for a dear.[101]

Holofernes is also keenly on the lookout for false Latin.

> *Clowns:* Goe to, thou hast it ad dungil, at the finger ends, as they say.
> *Peda:* Oh, I smell false Latin, dunghel for unguam.[102]

Furthermore he now and then falls into Italian as in his apostrophe to Mantuan, " Ah good old Mantuan, I may speake of thee as the traveller doth of Venice, 'Venetia, Venetia, chi non te vede, non te pregia.' " [103]

The verbal affectations and flourishes of Holofernes in the use of his mother-tongue are of definite sorts. In the first place he shows his mastery of a vocabulary by uttering on every possible occasion a mass of synonyms. He says that the braggart is " too picked, too spruce, too affected, too odde, as it were, too peregrinat." He comments as follows on Don Armado's use of the term " posteriors of this day " for afternoon as follows: " The posterior of the day, most generous sir, is liable, congruent, and measurable for the afternoone: the word is well culd, chose,

[100] Act IV, Sc. ii.
[101] Act IV, Sc. ii, ll. 10 ff.
[102] Act V, Sc. i, ll. 75–77.
[103] In the Folio text this is written as gibberish: " Venice, venchie, que non te unde, que non te perreche." Theobald was the first to discern the Italian proverb in this hash. Scherillo (*La Via italiana nel seicento,* p. 336) finds this like similar speeches of the Dottore Gratiano, the pedant in the Gelosi company.

sweet and apt. I doe assure you."[104] He speaks of his own talent in making rhymes in the following way: "This is a gift that I have simple: simple, a foolish extravagant spirit, full of forms, figures, objects, ideas, apprehensions, motions, revolutions."[105]

In the second place, Holofernes indulges a passion for over-ingenious etymologies. He exclaims pompously, "But for elegancy, facility and golden cadence of poesie, caret. Ovidius Naso was the man. And why indeed Naso, but for smelling out the odoriferous flowers of fancy, the jerks of invention."[106] He answers Jaquenetta's "God give you good morrow, Master Parson," in the following jocose fashion: "Master Parson, quasi pers-on. An if one should be pierced, which is the one?"[107]

In the third place, he is sometimes given to false pronunciations. For example, he says to Nathaniel, after he has read the love letter, "You find not the apostrophas and so miss the accent. Let me supervise the cangenet (canzonet)."[108]

The following somewhat puzzling passage, in which Holofernes comments on Don Armado's pronunciation, is also an indication of bookish ignorance of the spoken idiom: "He clepeth a Calf; Caufe halfe, haufe; Neighbour vocabitur nebour: neigh abbreviated ne: this is abhominable, which he would call abbominable."[109] To assume that the pedant here is talking merely as a purist is to attribute to him a subtlety of humor not in harmony with his character as drawn elsewhere in the play. He is rather presented in this speech as a man essentially

[104] Act V, Sc. i, ll. 14–15.

[105] Act V, Sc. i, ll. 87–90.

[106] Act IV, Sc. ii, ll. 80–83.

[107] Act V, Sc. i, l. 25. This speech is given to Nathaniel in the Folio, but obviously belongs to Holofernes, as Theobald was the first to see. After the first eighty lines of this scene there is much confusion in the attribution of speeches to Holofernes and Nathaniel. Fleay first (*Life,* p. 203) finds the origin of the confusion in the hurried retouching of the scene for a court performance. Later (*Anglia,* VII. p. 229) he says that in the first draft of the play Holofernes was curate and Nathaniel the pedant. Dr. Furness (Variorum, p. 136) prefers the traditional scapegoats, — the compositors or compositors' reader. I follow the attribution of the Cambridge editors.

[108] Act IV, Sc. ii, l. 135.

[109] Act V, Sc. i, ll. 24–26.

bookish, who has learned his words from a printed page, and is oblivious and contemptuous of their career in the living speech. His own mispronunciation of "abominable," based upon a false etymology, gives satiric emphasis to his ponderous ignorance of idiomatic pronunciation.

Now every one of these verbal affectations of Holofernes, with the necessary exception of his use of Italian, is a recognized convention of the pedantic doctor in the *Commedia dell' Arte,* and particularly of the rôle as played by Ludovico Bianchi of the Gelosi troupe. This *dottore,* generally called Graziano, is usually from Bologna, and his humors are exactly the same as those just catalogued. Rasi thus enumerates his foibles: "The doctor is always the invariable ignoramus and pedant, who utters wise saws in the inevitable mixture of macaronic Latin, of foolish quotations and absurd etymologies . . . clear proof that the true type of Graziano had, in the eyes of the public, as distinctive and fundamental characteristics, ignorant pretension to learning, stupid etymologizing, grotesque mispronunciation of words and the buffoonery of Latin quotation." [110] Later Rasi mentions the doctor's penchant for synonyms and gives as an example the following: Pero essend' tra un allegad et culigad la grazia, l'affabilita, la benignita, l'allegrezza, and so on for forty-eight synonyms.[111]

In this record of the practice of an actor in the Gelosi troupe are to be found all of the verbal extravagances of Holofernes: the inevitable medley of macaronic Latin, the whimsical etymologies, the mispronunciations, and the interminable lists of synonyms.

This doctor is a pedant, though not expressly so called. In Scala's Collection at least once the pedant is introduced by that knew. But the solidity of framework which this group gave

[110] Rasi, I. 407: Il Dottore è sempre il solito ignorantone, saccentone, che sputa sentenze, con mescolanza inevitabile di latino maccheronico, di citazioni spropositate, di etimologie bislacche. . . . Segno evidente che il tipo vero del Graziano ebbe al cospetto del pubblico per base unica la saccenteria ignorante, la etimologia insula, la storpiatura grottesca di vocaboli, la buffoneria delle citazioni latine.

[111] *Ibid.*, p. 412.

name.[112] This Cataldo is also a tiresome Latinate pedant, but is primarily a hypocrite. Under cover of giving Isabella, the beautiful young wife of Pantalone, the counsel that she needs to keep her from betraying her husband with the captain, he attempts to seduce her himself. Isabella traps, and exposes him, and so holds him up to ignominy and ridicule. Cataldo is thus a sort of skeleton for Tartuffe. This aspect of the pedant was not uncommonly treated in Italian comedy. Indeed several passages in *Love's Labour's Lost* show that Holofernes was sometimes under the sway of similar wanton desires.[113] This Shakespearian pedant thus seems to exhibit most of the absurdities conventionally the humorous property of the *Commedia dell' Arte* pedant.

The attempt to find any specific dramatic figure who served as a definite literary prototype for Holofernes is probably futile. These characteristics of the *dottore* did not join in any figure before Holofernes in a combination enough like his own to furnish Shakespeare a serviceable model. In English literature before *Love's Labour's Lost,* the pedant played a comparatively insignificant rôle. Rombus in Sidney's *Lady of May* is one of the few. He exhibits many of the characteristics of the Italian type in his predilection for Latin quotation and his grandiloquence in his native idiom. However he is ridiculous principally because he is excessively prone to formal rhetoric and the forms of the syllogism. He is a belated scholastic. Churchill and Keller, in the article already cited,[114] suggest that Shakespeare might naturally have known the Cambridge University play *Paedantius*[115] and have used the comic protagonist there, as a

[112] *Il Pedante, Giorno XXXI.*

[113] Compare the following speech of Holofernes: "Me hercule, if their Sonnes be ingennuous, they shall want no instruction. If their daughters be capable, I will put it to them. But *vir sapis qui pauca loquitur.*" Numerous editors, beginning with Steevens and Malone, have caught a *double entendre* in these lines. In spite of good Dr. Furness's irritation at the ignoble minds of the critics, the double meaning seems to be in the text.

[114] *Shakespeare Jahrbuch,* XXXIV (1898), 256 ff.

[115] Sir John Harington in his *Apology for Poetry,* written in 1591, speaks of the play, so that it was performed before this date.

model for Holofernes. However none of the similarities between the two lie in common deviations from the type figure, so that this assumption is hardly warranted. The pedant in *The Two Italian Gentlemen* is much more like Holofernes than either of these figures; doubtless because he bears a closer relationship to the Italian figure.

These facts pretty clearly establish the truth that Holofernes left a home in popular Italian comedy to travel with his clownish associates into Shakespeare's workshop. Naturally the English dramatist has transformed the figure in many ways. Some of his new traits may well have been derived from country schoolmasters whom he had known, but they never obscure Holofernes' relationship to the Italian type figure.

Nathaniel is a parasite who, like hundreds of his prototypes from classical comedy down, flatters and toadies to the person to whom he attaches himself, so that he may satisfy his insatiable appetite for food.[116] It is only in Italian comedy, however, that the parasite attaches himself to the pedant. Moland [117] says that it is only in the *Commedia dell' Arte* that he is thus placed, but in *The Supposes* Pasiphilo divides his allegiance between Erostrato and the pedant Cleander.[118] Nathaniel is, of course, a character of very minor importance. Yet the slight indications that the author has given us prove that he is a representative of the parasite in the form that he came to assume in Italian comedy.

Even Dull has a prototype in the Italian comedy. A stupid

[116] Churchill and Keller (*op. cit.*) think that the presence of a second pedant Dromodotus in the school-comedy *Paedantius* proves that Shakespeare had this situation in this Latin play in mind when he introduced both Holofernes and Nathaniel into *Love's Labour's Lost*. Dromodotus is called Philosophus and is a scholastic ridiculously wedded to his medieval jargon. Nathaniel is not a second pedant; he is a lightly-sketched parasite or "affamato," as he was called in Italian Comedy. Only in the confused attribution of speeches in Act IV, Sc. ii, of the Folio text does he seem to be a second pedant.

[117] *Molière et la Comedie Italienne,* 2d ed., Paris, 1867.

[118] *Supposes,* I. 3: "I am of the householde with this scholer Erostrato (his rival) as well as with Domine Cleander; now with the one, and then with the other, according as I see their caters provide good cheere at the market."

magistrate was one of Francesco Andreini's most successful rôles. In one of Bartoli's scenari, *La Regina d'Inghilterra,* Trappola plays an officer with the same portentous stupidity as does Dull. In *The Two Italian Gentlemen,* described above, there is a representative of the same type-character in Sberri, captain of the watch. Examples could be multiplied. Even the presence of the multiform love story may be due to *Commedia dell' Arte* influence. There were nearly always, in these plays, a *prima donna* and a *secunda donna.* Each of these ladies had to be provided with a lover. Occasionally there was even a third lady who made a like demand of the author. This was in addition to the inevitable love-making among the servants and clowns. Shakespeare's multiform love stories in this comedy and elsewhere may be regarded as a natural expansion and complication of this structural feature of Italian comedy.

The *capitano,* upon examination, seems to have brought all of his Italian familiars with him into *Love's Labour's Lost.*[119] Certain members of this famous group had appeared in plays in English before this one, but this is the first English comedy in which the entire group appears as a veritable *société joyeuse.*

The young dramatist evidently felt that the clever courtly badinage of Lyly-like ladies and gentlemen, even when associated with a more natural and sincere love story than any that Lyly had ever presented, did not give enough comic substance to his play, which we have agreed to regard as a sort of dramatic Progress. Accordingly, turning for material to the enormously popular characters of contemporary Italian Comedy, he imported thence not isolated figures, but the entire group of clownish masks. Their mere presence gave his comedy a firm foundation for laughter. He forced them moreover to meet some of the structural needs of his drama, as when he assigned to them the presentation of the burlesque pageant of *The Nine Worthies.* Each one of them was also modified as a result of Shakespeare's observation of contemporary life, and perhaps occasionally by his impulse to satirize certain ridiculous individuals whom he

[119] Birowne enumerates them all except the constable (V. ii. 545), "The Pedant, the Braggart, the Hedge-Priest, the Foole, and the Boy."

knew. But the solidity of framework which this group gave his tenuously connected episodes and the perennial mirth which it aroused must have been their main recommendation to the young dramatist.

Love's Labour's Lost, therefore, proves to have had a somewhat complicated history of construction. The nature of the play shows clearly enough that even in its earliest form, it was connected in some way with the English court. Indeed its central plot reveals such an intimate familiarity with nearly contemporary events and social conditions at the court of Navarre as the author could scarcely have gained from his own personal experience. This fact points to Shakespeare's association with some gentleman of the court in the composition of this *Love's Labour's Lost.* Who he was or what his purposes were in this collaboration will probably never be known. To a student of Shakespeare's early methods of composition, these interesting personal questions are of only minor importance. Once given his central idea, the playwright invested it with vitality and diversity by bringing to it constructive principles and comic motifs from three sources clearly within the range of his knowledge, — the progresses of Queen Elizabeth, the court comedies of John Lyly, and Italian comedy, particularly the *Commedia dell' Arte.*

We find Shakespeare then, at the outset of his career as a writer of comedy, not, as Bond asserts, having one master and one only, — John Lyly. Nor do we find him working carefully in imitation of this one author in an effort to discover what qualities of his own would emerge during this process. Such a method is scarcely calculated to develop the great versatility in comic composition which Shakespeare shows early in his career. What he seems actually to have done is to have found dramatic suggestions for his own practice in many places. Fortunately his imagination kindled at many smouldering fires.

Moreover each one of his borrowed ideas he developed with a joyous creative exuberance. He was not to be satisfied with one love story in this play or even with two. He arranged four or five. He developed, intensified, and diversified Lyly's courtly conversation until it became a veritable dramatic symphony on the theme of Euphuistic speech. He introduced into it not single figures from Italian comedy, but all of the comic masks at once and made each one of them contribute his traditional humor, in a sublimated form, to the gorgeous Progress given by the King of Navarre to his royal guests.

This imaginative abundance appears in all of Shakespeare's early plays, — tragedies and historical. It is the temper of *The Comedy of Errors,* of *Titus Andonicus,* and of *Richard III.* May we not say it is the universally approved and natural method of all youthful genius?

THE TWO GENTLEMEN OF VERONA
AND ITALIAN COMEDY

THE TWO GENTLEMEN OF VERONA AND ITALIAN COMEDY

O. J. CAMPBELL

SHAKESPEARE'S *The Two Gentlemen of Verona* occupies an important position in the history of English drama. It is usually regarded as "the earliest surviving romantic comedy of England and almost of Europe."[1] At all events in this play, so the approved criticism runs, the distinctive qualities of Shakespeare's romantic comedy appear for the first time. "In this play," writes Mr. Warwick Bond, "he opens the vein he worked so richly afterwards — the vein of crossed love, of flight and exile under the escort of generous sentiments; of disguised heroines, of sufferings endured and virtues exhibited under their disguise; and of Providence kinder than life, that annuls the errors and forgives the sin; and here first he lays the scene in Italy."[2]

The sources and provenience of a play of so great importance in the history of English drama are of more than ordinary interest. Yet the relations of this comedy to the continental drama contemporary with it and immediately anterior to it have, I believe, never been properly understood.

The commonly accepted notion is that the story of Julia and Proteus was derived, in all of its characteristic features, from the tale of Felix and Felismena in the romance *Diana Enamorada*, written in Spanish by the Portuguese poet Jorge de Montemayor, and first printed at Valentia in 1542. That story runs as follows. Felismena is wooed by the gentleman Don Felix, whose advances she at first repulses but later receives with pleasure. His father disapproves their love and sends his son away to court.

[1] This phrase comes from the work of R. Warwick Bond, the Arden edition of *The Two Gentlemen of Verona* (London, 1906), p. xxxii.

[2] *Ibid.*

Felismena, disguised as a page, follows him thither. The first night that she spends in the city, the host of her inn takes her to a place where she may hear music. He conducts her to a spot not far from the inn where she listens to a passionate serenade addressed by the false Felix to the lady Celia. Felismena next day sees him at court gorgeously arrayed in the colors of this new mistress. The deserted maiden enters his service as a page and bears his messages and gifts to Celia. This lady falls in love with Felismena, and realizing that it is impossible to win her love, she dies of a broken heart. Felix then mysteriously disappears and is thought to have died also of grief. Felismena becomes a shepherdess. One day long after she beholds an unknown knight pursued and hard pressed by three foemen. Through almost miraculous skill in archery she slays the pursuers and rescues the knight, and then discovers that he is her lost Felix. His love for her immediately revives and they are united.

The general similarities between this romantic tale and the story of Julia and Proteus are evident. At two points the likenesses extend to comparatively unimportant details. These are the effort of the lady's maid to deliver the lover's first letter to her mistress and the circumstances under which the girl-page overhears the serenade given by her faithless lover to his new flame. In Montemayor's romance Rosina's first attempt to deliver Felix's declaration of love is met by an angry rebuke by Felismena. The next morning, however, the maid allows the letter to fall, as if by accident, in the lady's chamber. Felismena, by this time eager to see the missive, pretends not to know what the dropped article is, and insists upon seeing it. Lucetta, in *The Two Gentlemen of Verona,* also lets the love letter fall where it will be certain to attract the attention of her mistress. Julia affects to believe it a missive from one of the maid's lovers, and insists upon seeing it. After she has it in her possession, she tears it into pieces. Then dismissing Lucetta, she eagerly gathers the fragments from the floor and pieces them together in an effort to recover some of its precious love-phrases.

The second point of similarity in detail between the two plays is to be found in the page's overhearing of the serenade. Felismena, at the suggestion of the host of the inn at which she is staying, goes to a spot where she hears Felix serenade Celia. Similarly it is the host in *The Two Gentlemen of Verona* who takes Julia to hear the serenade arranged by Thurio and incidentally to learn of her lover's infidelity.

The consensus of critical opinion seems to be that such points of similarity in unessential details make Shakespeare's knowledge of Montemayor's tale practically certain. Shakespeare, however, probably did not know Spanish. Scholarly ingenuity has therefore been severely taxed to discover a form of tale which he might have read. The facts are these. *The Two Gentlemen of Verona* was written certainly no later than 1592, while the first English translation of *Diana Enamorada,* that made by Bartholomew Yonge, was not printed until 1598.[3] To be sure, the translator says in his preface that the work had existed in manuscript for more than sixteen years, that is since 1582. There is no reason to suppose, however, that Shakespeare saw this document. Another translation was dedicated by Thomas Wilson to the Earl of Southampton in 1596. There was a French translation of the work made in 1578, which was reprinted with additions in 1587 and re-issued in 1592.[4] This French translation Shakespeare might conceivably have seen, although he was apparently not an habitual reader of French. The English version most apt to come within the range of Shakespeare's notice was that probably contained in the lost play *Felix and Philiomena,* which we know was acted before the queen on January 3, 1584–85.[5]

The assumption that the tale of Felix and Felismena, in the form which it assumes in Montemayor's romance, is the

[3] *Diana* (with a second part by A. Perez and also a continuation entitled *Enamoured Diana* by G. Gil Polo), translated out of Spanish by B. Yong. E. Bollifant: Imprensis G. B., London, 1598.

[4] *Le Diane* de G. de Montemayor. Divisée en trois parties . . . e traduites d'Espagnol en François (Pt. I by N. Colon, Pts. II and III by G. Chapuis.

[5] Feuillerat, Albert, *Documents relating to the office of the Revels in the Time of Queen Elizabeth,* p. 365. Bangs, *Materialien,* Vol. XXI.

sole source for the central story in *The Two Gentlemen of Verona* has led to two sorts of rather extreme views about this comedy. The first is that of Bond, part of which I have quoted above. He believes that Shakespeare is practically the inventor of most of the distinctive comic traits of this play and therefore of Elizabethan romantic comedy. It is undoubtedly true that the part played by Shakespeare in giving to this type of play its poetry and imaginative reach cannot be overestimated; yet the essential nature of this aspect of his genius and the interesting course of its development have been partially obscured by the belief that romantic comedy as a type sprang full-grown from his brain.

Professor George P. Baker's critical opinion of this play, which is based on the same notion of its inception and growth, is quite different from that of Bond. He assumes that the entire comedy, with the exception of the Proteus-Julia story, is Shakespeare's invention and so to be studied as evidence of his power to construct a complicated plot. Thus regarded *The Two Gentlemen of Verona* proves to be a weak and tentative effort. Shakespeare now recognizes the value of a complicated plot, Professor Baker believes, but he cannot develop with any firmness, the story that he has so constructed. He also realizes the need of creating suspense in his audience, but he does not know how to satisfy the suspense when once he has aroused it. Consequently the critic believes that the dénouement of the play is a "complete confession of dramatic ineptitude." [6]

These two somewhat contradictory views of the work, each one rather extreme, are at least partly the result of a narrow view of the origin of *The Two Gentlemen of Verona,* and of its relation to similar drama on the Continent, — particularly to that of Italy. There are, to be sure, other critics of the comedy who have recognized that parts of it other than the Proteus-Julia story smack of Italian ingenuity. Some scholars have pointed out certain definite Italian plays which Shakespeare may have had in mind when he composed this comedy. Sir

[6] Baker, George P., *The Development of Shakespeare as a Dramatist* (1907), p. 120.

Sidney Lee believes that the dramatist "had clearly studied *the pleasant and conceited comedy of Two Italian Gentlemen,* issued anonymously in London in 1584."[7] Klein asserts that Shakespeare took the elopement and double wooing from Parabosco's *Il Viluppo,* 1547,[8] a knowledge of which on Shakespeare's part would have been a kind of miracle. In 1817 Treck pointed out[9] a resemblance between *The Two Gentlemen of Verona* and a German drama called *Tragoedia von Julio,* published first in 1620 as one of the collection entitled *Englishe Comoedien und Tragoedien.*[10] Finally Max Koch has suggested[11] that the source of Shakespeare's play is a popular Italian comedy, *Flavio Tradito.* A scenario of this play is number five in Flaminio Scala's collection of scenarios of the *Commedia dell' Arte* published in 1611.

Resemblances certainly do exist between all of the Italianate comedies suggested by these learned critics and *The Two Gentlemen of Verona.* However, they occur, without exception, in situations which are commonplaces of Italian comedy as a type, both of the literary and popular sort. This form of drama, it will be remembered, possesses rigid conventionality of both plot and incidental device. Characters and situations recur indefinitely. This fact suggests the difficulty of finding the one Italianate play among those still extant which was the source of *The Two Gentlemen of Verona.* A search for time-worn commonplaces of Italian comedy in this drama, however, has convinced me that practically all its important structural elements are patterned after recurrent features of "Italian comedy."[12]

If this be true, certain general truths in regard to the inception of *The Two Gentlemen of Verona* become evident. If, for

[7] *A Life of William Shakespeare* (1922 edition), p. 107. This play is commonly assigned to Anthony Munday.

[8] *Geschichte des Dramas* (1866), IV. 785–791. Some of the similarities in detail are rather close.

[9] *Deutsches Theatre* (Berlin, 1817), I, xxiii–xxvii.

[10] It is possible that this drama may represent Henslowe's lost play, *Phillipo and Hewpolyta,* marked as old under date of July 9, 1594.

[11] *Shakespeare Jahrbuch* (1910), p. 10.

[12] For meaning of this term, see *"Love's Labour's Lost" Re-studied,* p. 26.

example, Shakespeare possessed a definite dramatic source for this comedy, such as the lost *Felix and Philiomena,* that must have been a thoroughly Italianate play. If, on the other hand, he had only a slender thread of story, such as that in Montemayor's *Diana,* upon which to build, he must have made all his additions to it from devices chosen from the wide-spread traditions of Italian comedy. In either case we shall have to recognize Shakespeare's contributions to the growth of romantic comedy, not in new forms of dramatic ingenuity, but in the emotional deepening of elements taken bodily from a drama which was at once comedy of intrigue and high complicated farce.

The plot structure of *The Two Gentlemen of Verona* is modelled on that of a typical Italian comedy. Ideally the play is a conflict between love and friendship illustrated by the love of two friends, Proteus and Valentine, for the same girl, Silvia. In the story Proteus, faithless to his friend, supersedes him in the favored position of suitor. Silvia's father prefers a third wooer, the foolish Thurio, a sort of braggart captain.[13] Eventually Proteus finds himself in danger of death, whence he is rescued by Valentine. Whereupon he repents, surrenders his claim to Silvia, and takes for his wife his first love Julia, who has followed him from Verona and served him in the disguise of a page. The various scenes in this double story are interrupted by intermezzi of verbal wit and horseplay carried on by two clowns, one intensely keen-witted and verbally adroit,—Speed; the other loutish and stupid,—Launce.

All of these elements are commonplaces of Italian comedy. Many of them appear in the play of Scala's collection mentioned above, *Flavio Tradito.* In this scenario Flavio, a Florentine gentleman, is in love with Isabella, the daughter of Dr. Gratiano. Oratio, his sworn friend, falls in love with the same girl. Thus is precipitated in the latter's mind a struggle like that of Proteus. The intellectual strife between love and friendship was a favorite

[13] *The Two Gentlemen of Verona,* V. iii. 15 ff.
Thurio: "How likes she my discourse?"
Proteus: "Ill when you talk of war. . . ."

theme of debate in all the bourgeois academies of Renaissance Italy; and this subject naturally became the intellectual substance of comedies composed by the cultivated members of the Gelosi troupe.[14] Isabella, like Silvia, has a third lover, the Capitano Spavento, who, like Thurio, is favored by her father, the Duke of Milan. This contest of the three rivals, two young men and one clown, invariably the father's favorite, for the hand of the *prima donna,* is a time-worn convention of Italian comedy. It is one of the commonest variations of the multiform love story which is a constant feature of both sorts of Italian comedy and particularly of the *Commedia dell' Arte.*[15]

Oratio in *Flavio Tradito,* renouncing the obligations of friendship, contrives to make Flavio believe that Silvia has been false to him, with the result that he abandons her.[16] Flavio learns of his friend's falseness through the craftiness of a servant, but bides his time for unmasking Oratio and exposing his treachery. His opportunity comes one day when the false friend is defeated in a duel and about to be slain. Flavio exhibits his unswerving friendship by rescuing him from this pressing danger. This generous act fills Oratio with so great remorse that he forthwith gives up Isabella to Oratio and consoles himself immediately with the ever willing Flaminia. Friendship thus triumphs, as it should in the soul of a Renaissance gentleman. However, Oratio, by quick thinking and equally quick acting, enables the comedy to close with the rigorously prescribed double marriage.

This dénouement is like that in *The Two Gentleman of Verona.* Valentine arrives in the nick of time to rescue Silvia from the unwelcome embraces of an outlaw, who proves to be the false Proteus. As soon as the mutual recognition takes place, Proteus immediately asks, and as immediately receives, forgiveness. Then follows a generous passing back and forth of the

14 See "*Love's Labour's Lost*" *Re-studied,* p. 25.

15 Two extant Italianate plays evidently known in some form to Shakespeare contain this feature. In *The Two Italian Gentlemen* there is presented the rivalry of Fortunio, Fedele and Captain Crackstone; in *Gl'Ingannati* that of Fabrizio, Flaminio and Gherardo. This is also an aspect of some of the comedies in Scala's Collection. In *Il Ritratto,* two old men and the Capitano seek the favor of the *Comédienne.*

16 Exactly the same situation appears in *The Two Italian Gentlemen.*

ladies without any regard for their wishes. This naturally seems to a modern critic like Professor Baker "complete dramatic ineptitude." To the author of this sort of Italianate comedy, it was the expected indisputable proof of the complete victory of friendship in its mortal struggle with love. Moreover it precipitated neatly the situation demanded for the proper ending of a *Commedia dell' Arte.* The *prima donna* and the *secunda donna* had each to be provided with a husband before the final curtain. Consequently when the author's attention had been largely devoted to his intrigue, the husbands were thrust upon the ladies almost *all' improviso,* utterly without psychological preparation for the author's beneficence.[17]

The larger features even of the Julia-Proteus plot are also conventions of the Italian drama. The male disguise of the girl was the authorized solution of a universal problem of stage realism. The scene of all the action in Italian comedy, both learned and professional, was a public place. But Italian customs of the cinquecento forbade the appearance of a respectable citizen's daughter on the street with the men.[18] If the girl, therefore, was to have any sort of extended speech with the men in these comedies, she had either to talk to them from a window or a balcony, or to assume some sort of male disguise. Consequently, all Renaissance comedy is filled with these two situations.

As the writers of the comedies became more skillful in giving their plots unity, they naturally wished the disguised girl to bear some intimate relation to the love intrigue. The disguise of page was hit upon as solving most successfully this problem of unity. A girl could most realistically impersonate a page and in this character she could naturally attach herself to one of the *amorosi.*

In at least three of Scala's collection of scenarios, the heroine

[17] Cf. also *The Two Italian Gentlemen.*

[18] R. Warwick Bond in his *Early Plays from the Italian* (Oxford: The Clarenden Press, 1911) quotes on page xxxix the following passage from Geraldi Cinthio's *Sulle Comedie* (p. 103): "Serva, messer Giulio, la comedia una certa religione che mai giovane vergine, o polzella, non viene a ragionare in iscena."

is disguised as a page. In two of these, *Il Ritratto* and *La Fortunata Isabella,* she follows her errant lover to a distant city where he has fallen in love with another girl. In *Il Ritratto,* written before 1578, Silvia follows her former lover, in this case the *capitano,* from Milan to Parma. There she assumes the name and guise of a page Lesbino and becomes the captain's servant. Act II, Scene XV, is a discussion, carried on by these former lovers, of the man's recent infatuation for *la Comédienne.* A significant sentence in the *scenario* reads, "She asks him if he has never loved before. The captain replies that he has loved at Milan a very beautiful young girl named Silvia."[19] A situation in *The Two Gentlemen of Verona* (Act IV, Scene V, ll. 75 ff.) between Julia and Proteus exactly similar to this one displays Julia in one of her most charming and wistful moments.

The girl who disguises as a page and takes service in that capacity with the lover is an equally common figure in the *commedia crudita.* Parabosco's *Il Viluppo,* 1547, Ceechi's *I Rivali,*[20] the same author's *Le Pellegrine,* 1567, and *Gl'Ingannati,*[21] written by the Intronate of Siena, are some of the best known of a large number of plays in which the heroine assumes some form of masculine disguise. In the two last mentioned she serves as the page of her lover. In *Gl'Ingannati,*[22] some version of which is now commonly supposed to be the source of the serious part of *Twelfth Night,*[23] Lelia disguises herself

[19] It is perhaps significant that one *amorosa* in each of these plays is called Silvia.

[20] Winnifred Smith in *The Commedia dell' Arte,* p. 98, note 56, says that this play and *Gl'Ingannati* are the best known of "innumerable written plays in which the heroine resorts to masculine disguise."

[21] Furness in the Variorum edition of *Twelfth Night* suggests that the Italian company led by Drusiano which played in London in 1577–78 (cf. "*Love's Labour's Lost*" Re-studied, p. 28) may have brought this popular play to England. This seems hardly probable.

[22] *Commedia dell' Arte* companies did sometimes play *Commedie erudite* in Italy, but practically never when touring abroad. The play was first performed in Siena in Carnival week of 1531 and printed first in 1537. The drama is undoubtedly the source for Bandello's novella of Nicuola and Lattanzio, which is Number XXXVI of *Le Novelle* in *Scrittori d'Italia,* Bari, 1911, Vol. I, Part. II, pp. 252 ff.

[23] A Latin version of the play called *Laelia* has sometimes been re-

as the page and takes service with her faithless lover Flaminio. In this disguise she carries on a conversation with Flaminio about his first love[24] even more like the scene in which Julia reproaches Proteus than the one from *Il Ritratto* mentioned above. Julia's grief-evoked "alas" and her subsequent swoon are paralleled in Lelia's actions when Flaminio urges her to press his suit upon Isabella.

> *Flam:* I will give Isabella to understand that I love Lelia no longer, rather that I hate her, and cannot bear to hear her named, and will pledge my faith never to go where she may be. Tell Isabella this as strongly as you can.
>
> *Lelia:* Oh, me.
> *Flam:* What has come over you? What do you feel?
> *Lelia:* Oh, Me.
> *Flam:* Lean on me. Have you any pain?
> *Lelia:* Suddenly. In the heart.[25]

These examples should be sufficient to show that all the structural points of similarity between the Proteus-Julia story and that of Felix and Felismena are commonplaces of Italian comedy. Indeed, one might pronounce them the most frequently recurrent features of that drama. Only the circumstances attendant upon the dropping of the love-letter and the conditions under which the disguised page overhears the serenade remain as evidence of a direct relationship between the plot of *The Two Gentlemen of Verona* and the story from the *Diana Enamorada*. To these details I shall recur later.

Still other conventions of Italian comedy appear in the play. Critics have remarked the large number of Petrarchan conceits and of the half-lyrical *tirades* on love and on the conflict between

---

garded as the direct source of Churchill, Geo. B., *Die lateinischen Universitäts-Dramen Englands in der Zeit Königen Elisabeth, Shakespeare Jahrbuch,* XXXIV (1898), 286.

[24] Act II, Scene i.

[25] Quoted from the translation of T. L. Peacock called *The Deceived* (*The Works* [London, 1875], III. 284). This situation between the *amorosa* and his abandoned and disguised mistress is indicated as a recurrent one by its appearance in collections of conceits written in dialogue form. There is one in the collection of Domenico Bruni, in which the man agrees with his former love, who is now disguised as his page, that his present lady is fairer and worthier than his first one. (Cf. Rasi, I. 521 ff.; also Smith, *The Commedia dell' Arte,* p. 90.)

love and friendship in which this drama abounds.[26] This curious mixture of sincere emotional exaltation and mere imaginative ingenuity, sometimes called Petrarchism, permeated the lyrical poetry of nearly every nation of Europe during the years of the sonneteering vogue. Shakespeare's non-dramatic works written about the same time as *The Two Gentlemen of Verona,*— *Venus and Adonis, The Rape of Lucrece* and *The Sonnets* are filled with this sort of lyrical decoration. Though widely diffused, in no drama of the time did it assume a form so close to that employed in *The Two Gentlemen of Verona* as in the love tirades contributed by Isabella Andreini to the *Commedia dell' Arte* as played by the Gelosi troupe.[27] Her letters,[28] a series of carefully wrought literary exercises, preserve these tirades in a form very like that which they must have assumed in the plays.[29] Here appear the subtle sentimentalities of the sonneteers expressed in a slightly inflated style. Here are the elaborate puns, the conventional love-laments and the fine-spun debates on the nature of love and on its distracting conflicts with friendship.

The vogue of this intellectual exercise was so wide-spread that verbal parallels between the *tirades* of Isabella, the *amorosa,* and the speeches of characters in *The Two Gentlemen of Verona* would not prove a direct relationship between the two. The significant fact is that the nature of the dramatic conversations about love in this play of Shakespeare's — the very essence of romantic comedy — is of exactly the same sort as the similar dialogue of the most highly developed form of *Commedia dell' Arte* that was composed in Shakespeare's time. The romantic story of *The Two Gentlemen of Verona,* then, and the dramatic form which it assumes are close reflections of the narratives of Italian comedy.

[26] For a list of such conceits cf. Bond, *op. cit.,* p. xxxi.

[27] Cf. *"Love's Labour's Lost" Re-studied,* p. 25.

[28] Andreini Isabella: *Lettere d'Isabella Andreini. Comica Gelosa, et academica intenta, nominata l'Accesa, Venetia,* 1607.

[29] As I have explained in my study of *Love's Labour's Lost,* certain fixed and typical speeches made by the characters were not left to the invention of the moment, but were carefully composed and committed to memory. The *tirades* of Francesco Andreini spoken in his rôle of Capitano Spavento (cf. *"Love's Labour's Lost" Re-studied,* p. 25) were also of this sort.

The fun provided by Speed and Launce in their *intermezzi* is of the essence of this comedy, particularly of the *Commedia dell' Arte*. The traditional view is that these clowns bear at least a general likeness to Lyly's pages. Courthope states definitely that they are modelled on the characters of Licio and Petulus in *Mydas*.[30] He also asserts that the dialogue between Launce and Speed, in which the latter gives a catalogue of his mistress's qualities and Launce makes a feebly witty comment upon each item,[31] is founded on a similar conversation between Licio and Petulus.[32] This latter fact seems highly probable, inasmuch as it is certain that Shakespeare when writing these early comedies imitated the dramatic style of Lyly.[33] In these encounters between Launce and Speed, however, Shakespeare develops and emphasizes the amusing contrast between the quick-witted rogue and the slow-minded rustic which he presented only tentatively in *Love's Labour's Lost*,[34] but which Lyly does not suggest. Even in the scene under discussion in which the conventional form of the dialogue obscures a little the firm outlines of Launce's character as established elsewhere in the play, his replies do not ever display the ingenuity of those habitual to Petulus. On the contrary, they are pretty consistently heavy-footed and stupid.

In the *Commedia dell' Arte,* however, by the end of the sixteenth century, this relationship had become one of its firmest traditions.[35] The books of dramaturgy laid down the conventions which had to be observed in conceiving and presenting these characters. Both Moth and Costard, and Speed and

[30] *A History of English Poetry* (London, 1903), IV. 89.

[31] *The Two Gentlemen of Verona,* Act III, Scene ii. 281 ff.

Speed: Item, She can wash and scour."

Launce: "A special virtue: for then she need not be washed and scoured."

[32] *Mydas,* Act II, Scene i.

Licio: "Well, she hath the tongue of a parrot."

Pet: "That's a leaden dagger in a velvet sheath, to have a blacke tongue in a fair mouth."

[33] *"Love's Labour's Lost" Re-studied,* p. 21.

[34] *Ibid.,* p. 35.

[35] *Ibid.,* pp. 34 ff., for the development of these two figures in the *Commedia dell' Arte.*

Launce conform closely to the types. The dramatic possibilities of the two contrasted clowns are naturally more thoroughly realized in the later play. There, also, the nationalization of the booby's stupidity has proceeded further, so that Launce seems a typical English country lout whose Italian origin is never obvious.

Launce's immortal dog, who gives occasion to much "unforced unageing humor" seems to be English to the core. Yet even he may have escaped from some Italian scenario. At least live animals of all sorts, particularly dogs, were often introduced upon the stage of the *Commedia dell' Arte* and very seldom elsewhere. I have not forgotten Balaam's ass and the boisterous comedy that he provoked in both French and English Miracle plays.[36] However, other live animals seem not to have found their way upon the English stage in his company; but the farcical atmosphere of the *Commedia dell' Arte* was very congenial to the incalculable improvisation in which animals might indulge. In Scala's collection they appeared frequently. In *La Caccia* we have the following extraordinary directions: "Enter Graziano with a live cock on his wrist for a sparrowhawk. Claudione with a cat on a leash. Burattino with an ape on a leash."[37] Among the properties required for another one of Scala's scenarios were "a live cat, a live cock and four hunting dogs." Occasionally live animals are introduced into a *Commedia erudita,* where they obviously harmonize less naturally with the comic temper of the play. In Luigi Grotto's *Il Tesoro* (1590), for example, when the old woman Donnola goes to consult a lawyer, she is informed that he is conferring with the gentlemen. Upon being admitted she finds him playing with two kittens which are on his lap.

In the dialogue on scenic performances composed by Leone de Sommi, and referred to above,[38] one of the directions given

[36] Prof. Gayley remarks that "Once the donkey thrust his head within the church door, liturgy and drama were lost in the stupor of his ears or the bathos of his braying." — *Plays of Our Forefathers* (N. Y., 1901), p. 33.

[37] Giorn., 36: "Graziano che viene con un gallo vivo in pugno per sparviere, Claudione con una gatta alla lassa, Burattino con una scimmia alla lassa."

[38] P. 34.

to actors is the following: "If the poet brings in a cowherd, let him wear rustic clothes that he may appear peasantlike — and it adds much pleasure if the shepherd have with him at times one or more dogs, so also would it please me if the nymphs, too, had some, but gentler with pretty collars and delicate little coats."

The rustic or stupid clown in Italian comedy, if he follows the authoritative directions of Leone di Sommi, would as often as possible bring his live dog with him. Launce, inheriting the rôle of this Italian figure, inherited his cur also and brought the beast with him into *The Two Gentlemen of Verona,* to the delight of every reader of Shakespeare's comedy.

These parallels between essential situations and mere incidental comic devices of *The Two Gentlemen of Verona* and Italian comedy show with reasonable certainty that Shakespeare's source was some thoroughly Italianate play. If that was by chance the lost *Felix and Philiomena,* we may assume that this drama was a conventional Italian comedy into which some of the details of the Spanish story had been inserted to give the play its distinctive features.[39] In these Italian plays, particularly in the *Commedia dell' Arte,* it was the new or unusual element in its which determined its title. That was obviously the thing to advertise. This method of naming comedies was that employed by Menander [40] and by authors of every sort of so-called "new comedy." Indeed, this is the inevitable method of choosing titles for plays in any sort of drama in which the stable, unchanging element was as large as it was in most forms of Italian comedy.

By being thus able to assume that this *Felix and Philiomena,* or whatever the play that served as the source of *The Two Gentlemen of Verona,* supplied Shakespeare with many more

[39] The writers of scenarios took plot material avidly from every sort of available source and naturally often from novella and romance. Sometimes, to be sure, the borrowing was in the opposite direction, from the play to the novella. For the purpose of this argument the exact history of this relationship does not need to be determined.

[40] Cf. Post, C. R., *The Dramatic Art of Menander, Harvard Studies in Classical Philology,* XXIV. 116.

elements of his comedy than has hitherto been suspected, we are able to revise the traditional opinion in regard to Shakespeare's contribution to the development of Elizabethan romantic comedy. He can no longer be regarded as having invented the type in all of its distinctive features. Nor can he be regarded as an experimenter attempting to graft foreign material upon a slender romantic story and producing an ill-constructed play.

His method must be conceived, rather, as much more nearly analogous to that which he applied to the development of other types, such as Senecan tragedy and Chronicle history. He found in his source his plot in all its constructive elements, and he found there many of the type-figures needed to animate it ready to his hand. This perfectly conventional material occasionally appears in *The Two Gentlemen of Verona* in its original stiff caricature of reality, as in the hurried dénouement. Usually it is made to assume new forms of authentic life through Shakespeare's creative sympathy with youthful emotion, particularly in the soul of the woman. This interest expressing itself in dramatic form completely changed the spirit of Italian comedy. It released the love story from its bondage to the intrigue and gave it the central point of interest through its revelation of the beauty and the poetry of youthful love. The result was a comedy, new in kind, which was to develop into one of the most characteristic manifestations of Elizabethan art.

The formative influence of Italian comedy upon *Love's Labour's Lost* and *The Two Gentlemen of Verona,* which these two essays have tried to reveal, is but an example of its effect upon much of Shakespeare's early work in comedy. To a study of its influence upon *The Taming of the Shrew, The Comedy of Errors* and *The Merry Wives of Windsor,* I shall turn in the near future.

SHAKESPEARIAN PUNCTUATION

SHAKESPEARIAN PUNCTUATION

CHARLES C. FRIES

EDITORS of the text of Shakespeare have hitherto cast aside as utterly worthless the punctuation of the early Quartos and of the 1623 Folio. The usual attitude has been that expressed by the editors of the Cambridge edition of 1894–1895,

> . . . in many places, we may almost say that a complete want of points would mislead us less than the punctuation of the Folios. The consequence is that our punctuation is very little dependent upon the Folios and Quartos, but generally follows the practice which has taken possession of the text of Shakespeare, under the arrangement of the best editors, from Pope to Dyce and Staunton.[1]

And the principle underlying this practice could almost be summed up in the words of Dr. Samuel Johnson,

> In restoring the author's (Shakespeare's) works to their integrity, I have considered the punctuation as wholly in my power. . . .[2]

On the other hand, the editors of the new *Cambridge Shakespeare* (1921–), Sir Arthur Quiller-Couch and Mr. John Dover Wilson, in their "attempt . . . at a complete recension of Shakespeare's text"[3] have daringly adopted a punctuation of their own which aims "to translate into symbols convenient to the modern eye"[4] the pointing of the 1623 Folio. This revolutionary point of view cannot help arousing discussion with the appearance of each volume of the new edition,[5] and a question-

[1] Preface, p. xxi.

[2] *Preface to Shakespeare, The Works of Samuel Johnson* (Oxford, 1825), 5. 148.

[3] *The Tempest, General Introduction,* p. vii.

[4] *Ibid., A Note on Punctuation,* p. lvii.

[5] *The Tempest* and *The Two Gentlemen of Verona* appeared in 1921; *Merry Wives of Windsor,* in 1922; *Much Ado About Nothing,* in 1923.

ing of the grounds upon which the practice of two centuries has been repudiated.

The statements of the new theory of the reliability of the punctuation of the Folio and the early Quartos and the evidence upon which it rests are contained in a number of articles published during the last twenty-five years.[6] In the views of those who have argued for the new theory there seems to be considerable diversity.

The suggestions of the first two, Mr. Wyndham and Mr. Thistelton, substantially agree. The substance of their view is as follows:

(*a*) There is an order and system, not chaos, in the punctuation of the early Quartos and the 1623 Folio;

(*b*) There are two possible principles of punctuation: one based upon elocution, indicating pauses for delivery; the other

[6] The most important contributions to the discussion of Shakespearian punctuation are the following:

George Wyndham, *The Poems of Shakespeare* (1898), Notes on the Sonnets, pp. 265–268.

A. E. Thistelton, *Textual Notes on Measure for Measure* (1901), pp. 43–46.

———, *Textual Notes on Cymbeline* (1902), pp. 52–56.

———, *Textual Notes on A Midsummer Night's Dream* (1903), pp. 80–87.

Percy Simpson, *Shakespearian Punctuation* (1911).

A. W. Pollard, *Shakespeare's Fight with the Pirates, . . .* (1917), pp. 91–97.

———, 2d edition (1920), *Introduction*, pp. xv–xxi.

———, Introduction to *A New Shakespeare Quarto, the Tragedy of King Richard II, printed for the third time by Valentine Simmes in 1598*, edited by William A. White (1916).

Sir Edward Sullivan, *Punctuation in Shakespeare* (1921), *The Nineteenth Century*, 90. pp. 995–1006.

John Dover Wilson, *The Tempest* (1921), Textual Introduction, and a Note on Punctuation, pp. xxxvii, lvii.

William Poel, *Shakespeare's Prompt Copies* (1921), *London Times Literary Supplement*, Feb. 3, 1921, pp. 75, 76.

Sir Sidney Lee, *A Life of Shakespeare* (1922), Preface, pp. xiii–xvi.

Percy Simpson (A letter replying to the objections offered by Sir Sidney Lee), *London Times Literary Supplement*, July 13, 1922, p. 476.

As this paper was going through the press there appeared in the *Publications of the Modern Language Association* (XXXIX. 555–580) an article by the late Professor Raymond M. Alden, entitled *The Punctuation of Shakespeare's Printers*. Professor Alden examines with care the claims of the "elocutionary theory" in the light of the actual practice of the Folio and the early Quartos and concludes that the case for the new theory, so far as the evidence goes, has not as yet been proved.

based upon construction to distinguish structural additions to the sentence;

(*c*) In Shakespeare's work *both* principles are employed. The stops mark the syntax but they also frequently indicate elocutionary pauses unrelated to syntax. In the somewhat unsettled punctuation of the times the two principles seem to be striving for mastery.

The next four, Mr. Percy Simpson, Mr. A. W. Pollard, Sir Edward Sullivan, and Mr. John Dover Wilson, accord with the view just given in respect to denying the chaos and affirming the soundness and reasonableness of the punctuation of the Folio and the early Quartos. They differ, however, in objecting to the essential relation of the grammar and the syntax to the punctuation and insist upon the rhythmical or elocutionary principle as *the* guide to its interpretation. Even with these men there is considerable diversity between the cautious statement of Mr. Pollard,

> In Shakespeare's day . . . all the four stops, comma, semicolon, colon, and full stop, could be, and (on occasion) were, used simply and solely to denote pauses of different length irrespective of grammar and syntax. . . .[7]

and the unconditional assertion of Mr. John Dover Wilson, that

> . . . this punctuation is dramatic . . . a question of pause, emphasis and intonation; and is quite independent of syntax. . . . The stops, brackets, capital letters in the Folio and the Quartos are in fact stage directions, in shorthand. They tell the actor when to pause and for how long, they guide his intonation, they indicate the emphatic word, often enough they denote stage business.[8]

Among those who have supported this view of dramatic punctuation there seems to be fairly general agreement that the punctuation of the Folio and the early Quartos reproduces with substantial fidelity the pointing of Shakespeare's manuscript. In this respect even Mr. Pollard becomes so enthusiastic for the rhythmic effect of certain marks of punctuation that he feels that the " colons and commas [of one set speech of Richard

[7] A. W. Pollard, *Shakespeare's Fight with the Pirates* (1917), p. 92.
[8] John Dover Wilson, *The Tempest,* pp. lvii, xxxvii.

II] take us straight into the room in which *Richard II* was written and we look over Shakespeare's shoulder as he penned it."[9] A more cautious statement of the significance attached to the new theory comes from Sir Edward Sullivan,

> . . . there is thus a high probability that the long derided punctuation of the First Folio gives us a very fair idea of how Shakespeare's lines were being spoken within a few years of his death by actors who had been, directly or indirectly, in close touch with him.[10]

In support of this very interesting theory that Shakespeare by means of punctuation in his manuscript endeavored to instruct actors in the elocutionary or dramatic delivery of his lines there is offered very little tangible evidence; nothing, indeed, except a rather large number of instances given by Mr. Thistelton to fit his "rules," and by Mr. Simpson in forty-two roughly classified groups. Of the other men, Sir Edward Sullivan and Mr. Pollard also set forth and analyze a few additional instances of noteworthy "elocutionary" pointing. No attention is paid to instances which do not fit the classifications or the theory proposed.[11] One ought also to remark in passing that, although Mr. Simpson is attempting to prove by his accumulation of instances that the Shakespearian punctuation was based upon rhythmical rather than grammatical or logical considerations, of the forty-two classes in which these instances are grouped, at least eighteen are formed on the basis of the grammar of the sentence and seven others have a logical basis. No more than twelve of the classes given seem to rest on rhythmical or logical considerations.[12] So far as I am aware, such instances

[9] A. W. Pollard, *Shakespeare's Fight, etc.* (2d edition, 1920), p. xxi.

[10] Sir Edward Sullivan, *Punctuation in Shakespeare, Nineteenth Century,* 1921, p. 998.

[11] Mr. Simpson seems to consider this system of punctuation so flexible that no *negative* instances are possible. See his reply to Sir Sidney Lee, *London Times Lit. Suppl.,* July 13, 1922, p. 476.

[12] The following classes seem to rest on grammatical considerations. I give the numbers and titles as they appear in Mr. Simpson's book:

2. Vocative followed, but not preceded by a comma.
10. Comma marking logical subject.
11. Comma marking off adverbial phrase and clause.
14. Comma before a noun clause.

constitute the whole of the evidence upon which the case for the theory of elocutionary and dramatic punctuation rests.

On the other hand, both Mr. William Poel and Sir Sidney Lee present a negative argument of three objections:

---

15. Comma before the defining relative.
22. Comma with inversion.
23. Relative followed by a comma.
24. Comma marking ellipse of copula.
25. Comma marking the omission of the relative.
27. Semicolon with preliminary clauses.
34. Colon introducing reported speech, etc.
12. Comma between accusative and dative.
13. Comma between object and complement.
39. Brackets "mark off words, phrases, or clauses which interrupt the direct grammatical construction."

The following classes rest on grammatical considerations, but differ from those above in having no marks of punctuation:

3. Vocative without comma.
4. Imperative without comma.
5. Appositional phrase without comma.
41. Absence of punctuation to mark an interruption.

The following are the classes referred to above as having a logical basis for the grouping:

8. Comma equivalent to a dash.
16. Comma before "as."
17. Comma before "but" (= "except").
18. Comma before "than."
19. Comma before "and," with no comma after.
20. Comma before "or" and "nor," with no comma afte
21. Comma before "not," with no comma after.

The following classes accord more or less with a rhythmical basis for the grouping:

1. Light stopping.
6. Comma marking a metrical pause.
7. The emphasizing comma.
9. Comma marking interrupted speech.
28. Semicolon marking interrupted speech.
29. The emphasizing semicolon.
31. Colon marking an emphatic pause.
32. Colon marking an interrupted speech.
33. Antithetic colon.
35. The full stop in an incomplete sentence.
36. Full stop ending an interrupted speech.
38. The metrical hyphen.

(*a*) The avowed practice of actors is and has been against the usefulness of such punctuation in the manuscript of an author.[13]

(*b*) The punctuation of the Folio and the Quartos when followed in accord with this elocutionary theory often indicates a word as the key-word of a passage which is impossible in the light of the whole context.[14]

(*c*) It is unlikely that such a system of punctuation could have been employed by Shakespeare with no knowledge or mention of it among contemporaries.[15]

In support of these negative contentions the evidence offered is also exceedingly meager.

From this discussion of Shakespeare's punctuation three questions arise upon which it seems possible to offer some definitely objective evidence:

[13] William Poel, *Shakespeare's "Prompt Copies," London Times, Literary Suppl.*, Feb. 3, 1921, pp. 75, 76.

Mr. Poel quotes two actors' opinions:

Coquelin: "When I have to create a part, I begin reading the play with the greatest attention five or six times."

———: "I pay no attention to punctuation, because this would impede the natural movement of the voice from expressing the various shades of thought and feeling which are indicated by the sliding of the voice up and down."

———: "Before a passage can be tuned, the key-word to its meaning must be found. Find that and bring it out forcibly, and the other words will take care of themselves."

Talma: "The hunting for the key-word gives you the eyes of a lynx in searching all the corners of the sentence, and compels you to study closely the thought of the author and to weigh all his words."

[14] Mr. Poel objects to the illustration Mr. Pollard offers as an excellent example of rhythmical pointing in these words: "If, like Coquelin, Mr. Pollard had read the scene over, in which the quotation appears, five or six times, he might then, perhaps, have discovered a more suitable key-word than the one he thinks Shakespeare has indicated. . . . The scene does not deal with the question of Mowbray's treasons, but with that of who is the traitor, Bolingbroke or Mowbray. If so, the colon after the word 'treasons' has no elocutionary value."

[15] Sir Sidney Lee rests this contention on the ground that "Jonson, who was as well acquainted with the technique of the drama and the customs of the stage as any contemporary, knew nothing of any 'rhetorical' or 'elocutionary' mode of Elizabethan or Jacobean punctuation, which should convey to actors the dramatist's conception of emphasis." And he refers to the treatment of punctuation in Jonson's *Grammar* as evidence.

(1) Was there an *accepted system* of punctuation at the end of the sixteenth and the beginning of the seventeenth century?

(2) What connection existed between the marks of punctuation used and the structure and syntax of the sentence, and between the punctuation and oral reading?

(3) In what respects does the use of punctuation in the sixteenth and seventeenth centuries differ from the modern theory of punctuation?

Upon these questions a search of the grammars, rhetorics, and books to teach reading and speaking, published during the late sixteenth and early seventeenth centuries, yields some facts worthy of consideration.

On mere a priori grounds it would seem necessary that whenever or wherever punctuation is generally used in printed texts there must exist something of an accepted or general interpretation of its use. A peculiarly individual system of pointing without a key could have no meaning for others than the author. It seems very difficult indeed, therefore, to accept Mr. John Dover Wilson's assertion, " Punctuation, spelling, and the use of capitals were, in Shakespeare's day, personal matters, subject solely to the individual practice of a particular author,"[16] or to reconcile such a view with either of the two theories of punctuation, even that which insists that Shakespeare used his punctuation to convey stage directions or delivery hints to readers of his lines.

Against the idea of a generally *accepted system* of Elizabethan punctuation, however, and in harmony with Mr. Wilson's assertion, might be urged (1) the silence of a number of the books of grammar, rhetoric, and the art of reading, in which we should expect to find the subject of punctuation treated,[17] and (2) the

[16] John Dover Wilson and A. W. Pollard, *The " Stolne and Surreptitious" Shakespearian Texts, London Times Literary Suppl.,* Jan. 16, 1919, p. 30.

[17] The following books contain no statement of the use of punctuation:
Thomas Smith, *De recta & emendata Linguae Anglicae Scriptione,* 1568.
J. B. Gen. Ca., *Le Maistre d'Escole Anglois,* 1580.
W. Bullokar, *Bullokars Booke at large, for the Amendment of Orthographie for English speech,* 1580.
———, *Bref Grammar,* 1586.

fact that printers even as late as the eighteenth century regarded punctuation as a matter of so little consequence that neither the " Corrector " nor the " Compositor " was expected to refrain from " changing and thrusting in Points, capitals, or anything else that has nothing but fancy and humour for its authority and foundation."[18]

On the other hand not only does Shakespeare himself mention

P. Gr., *Grammatica Anglicana,* 1594.
George Mason, *Grammaire Angloise,* 1622.
John Wallis, *Grammatica Linguae Anglicanae,* 1653.

Nor does any mention of punctuation appear in
Thomas Wilson, *The Arte of Rhetoryke,* 1553.
Leonard Cox, *The Arte or Crafte of Rhethoryke,* 1532.

[18] P. Luckombe, *The History and Art of Printing,* 1771, p. 441:

" But where a Corrector understands the language and characters of a work, he often finds occasion to alter and to mend things that he can maintain to be either wrong or else ill digested. If therefore a Corrector suspects Copy to want revising, he is not to postpone it, but to make his emendations in the Manuscript before it is wanted by the Compositor, that he may not be hindered in the pursuit of his business; or prejudiced by alterations in the proof, especially if they are of no real signification; such as far-fetched spelling of Words, changing and thrusting in Points, Capitals, or any thing else that has nothing but fancy and humour for its authority and foundation."

Ibid., p. 263: " 'Tis true, that the expectation of a settled Punctuation is in vain, since no rules of prevailing authority have yet been established for that purpose; which is the reason that so many take the liberty of criticizing upon that head; yet when we compare the rules which very able Grammarians have laid down about Pointing, the difference is not very material; and it appears, that it is only a maxim with humourous Pedants, to make a clamour about the quality of a Point; who would even make an Erratum of a Comma which they fancy to bear the pause of a Semicolon, were the Printer to give way to such pretended accuracies. . . . It must be allowed, that all Matter is not pointed alike; for some require more stops than others. Thus, Historical and Narrative subjects do not take up so many points as Explanatory Matter; and that, again, not so many as English Statute Law —— But, happy! that Mispointing is not of the same consequence with Misnomer; otherwise, Where would be the end of Law-quibbles!

" It must likewise be owned, that every Compositor is not alike versed in pointing; and therefore such as are dubious whether they can maintain their notion of Pointing, ought to submit to the method, or even humour, of Authors, and authorized Correctors, rather than give them room to exclaim about spoiling the sense of the subject, because the Points are not put their right way. . . ."

punctuation and use pointing as a source of humor,[19] but a definite treatment of the uses of punctuation does appear in each of the following:

George Puttenham, *The Arte of English Poesie,* 1589.
Alexander Gil, *Logonomia Anglica,* 1619, 1621.
Charls Butler, *The English Grammar,* 1633.
Ben Jonson, *The English Grammar* (written before 1637).
Simon Daines, *Orthoepia Anglicana,* 1640.

The character of the discussions in these five books (set forth below, pages 76–79) with their points of similarity provides fairly safe ground for the conclusion that there was in the late sixteenth and early seventeenth centuries something of a *generally accepted system* of punctuation. The attitude of the printers, however, and the silence of some grammarians, or rather the few statements of the uses of punctuation which appear, point to two equally important provisions: that this system must have been loosely and somewhat variously applied and considered of rather small importance; and that the pointing of any printed book of this period cannot be assumed to be the author's without definite and unmistakable evidence.

II

That punctuation should serve as a guide to oral reading and indicate to the eye places of pause has been true throughout its history. Books and teachers of reading have all emphasized and still do insist that a reader should observe the pauses indicated by the commas and periods; that he should sustain the tone of his voice at the former but drop it at the latter. Many have objected to the system of punctuation as an inadequate guide to the pauses of oral reading, but throughout the last three centuries practically all agree that the two are essentially related.[20]

[19] See examples given below, pages 81–82.

[20] J. F. Genung, *The Working Principles of Rhetoric* (1900), p. 333: " By way of premise it should be borne in mind that, well furnished as it is, the existing scale of punctuation is by no means a complete represen-

The question at issue in this discussion of punctuation is whether the pauses indicated by the punctuation have been placed as dictated by the syntax and structure of the sentences or whether they are dramatic pauses indicating elocutionary emphasis and placed with no relation to structural divisions. On this question we have as evidence, first of all, the five summaries of the practice of the times listed above (page 75) — all by contemporaries of Shakespeare. The most important parts of these summaries of the uses of the four marks indicating pause are the following.

George Puttenham, *The Arte of English Poesie,* 1589:

" it is therefore requisit that leasure be taken in pronuntiation, such as may make our wordes plaine & most audible and agreable to the eare; also the breath asketh to be now and then releeued with some pause or stay more or lesse; besides that the very nature of speach (because it goeth by clauses of seuerall construction & sence) requireth some space betwixt them with intermission of sound, to th'end they may not huddle one vpon another so rudly & so fast that th'eare may not perceiue their difference. For these respectes the auncient reformers of language inuented three maner of pauses, one of the lesse leasure then another, and such seuerall intermissions of sound to serue (besides easment to the breath) for a treble distinction of sentences or parts of speach, as they happened to be more or lesse perfect in sence. The shortest pause or intermission they called *comma,* as who would say a peece of a speach cut out of. The second they called *colon,* not a peece, but as it were a member for his larger length, because it occupied twise as much time as the *comma.* The third they called *periodus,* for a complement or full pause, and as a resting place and perfection of so much former speach as had bene vterred, and from whence they needed not to passe any further, vnless it were to renew more matter to enlarge the tale. . . . I will say no more in it then thus, that they be vsed for a commodious and sensible distinction of clauses in prose, since euery verse is as it were a clause of it selfe, and limited with a *Cesure* howsoeuer the sence beare, perfect or imperfect, which difference is obseruable betwixt the prose and the meeter." [21]

---

tation of the pauses actually made in speaking or reading aloud. In every sentence there are rhetorical pauses that go unmarked and need no marking; they make themselves. And the more lucid and well organized the sentence, the more safely these pauses may be left to the reader. In a well-written passage the syntax dictates the place of the stops, and is not dependent on them. When a pause has to be lugged in to bolster up the construction, and above all when without the pause it would be left ambiguous or uncertain, the sentence itself is wrong, — it needs amendment."

[21] Book II. iv (v), pp. 77–80.

Alexander Gil, *Logonomia Anglica,* 1619, 1621:

"Accentui inseruiunt interpunctiones: quia illae ut sensũ aperiunt, ita quantũ possunt accentui viam sternunt. Eaedē sunt nobis quae Latinis, & usus idem: sunt autem κόμμα siue incisum (,), ποδιαστολή aut subdistinctio (;), κῶλον siue membrum (:) περίοδος siue sententiae & sensus. integra complexio (.)" [22]

Charls Butler, *The English Grammar,* 1634:

(The *special* symbols of Butler's phonetic spelling are here changed to the usual letters of normal spelling.)

"Points serving for the better understanding of Woords ar either Primari, or Secondari.

"Primari Points, which shew their Ton', Sound, and Pauses, ar eight: 4 simple and mor' common; Period, (.) Colon, (:) Semicolon, (;) Comma; (,) and 4 mixt and les freqent.

"Period is a point of perfect sens, and perfect sentenc': which, in the last woord, falleth the Ton' of the voic' below its ordinari tenour, with a long paus.

"Colon is a point of perfect sens, but not of perfect sentenc': which falleth the Ton' of the voic', with a shorter paus.

"Colon beeing a point of imperfect sentenc', the part following soomtim' dooth perfect the sam' . . . soomtim' it on'ly maketh perfect sens; (as the former part) but dooth not perfect the sentenc': so that ther' may bee many Colons in on' Period: . . . But wher' such perfect members ar both many and short; Semicolon dooth wel suppli' the Colons room': . . . And wher' they go' by par's, answering on' an other; . . . every second member is noted with a Semicolon, and every first with a Comma; . . .

"Semicolon is a point of imperfect sens, in the midle of a Colon, or Period: commonly, when it is a compound axiom; whos' parts ar joyned together, by a dubble, and soomtim' by a single, conjunction: . . . and it continueth the tenour or ton' of the voic' to the last woord, with a Colon-paus: . . .

"Comma is a point of mor' imperfect sens, in a simple axiom, or in either part of a compound: which continueth the tenour of the voic' to the last, with the shortest paus.

"Many single woords, of the sam' sort, cooming together, ar distinguished by Commas: . . . But if they bee *antitheta* answering on' another; every second, for distinction of the par's, is fitly pointed with Semicolon." [23]

Ben Jonson, *The English Grammar* (written before 1637):

"For, whereas our breath is by nature so short, that we cannot continue without a stay to speak long together; it was thought necessary as well for the speaker's ease, as for the plainer deliverance of the things spoken,

[22] P. 135.
[23] Pp. 58, 59.

to invent this means, whereby men pausing a pretty while, the whole speech might never the worse be understood.

"These distinctions are either of a *perfect* or *imperfect sentence.* The distinctions of an imperfect sentence are two, a *subdistinction* and a *comma.* A *subdistinction* is a mean breathing, when the word serveth indifferently, both to the parts of the sentence going before and following after, and is marked thus (;).

"A *comma* is a distinction of an *imperfect* sentence, wherein with somewhat a longer breath, the sentence following is included; and is noted with this shorter semicircle (,). . . . The distinction of a *perfect* sentence hath a more full stay, and doth rest the spirit, which is a *pause* or a *period.*

"A *pause* is a distinction of a sentence, though perfect in itself, yet joined to another, being marked with two pricks (:).

"A *period* is the distinction of a sentence, in all respects *perfect,* and is marked with one full prick over against the lower part of the last letter, thus (.). . . . These distinctions (whereof the first is commonly neglected,) as they best agree with nature, so come they nearest to the ancient stays of sentences among the Romans and the Grecians." [24]

All four thus far quoted show remarkable agreement concerning the point at issue. One cannot mistake the basis of their theory of punctuation. The pauses, comma, semicolon, colon, and period, with their graded values are to be placed according to the "sense" or structure of the sentence, with a discrimination of a more or less "imperfect sense" or a "perfect sense." In the views expressed in these summaries, the placing of the marks of punctuation which indicate pause is to be determined upon a structural basis, with no hint of an elocutionary system.

The basis of the directions given by the fifth author, Simon Daines, seems at first somewhat less certain.[25] One cannot at

[24] Pp. 144–147.

[25] Simon Daines, *Orthoepia Anglicana,* 1640, pp. 69–74.

The full statement of the uses of these marks of punctuation as given by Daines follows:

". . . it onely remaines, that we say somewhat of the stops, or pauses, between sentence and sentence, for the more renable (as we call it) and distinct reading . . . the knowledge of these stops or points is no lesse conducible and hypothetically necessary to distinct and ready reading (the perfection of Orthoepie) than to Orthographie, or right writing: though I will not further inferre, knowing it so requisite to both.

"These stops therefore are by the Latines termed *Comma; Comma-colon; colon; periodus; Interrogatio; Parenthesis; Exclamatio; Apostrophe, sive contractionis nota, vel signum.*

"Their number (you see eight) their figure and use ensues.

"The *Comma* hath its place at the foot of the line, . . . The use onely once definitely conclude that he agrees with the others in making structure determine the stops, although the following statements do look in that direction:

This [the period] is altogether used at the end of every speech or sentence, as the name it selfe implies . . . and signifies *conclusion.*

It [the colon] is chiefly used in the division of sentences, and exacts halfe the pause of a Period.

The *Comma-colon* . . . to make some short deliberation as it were of little sentences, as the *Comma* doth of words.

Even the following remark concerning the comma,

---

in long sentences, in the most convenient places to make a small pause for the necessity of breathing; or in Rhetoricall speeches (where many other words are used to one effect) to make a kind of Emphasis and deliberation for the greater majesty or state of Elocution.

" The *Comma-colon,* as you see by the name, participates of both the *Comma* and the *Colon;* . . . This to the Ancients was not knowne; but now in no lesse use than estimation, especially among Rhetoricians. Who in their long winded sentences, and reduplications, have it as a constant pack-horse, to make some short deliberation as it were of little sentences, as the *Comma* doth of words; the time of pause about double that of the *Comma* generally, which yet is very small.

" The *Colon.* . . . It is chiefly used in the division of sentences and exacts halfe the pause of a *Period;* and halfe as much againe as a *Comma Colon.*

" The *Period.* . . . This is altogether used at the end of every speech or sentence, as the name itselfe implies (being derived from the Greek) and signifies *conclusion.* The pause or distance of speaking hereto appropriate is sometime more, sometime lesse: for . . . when in the middle of a line it cuts off any integrall part of a complete Tractate, which goes not on with the same, but begins a new line, it requireth double the time of pause, that it doth when the Treatise persists in the same line: being then foure times as long as a *Colon,* which in the same line is but twice.

" I remember my singing-Master taught me to keep time, by telling from 1, to 4, according to the nature of the time I was to keep, and I found the practice thereof much ease and certainty to me, till I was perfect in it. The same course I have used to my pupils in their reading, to inure them to the distinction of their pauses, and found it no lesse successefull."

One sentence from the example given to illustrate the use of the points follows. This sentence is the shortest one that contains all four points.

" Travellers, Merchants, Historiographers, report, assure, relate, partly what themselves have seen; partly what approved in their wofull companions, left to be entombed in the bellies of those monsters: while they themselves with much adoe escaped, onely to be the dolefull narratours of so sad a story."

The use onely in long sentences, in the most convenient places to make a small pause for the necessity of breathing; or in Rhetoricall speeches (where many other words are used to one effect) to make a kinde of Emphasis and deliberation for the greater majesty or state of Elocution,

which, indeed, comes nearest to the elocutionary-emphasis theory of punctuation, indicates the separation of words in a series "where many other words are used to one effect," a structural relation, as the peculiar function of this point. But when these statements of the uses of the points are completely analyzed and viewed in connection with the example "annexed [by Daines] to exemplifie further the use of the precedent Points in their severall kinds" there seems to be little doubt that this grammarian also would place the pauses on the basis of structural considerations.

Some significance attaches to the fact that all five grammarians refer to the use of these terms, *comma, colon,* and *period* in classical rhetorical theory. Indeed, Alexander Gil (1619) definitely insists, "Eaedē sunt nobis quae Latinis, & usus idem." In Aristotle, in Cicero, in Quintilian, these names refer not to punctuation but to parts of the sentence.[26] The *period* is a

[26] Aristotle, *Rhetoric,* III. 9. 4, 5, 6: δεῖ δὲ τὴν περίοδον καὶ τῇ διανοίᾳ τετελειῶσθαι, καὶ μὴ διακόπτεσθαι . . . . . περίοδος δὲ ἣ μὲν ἐν κώλοις ἣ δ' ἀφελής. ἔστι δ' ἐν κώλοις μὲν λέξις ἡ τετελειωμένη τε καὶ διῃρημένη καὶ εὐανάπνευστος, μὴ ἐν τῇ διαιρέσει ὥσπερ ἡ εἰρημένη περίοδος, ἀλλ' ὅλη. κῶλον δ' ἐστὶ τὸ ἕτερον μόριον ταύτης. ἀφελῆ δὲ λέγω τὴν μονόκωλον. δεῖ δὲ καὶ τὰ κῶλα καὶ τὰς περιόδους μήτε μυούρους εἶναι μήτε μακράς.

Cicero, *Orator,* 66. 222, 223 (referring to sentences just quoted): "Prima sunt illa duo, quae κόμματα Graeci vocant, nos *incisa* dicimus; deinde tertium κῶλον illi, nos *membrum;* sequitur non longa — ex duobus enim versibus, id est membris, perfecta comprehensio est et in spondios cadit."

Quintilian, *Institutionis Oratoriae,* IX. 4. 22. 122, 123: "At illa connexa series tres habet formas: incisa quae κόμματα dicuntur, membra quae κῶλα, περίοδον, quae est vel ambitus vel circumductum vel continuatio vel conclusio.

"Dicimus igitur esse incisa, membra, circuitus. Incisum (quantum mea fert opinio) erit sensus non expleto numero conclusus, plerisque pars membri. . . . Fiunt autem etiam singulis verbis incisa; *Diximus, testes dare volumus;* incisum est diximus. Membrum autem est sensus numeris conclusus, sed a toto corpore abruptus et per se nihil efficiens. . . . Quando ergo incipit corpus esse? cum venit extrema conclusio. . . . Itaque, fere incisa et membra mutila sunt et conclusionem utique desiderant. Periodo plurima nomina dat Cicero, *ambitum, circuitum, comprehensionem, continuationem, circumscriptionem.* Genera eius duo sunt, alterum simplex, cum sensus unus longiore ambitu circumducitur, alterum, quod constat membris et incisis, quae plures sensus habent."

complete sentence; the *colon* a member; the *comma*, a small part or phrase. Starting from this use in classical rhetoric these names for the parts of the sentence attached themselves to the particular points used to set them off. The word *period* thus not only means a sentence, but also the point (.) indicating its end; *colon* becomes the name of the " two pricks " (:) commonly used to separate the *cola* of a sentence; and *comma*, the name for the point (,) separating the *commata* or smaller parts of a sentence member. These names for the points thus indicate their earliest use, the separation of the structural parts of the sentence. That a structural basis should underlie the explanations of the uses of the marks of punctuation as set forth in the early grammars is thus to be expected, for these books depend upon classical grammar and rhetoric for their ideas and apparatus.

Although the practice of the times might easily not strictly conform to the theory of the grammarians (and very probably in any case only loosely conformed) it seems unlikely that that practice could have been consciously based upon another principle differing so fundamentally from that expressed in contemporary grammars and opposed to the early structural connection of the names employed.

If that were the case with Shakespeare we should at least expect his comments upon punctuation to accord with the principle of his practice. In the footnotes are given five instances from Shakespeare's plays and poems.[27] Of these, in *a* the word

[27]

a Timon of Athens, I. i. 39–50.

Poet: . . . My free drift
Halts not particularly, but moves itself
In a wide sea of wax. No levell'd malice
Infect one comma in the course I hold;
But flies an eagle flight, bold and forth on,
Leaving no tract behind.

b Hamlet, V. ii. 36–47.

Hamlet: . . . Wilt thou know
The effect of what I wrote?
Horatio: Ay, good my lord.
Hamlet: An earnest conjuration from the King,
As England was his faithful tributary,
As love between them as the palm should flourish,

comma is used in its original structural meaning of a short member of a sentence or period, a group of words less than a colon.

As Peace should still her wheaten garland wear
And stand a comma 'tween their amities,
And many such-like *as*-es of great charge,
That, on the view and know of these contents,
Without debatement further, more or less,
He should the bearers put to sudden death,
Not shriving time allow'd.

c *Midsummer Night's Dream,* V. i. 89–105.

Theseus: Where I have come, great clerks have purposed
To greet me with premeditated welcomes;
Where I have seen them shiver and look pale,
Make periods in the midst of sentences,
Throttle their practis'd accent in their fears,
And in conclusion dumbly have broke off,
Not paying me a welcome.

d *Lucrece,* 561–567.

Her pity-pleading eyes are sadly fixed
In the remorseless wrinkles of his face;
Her modest eloquence with sighs is mixed,
Which to her oratory adds more grace.
She puts the period often from his place;
And midst the sentence so her accent breaks,
That twice she doth begin ere once she speaks.

e *Midsummer Night's Dream,* V. i. 108–126.

Enter (Quince for) the Prologue.

Pro. If we offend, it is with our good will.
That you should think, we come not to offend,
But with good will. To show our simple skill,
That is the true beginning of our end.
Consider then we come but in despite.
We do not come as minding to content you,
Our true intent is. All for your delight
We are not here. That you should here repent you,
The actors are at hand, and by their show
You shall know all that you are like to know.

The. This fellow doth not stand upon points.

Lys. He hath rid his prologue like a rough colt; he knows not the stop. A good moral, my lord: it is not enough to speak, but to speak true.

Hip. Indeed he hath play'd on this prologue like a child on a recorder; a sound, but not in government.

The. His speech was like a tangled chain; nothing impaired, but all disordered.

The figurative use of a word *comma* in *b* seems to have no meaning in harmony with an elocutionary or stress principle of punctuation. In *c* and *d* the end of the sentence is recognized as the proper place for the period but under embarrassment or great emotional stress one may *break off* before the meaning is complete or make several false starts. Such " making a period in the midst of the sentence " seems to me to have structural significance rather than to be, as the elocutionary theory implies, the indication of a long pause of emphasis upon the word preceding the period. In *e* the humor of the mispointing and wrong pausing arises out of the changed meaning conveyed by the joining of wrong structural elements or the separation of essential parts of the sentences. If the punctuation here has significance only for stress and no relation to syntax and structure, the humor loses much of its point.

III

Those who support the elocutionary theory of Elizabethan punctuation insist that punctuation " has radically changed in the last three hundred years," in that (1) " modern punctuation is, or at any rate attempts to be, logical; the earlier system was mainly rhythmical," and (2) " modern punctuation is uniform; the old punctuation was quite the reverse . . . a flexible system . . . to express subtle differences of tone." [28] One who attempts to trace the development of our system of punctuation as that system is expressed in the grammars of the last three hundred years [29] receives an impression quite different from that

[28] Percy Simpson, *Shakespearian Punctuation* pp. 8, 10.

[29] In addition to the books referred to above, pages 73–75, the following texts were examined with considerable care:

C. Cooper, *Grammatica Linguae,* 1685, pp. 154–160.

J. Jones, *Practical Phonography,* 1701, pp. 141–144.

Anon. (Brightland) *English Grammar,* 1710, pp. 127 ff.

I. Watts, *The Art of Reading and Writing English* (6th ed., 1740), pp. 35 ff.

Robert Lowth, *A Short Introduction,* etc., 1762, pp. 177–193.

Thomas Sheridan, A *Prosodial Grammar* (prefixed to dictionary), 1780, pp. li–lv.

of these assertions. In all the grammars examined, dated from 1589 to 1900, the structural basis of placing the points of punctuation appears without exception. Changes during the last three hundred years have not shown themselves in the underlying general principles of the uses of the stops. Lindley Murray's general statement of the use of the comma,

> The Comma usually separates those parts of a sentence, which, though very closely connected in sense and construction, require a pause between them [30]

closely parallels that of Charls Butler (of 1634),

> Comma is a point of mor' imperfect sens, in a simple axiom, or in either part of a compound: which continueth the tenour of the voic' to the last, with the shortest paus

and that of J. F. Genung in 1900,

> *The Comma.* Just as the semicolon is the mark of the added clause, with its clear though appreciably remote logical relation, the comma is the mark of the closer dependent clause . . . and of the phrase or the word that does duty *as* a phrase. It is still a mark of separation, but not enough, ordinarily to break into the grammatical continuity of the passage.[31]

The difference in treatment from that of the early seventeenth century, however, shows itself in Lindley Murray's twenty specific rules for the comma in which he attempts to indicate very definitely all the applications of the general statement he first gives. If the grammars can be trusted as evidence, the development of our punctuation has not resulted in a changed

---

Anon. (Thomas Dodson), *Comprehensive Grammar,* 1780, pp. 155–173.
Ralph Harrison, *Rudiments of English Grammar,* 1783, pp. 67–78.
Charles Coote, *Elements of the Grammar of the English Language,* 1788, pp. 260–267.
Noah Webster, *An American Selection of Lessons in Reading and Speaking* (9th ed., 1794), pp. 3 ff.
———, *A Philosophical and Practical Grammar,* pp. 214–220.
William Hazlitt, *A New and Improved Grammar* 1810, pp. 145–148.
John Walker, *Rhetorical Grammar,* 1814, pp. 50–77.
Lindley Murray, *English Grammar* (1795, 5th ed., 1824), pp. 392–415.
A number of later 19th century texts were also examined, but with much less care.

[30] Lindley Murray, *English Grammar,* p. 392.

[31] J. F. Genung, *The Working Principles of Rhetoric,* 1900, p. 328.

basis or *theory* of its use, but rather in this attempt to make more definite and regular the application of the points in matters of detail. This particular tendency appears to have reached its highest point at the end of the eighteenth century and during the first half of the nineteenth. The best modern practice, according to Professor Genung,[32] probably tends to a much more flexible, artistic use of punctuation, more open to the individualities of style.

These facts in the history of punctuation have some significance for our immediate problem. If Elizabethan punctuation is based on the structure of the sentence, then it is directly in line both with the meanings of the names, comma, colon, and period, as these were used in classical rhetoric and with the theory of punctuation expressed in the grammars from 1589 to 1900. If, on the other hand, Elizabethan punctuation is based on elocutionary emphasis unrelated to syntax and structure, then there must be found some means to account for the development of that elocutionary principle out of the earlier structural applications of the names, comma, colon, and period, in classical rhetoric, and for the later progress from that elocutionary principle back to structural considerations after the Elizabethan era.

From the materials here presented one cannot by any means insist that an elocutionary system of Shakespearian punctuation is impossible. But when they are all gathered in a single view it seems much more reasonable to conclude that we have in Elizabethan books a structural punctuation, in line both with the modern principle of punctuation and with the earlier history

[32] *Op. cit.,* pp. 333, 334: "The modern tendency is to reduce punctuation: cutting down semicoloned relations, where possible, to the comma, and leaving many of the comma pauses to the unmarked rhetorical pause. . . . With this general reduction of punctuation the field is left clearer for special effects. Accordingly we find that in modern writing punctuation is a much more flexible thing, and more open to individualities of style, than was formerly the case. It may for greater stress be augmented,—that is, pushed up from comma to semicolon; it may also be attenuated for greater rapidity. It is this skilful employment of punctuation as a flexible, living, artistic thing which makes it so truly a cardinal factor in the organism of the sentence."

of the names for the points used.[33] One must add, however, that this early structural punctuation, especially that in the Quartos and the Folio, was much more loosely and variously applied than modern punctuation and represents so much possibility of printers' interference that it can have very slight value for our interpretation of Shakespeare.

[33] Not only is the elocution-emphasis theory of punctuation applied to the use of the stops but frequently also to the use of capital letters. Mr. Simpson's statement (*Shakespearian Punctuation,* p. 103) is typical: "Capitals emphasize: hence the implied courtesy in their use with proper names. When a word derived special significance from its context, it was the rule to use a capital."

Although the use of capital letters is treated even more frequently in Elizabethan grammars than is the use of the stops, there is no hint of such an emphasis use of capitals in any of these books. The statements, despite considerable variation, do not essentially differ from that contained in *Bullokar's Booke at large, for the Amendment of Orthographie for English speech,* 1580 (Section XXXV):

"Note farder, that capitall or great letters, are to be placed onely at the beginning of words, that begin a full, perfect, and seuerall sentence: or in the beginning of words, that signify great countries, nations, sects, & proper names of men, Cities, Castles, Sheres, Villages, Hils, Riuers, and other proper names which be specially notorious."

THE YOUTH OF MILTON

AN INTERPRETATION OF HIS EARLY LITERARY DEVELOPMENT

THE YOUTH OF MILTON

AN INTERPRETATION OF HIS EARLY LITERARY DEVELOPMENT

JAMES HOLLY HANFORD

THE part of Milton's life which falls between his eighteenth and his thirty-second years has never, I think, been made the subject of a special and independent critical study. Its various outward episodes — the residence at Cambridge, the retreat at Horton, the continental journey, the return to England — are presented in full detail by Masson and more interpretatively by Mark Pattison and other writers. Critical comment on the early poems, often of the most brilliant sort, of course abounds. What one misses in the discussions is a recognition of the fact that these years, comprising as they do the epoch of Milton's transition from boyhood to maturity and the first full cycle of his poetry, constitute, both from the psychological and from the literary standpoint, a unit.

Even the recent admirable study of the Latin poems by Professor E. K. Rand,[1] which greatly enriches our understanding of these remarkable compositions and is so full of suggestion to the Milton student, makes no systematic attempt to integrate them with other phases of the poet's early work or to set forth in detail their significance in relation to his personality. Outwardly the Latin verse is sharply distinguished from the contemporary English poetry as belonging to a different literary tradition, and, indeed, the whole product of Milton's youthful imagination has the appearance of being highly miscellaneous. More carefully considered, it is seen to be marked, not alone by the normal growth of his powers, but by a singularly coherent progression of experience.

[1] *Milton in Rustication, Studies in Philology,* April, 1922.

The failure of Milton students generally to interpret his development in what seem to me its most essential aspects results, I believe, from an overvaluation of known outward incident and historical circumstance as determining factors in the constitution of the poetic mind. The mass of biographical detail and the still larger mass of information regarding the setting of Milton's career presented by Masson is, after all, of little avail toward an understanding of the actual unfolding of his genius. These things are, of course, not to be neglected, but they can be used only tentatively and in subordination to the all-important evidence of the poet's self-expression. Such evidence, modestly interpreted, may yield us less, but what it yields will be definite and assured, whereas conclusions based on assumptions regarding the relation between biographical incident and the subjective consciousness of the artist remain at the mercy of conjecture. A recent important work, M. Denis Saurat's *La Pensée de Milton,* which aims to give a comprehensive map of the poet's mind, is frequently liable to objection on these grounds. A weight of inference is attached, for example, to Milton's first marriage, which, even if we possessed complete understanding of the facts, the episode will by no means bear. Another contemporary student, Heinreich Mutschmann (*Milton und das Licht*), who approaches his subject equipped with all the paraphernalia of psychoanalysis, is shipwrecked by a wild thesis concerning Milton's supposed physical degeneracy. Finally the able and industrious Liljegren in his *Studies in Milton* stakes everything on the demonstration of two facts, that Milton did not, as he claims, meet Galileo in Italy, and that he did, as his enemies affirmed, craftily insert the Pamela prayer into the *Eikon Basilike* for the purpose of finding it there, facts sensational enough, certainly, but of purely speculative relevance even if true. The present writer, while confessing himself, in his attempt to envisage Milton's personality more clearly, indebted to these works, even to that of Mutschmann, professes to avoid their waywardness by virtue of a stricter dependence on the poet's written words.

The proper use of these materials involves, first of all, a careful attention to their chronology. There have been errors here which it is now possible to correct. It involves also a due proportioning of emphasis. Milton critics have in the past inclined to center attention too much on the Horton period, to the comparative neglect of that which immediately preceded it. From the standpoint of literary values such an emphasis is natural enough; but for the comprehension of the mental processes and habits which underlie his creative activity and of the moulding effects of the intellectual and imaginative forces with which he was in contact, the significance of his less mature work, of his failures, even, and of documents not literary at all may be greater than that of the Horton masterpieces.

But the Horton period itself has not, I think, been altogether rightly understood. Romantic critics like Raleigh and Moody go to great lengths in idealizing Milton's " long vacation," painting it as a moment of sweet serenity in which the poet reflects without emotional disturbance the joyous spirit of the English Renaissance. Such a view is based too exclusively on the evidence of four poems, and, with regard to these poems, it fails to take account of the effects of a studied decorum, the result of a strong personal reserve and of the strict tradition in which Milton had so carefully schooled himself, which compelled him to conceal his more instinctive emotions under a mask of formal beauty. This is generally true of the poet's early work in verse; it is particularly so of that done between 1632 and 1637. The aesthetic objectivity of the Horton poems was in considerable degree an artificial thing.

Beneath it, and in the entire body of Milton's youthful writing, we may read the evidence of disturbing experiences and intimate reactions which belong characteristically to the period of adolescence. We may read also a part, at least, of the record of Milton's awakening to the potential influences of his intellectual and artistic environment. To indicate as definitely as possible the stages in this awakening and to trace the effects of the emotional and imaginative forces thus released in him upon the developing processes of his art, is the object chiefly aimed at in the present discussion.

The record of Milton's more individual experience does not begin significantly before the period of the Latin elegies. Of his really distinctive boyhood traits we know nothing directly. Even the untimely seriousness and ambition, the deliberate purpose to fulfill expectation by becoming something good and great, are, as regards his childhood, matters of inference. We may assume him to have taken his bent thus early, but it is only later that we can study his temperament at first hand. We have Milton's own later statement to the effect that his literary talents early attracted the attention of his elders. It would be interesting to know under precisely what conditions and stimuli his first compositions were written. Given the cultural tradition of the Renaissance, it was entirely natural that he should write verses before any powerful original impulses asserted themselves in him. Latin composition was an important feature of the curriculum in all the public schools of Milton's time, a "preposterous exaction," the poet describes it in the *Tractate of Education,* "forcing the empty wits of children to compose themes, verses, and orations which are the acts of ripest judgment, and the final work of a head filled by long reading and observing, with elegant maxims and copious invention." The writing of English verse was required at Westminster and may have been at St. Paul's.

Beside this we have the special influences of Milton's home environment. It should not be forgotten that to cultivate music meant, throughout the English Renaissance, to cultivate song, and that the known compositions of Milton's father are all settings of English words. This fact presumably determines the character of Milton's first approach to poetry, and it is of far-reaching importance in its effect upon his art. Particularly suggestive, in view of the fact that the father had contributed tunes to five of the Psalms in Ravenscroft's psalter of 1621, is the preservation of two metrical Psalm paraphrases written by Milton in his sixteenth year. One surmises collaboration between the musician father and the poet son. In any case some of the sweetest of his later verses — the *Song on a May Morning* and the lyrics in *Arcades* and *Comus* were composed for music.

Milton's own musical training and his sense of the analogy between the sister arts of music and poetry clearly underlie the conception of *L'Allegro* and *Il Penseroso.*

A less obvious result of this early influence is to be found in the aesthetic character of his enthusiasm for language. The terms in which he expresses in the poem *Ad Patrem* his gratitude to his father for his linguistic education suggest the meeting point in him of humanistic learning and the sense of beauty:

> Tuo, pater optime, sumptu
> Cum mihi Romuleae patuit facundia linguae,
> Et Latii veneres, et quae Iovis ora decebant
> Grandia magniloquis elata vocabula Graiis,
> Addere suasisti quos iactat Gallia flores,
> Et quam degeneri novus Italus ore loquelam
> Fundit, barbaricos testatus voce tumultus,
> Quaeque Palaestinus loquitur mysteria vates.[2]

His feeling for English is a home-felt delight, implying a still closer discrimination of the harmonies and ornaments of speech:

> Hail, Native Language, that by sinews weak
> Didst move my first endeavouring tongue to speak,
> And madest imperfect words with childish trips,
> Half unpronounced, slide through my infant lips,
> Driving dumb Silence from the portal door,
> Where he had mutely sat two years before. . . .
> But haste thee straight to do me once a pleasure,
> And from thy wardrobe bring thy chiefest treasure,
> Not those new-fangled toys, and trimming slight
> Which takes our late fantastics with delight;
> But cull those richest robes and gay'st attire,
> Which deepest spirits and choicest wits desire.[3]

There is no reason to suppose that these enthusiasms do not go back to the early years of Milton's schooling. They are, like

[2] "When, at your cost, dear father, I had mastered the tongue of Romulus and seen all the graces of it, and had learned the noble idiom of the magniloquent Greeks, fit for the great mouth of Jove himself, you persuaded me to add to these the flowers which France boasts; and the speech which the modern Italian pours from his degenerate lips, bearing witness in every accent of the barbarian tumults; and the language in which the singers of Palestine speak their mysteries." — W. V. Moody's translation, revised by E. K. Rand, Moody, *Milton's Complete Poems,* revised edition, 1924.

[3] *At a Vacation Exercise,* vv. 1 ff. The text employed for the quotations from the English and Latin poems is W. A. Wright's, *The Poetical Works of Milton,* Cambridge, 1903.

the born artist's love of color, his initial gift as a poet, and they antedate the need which he later felt to find an expressive medium for those

> naked thoughts that rove about
> And loudly knock to have their passage out.[4]

According to a statement made by Aubrey on the authority of Milton's brother Christopher he was already a poet at the age of ten and "composed many copies of verses which might well become a riper age."[5] The anonymous biographer, who is well informed regarding Milton's early life, says that in his school days he "wrote several grave and religious poems, and paraphrased some of David's Psalms."[6] The first of these experiments and exercises, of whatever sort they may have been, are lost, but the two Psalm paraphrases, the only pieces which survive from his school period, will serve as slightly more mature examples. They were preserved and printed in the 1645 edition of the *Poems,* not, presumably, for their own sakes but as evidences of the poet's early devotion to the Muse of his native land, and they bear accordingly the careful superscription "This and the following Psalm were done by the Author at fifteen years old." This would be in 1624, the year preceding his matriculation at the University. The choice of subject was dictated by a time when Psalm paraphrase was not merely a habit but an obsession. An illustrious line of poets had swollen the records of failure in this attempt. A pious and learned sovereign, who was not a poet, had magnanimously lent his hand. More directly responsible for Milton's endeavor in this common task were the elegant Latin versions of Buchanan, which he had doubtless studied at St. Paul's.[7]

[4] *Ibid.,* vv. 23–24.

[5] *Collections for the Life of Milton* reprinted in L. E. Lockwood's *Of Education,* etc., Riverside Edition, 1911, p. xl.

[6] *Op. cit.,* p. xxiv.

[7] There are perhaps eight or ten instances in which Milton clearly owes his turn of phrase to Buchanan's rendering. Thus in v. 3 of Psalm cxxxvi, where Scripture has simply "Lord of Lords" Buchanan paraphrases "Cui domini rerum submittunt sceptra tyranni," and Milton, with a similar republican touch, "That doth the wrathful tyrants quell." Buchanan's "auricomum solem" becomes "the golden-tressed sun;" his unscriptural

Milton was to return on two later occasions to Psalm paraphrases. In 1648 he undertook to supply the need of an accurate and doctrinally sound Puritan version to supplant the Sternhold and Hopkins Psalter for congregational singing. In 1653, when he had become blind, he did the first eight Psalms (on successive days) as a combined spiritual discipline and metrical exercise, probably in anticipation of a renewal of work on the composition of *Paradise Lost.* The two early pieces differ strikingly in character from these uninspired works of his maturity. The latter are severely plain in language, and the first set, at least, as nearly literal as Milton could make them. The early versions, on the other hand, are independent poems. They are characterized by a freedom of rhythm which marks them as the products of a genuine though immature poetical enthusiasm, and their original Hebrew substance is all but lost in the ornamental phraseology which Milton adopts from the religious verse of seventeenth century England. More specifically their stylistic inspiration is Sylvester, whose rich and elaborate though somewhat undignified language apparently satisfied Milton's youthful sense of verbal beauty.[8] The choice of the 114th and 136th Psalms and the manifest enthusiasm which Milton puts into the compositions is evidence also of a deeper sympathy with the poetic substance of Sylvester, whose broad and pious sense of the greatness and goodness of God as witnessed by the excellence of created nature Milton reproduces not ineffectively. We have here the beginning of a strain in Milton's poetry the importance of which, far more than any mere consideration of style, justifies the claim of Sylvester's *DuBartas* to be counted among the permanent

---

epithet for Og, "confisum viribus Ogum," is repeated in Milton's "large-limbed Og." In Psalm cxiv, "Pharian fields" goes back to Buchanan's "arva Phari" and the phrase "among their ewes," which is added to the literal rendering of v. 4, has its original in Buchanan's "ut dux gregis inter oves."

For the prevalent use of Buchanan's Latin Psalms as school texts see P. Hume Brown, *Buchanan as Humanist and Reformer,* 1890, p. 146; Foster Watson, *English Grammar Schools to 1660,* 1908, p. 472. I have no evidence that Buchanan was used at St. Paul's.

[8] See C. Dunster, *Considerations on Milton's Early Reading and the prima stamina of "Paradise Lost,"* 1800.

sources of his inspiration, a strain which reaches its culmination and full Miltonic glory in the morning hymn of Adam and Eve in the fifth book of *Paradise Lost.*[9]

In such a passage as this Milton has, of course, far transcended Sylvester's humbler muse. In it, too, more than in any attempt to reduce the Psalms to meter, does he approach their spirit, as he elaborates with his own imagery and in his own majestic idiom the great theme "The Heavens declare the glory of God." Yet the animating motive of the hymn and the quality of religious feeling manifested in it are essentially the same as in the work of his Puritan predecessor. It is an elevated and impersonal enthusiasm, having as its appropriate expression precisely the ornate magniloquence of which Sylvester is a humble and Milton the consummate master. Essentially literary in origin and developing naturally from boyhood tastes and influences this emotion and the style which attended it became characteristic of one whole phase of Milton's poetry, and of this phase the early Psalms are clear though faint precursors. With the more individual aspects of his genius, on the other hand — with such subjective experience as is embodied, for example, in the invocations in *Paradise Lost* and in the lyric parts of *Samson Agonistes,* the two paraphases have not the slightest discernible relation.

Of analogous significance in Milton's literary biography, is the poem *On the Death of a Fair Infant Dying of a Cough,* published along with other material which he apparently had not at first considered worth printing, in the edition of 1673, and dated "Anno aetatis 17." Allowing for Milton's peculiar usage in the Latin designation of his age and assuming that the poem was composed immediately after the event which it commemorates, the death, namely, of the infant daughter of his sister Anne Philips, its date would be between December 8, 1626, and the following spring, when Milton was in his second year of residence at the University. The piece was conceived in a mood of tender grief and sympathy, not untouched with a larger sense of the mystery of death and immortality, motives

[9] Lines 153–208.

toward which his mind had naturally been drawn by the ravages of the plague in London, even before they were brought home to him in a domestic sorrow. The literary influence under which his emotion characteristically shapes itself is the seventeenth century poetry of death. In style it belongs, as is evident both from its meter and its language, to the Spenserian tradition as represented particularly by Giles and Phineas Fletcher. The verbal conceits which chill the feeling in all but a few stanzas show Milton in the toils of a fashion which he was later to repudiate. There are, however, beyond this, some definitely marked Miltonic traits which suggest the beginnings of a more individual style. Such expressions as "the ruined roof of shaked Olympus," the "golden-winged host," "the middle empire of the freezing air," "thy heaven-loved innocence" surely enough reveal his touch. The lovely opening anticipates the delicate perfection of the Horton poetry:

> O fairest flower, no sooner blown but blasted,
> Soft silken primrose fading timelessly,
> Summer's chief honour, if thou had'st outlasted
> Bleak Winter's force that made thy blossom dry.

We have, too, the introduction of favorite motives which he was later to employ more happily. Thus lines 38–40,

> Tell me, bright Spirit, where'er thou hoverest,
> Whether above that high first-moving sphere,
> Or in the Elysian fields (if such there were),

establish the verbal form for *Lycidas,* 155 ff.,

> where'er thy bones are hurled,
> Whether beyond the stormy Hebrides, . . .

and the parenthesis, "if such there were," is the first of those conscientious reservations with which Milton checks himself in his instinctive use of classical mythology. Again, the allusion to Astraea in the eighth stanza, and the mask-like imaging of Mercy and "that crowned Matron, sage white-robed truth . . . let down in cloudy throne to do the world some good," while suggesting the Fletcherian personifications, anticipate familiar passages in the poem *On the Morning of Christ's Nativity,* and the references to the guardian spirit introduce a motive to which Milton returns again and again.

These things are specifically and characteristically Miltonic. Where, however, in Stanza V, he reaches for a moment the heights of poetic utterance it is on the wings of the great tradition of Elizabethan and Jacobean song:

> Yet can I not persuade me thou art dead,
> Or that thy corse corrupts in earth's dark womb,
> Or that thy beauties lie in wormy bed,
> Hid from the world in a low-delved tomb.

A striking parallel to these lines is to be found in the words of Christ in Book III of *Paradise Lost:*[10]

> Though now to Death I yield, and am his due
> All that of me can die, yet, that debt paid,
> Thou wilt not leave me in the loathsome grave,
> His prey, nor suffer my unspotted soul
> Forever with corruption there to dwell;
> But I shall rise victorious, and subdue
> My vanquisher, spoil'd of his vaunted spoil.
> Death his death's wound shall then receive, and stoop
> Inglorious, of his mortal sting disarm'd;
> I through the ample air in triumph high
> Shall lead Hell captive maugre Hell, and shew
> The powers of Darkness bound.

The poetic essence of this passage, apart from its theological implications, is something, one feels, which Milton has carried over from his youth. It shows that he could still respond with the full energy of maturity to the Christian sentiment of Donne's "Death, be not proud" or of Giles Fletcher's *Christ's Victory and Triumph.* But such moments in Milton's later work are rare. His mature spiritual life is normally ministered to by other emotions than those which associate themselves with the Resurrection, and it is only by reviving an old emotion and by falling back on his unfailing stylistic resources that he avoids the danger of mediocrity in dealing with this theme. The more striking, therefore, is its pervasiveness in the work of the Cambridge and Horton periods, where the idea of future bliss held,

[10] Lines 245–256.

as we shall see, an increasingly strong and glowing appeal to his imagination.

It is, I think, significant that the poems just described stand alone among Milton's works at this period of his career. There is nothing further in English before the *Vacation Exercise* of 1628 and the *Nativity* of 1629. On the other hand, we have no less than six Latin poems dated, like the English elegy, "Anno aetatis 17," a larger number than belongs to any other single year in his life. We may, perhaps, infer a deliberate postponement of further English composition in favor of an assault on the citadels of poetry in a medium dictated by the humanistic ideals of his day and rendered attractive by a growing sense of the rich beauties of Latin style.

Four of the poems, all written in the autumn of 1626, are laments occasioned by the deaths of dignitaries associated in one way or another with the University, namely, the Bishops of Winchester and Ely, alumni and former masters of Pembroke Hall, John Gostlin, the vice-chancellor, and Richard Riddle, the University beadle. The poem on the vice-chancellor is simply a meditation on the inevitableness of death, with praise of Gostlin's skill in medicine and the usual conceits regarding the failure of his art to procure him release from the common doom.

The elegies for the bishops are more elaborate and are constructed on an identical plan, having evidently been written within a short time of each other. The poet represents himself as in the act of exclaiming against Death when he is vouchsafed a vision of the abode of the blessed. In the earlier piece, *In Obitum Praesulis Wintoniensis,* Milton describes this vision in detail, painting in colorful imagery the landscape of Heaven, with its flowers, its silver streams playing over golden sands, its bejewelled angelic presences, its fanfare of celestial music. The passage anticipates both *Lycidas* and the *Epitaphium Damonis* and is the first of a series of Paradisiac pictures elaborated from antique models and enriched by the more luxuriant poetic tradition of the Renaissance, a series which culminates in the account of Eden in *Paradise Lost.* In the second piece he forbears to repeat the description of the Heaven of Heavens, but elaborates instead the journey on which he is borne by the Muse into the broad spaces of the sky, past Boötes and Orion, above the moon and the starry sphere, to the threshold of Olympus. The theme is an equally congenial one and foreshadows some of the best known and most characteristic passages in his mature poetry. The remaining elegy, *In Obitum Praeconis Academici Cantabrigiensis,* is a mere trifle, exhibiting the same conceitful humor, not untempered by kindliness, which marks the later English poems on the death of the old carrier Hobson. The attitude is oddly but appropriately expressive of the sentiments of young academic gentlemen toward those minor functionaries who are ridiculed during their lives and offices only to have it faintly remembered at their passing that they were human. In style it is, like the others, laden with verbal ornament. Milton is making himself free of the realm of classic vocabulary and allusion as, in the Psalms and the English elegy, he was free of seventeenth century poetic phrase. All three pieces are largely devoid of the personal note which characterizes Milton's expression of sorrow for the loss of his sister's child. Yet one feels that he has been sincerely moved by realization of the fact of death and that it costs him no effort to accept the obligation of celebrating these successive occasions of academic mourning. Witness the sober and beautiful opening of the elegy on the Bishop of Winchester:

Moestus eram, et tacitus, nullo comitante, sedebam,
  Haerebantque animo tristia plura meo:
Protinus en subiit funestae cladis imago
  Fecit in Angliaco quam Libitina solo;
Dum procerum ingressa est splendentes marmore turres
  Dira sepulchrali Mors metuenda face,
Pulsavitque auro gravidos et iaspide muros,
  Nec metuit satrapum sternere falce greges.
Tunc memini clarique ducis, fratrisque verendi,
  Intempestivis ossa cremata rogis;
Et memini Heroum quos vidit ad aethera raptos,
  Flevit et amissos Belgia tota duces.
At te praecipue luxi, dignissime Praesul,
  Wintoniaeque olim gloria magna tuae.[11]

[11] Sad and silent I sat, comradeless; and many griefs clung about my soul. Then suddenly, behold, there arose before me an image of the

Also the tenderly melancholy lines with which he brings to a close the lament for the vice-chancellor, dismissing his body to the grave and his spirit to the Elysian Fields:

> Colende Praeses, membra precor tua
> Molli quiescant cespite, et ex tuo
> Crescant rosae calthaeque busto,
> Purpureoque hyacinthus ore.
> Sit mite de te iudicium Aeaci,
> Subrideatque Aetnaea Proserpina,
> Interque felices perennis
> Elysio spatiere campo! [12]

These Latin poems, then, as clearly as the English elegy, are something more than mere poetic exercises or prescriptive tasks. They spring spontaneously enough from a mood of reflective melancholy forced upon the youthful poet by the ravages of the plague, and they definitely suggest the birth in him of a more inward poetic impulse than would have been natural in his earlier boyhood. Of rather less interest is the long hexameter poem, *In Quintum Novembris,* a miniature epic, written just after the Latin elegies and describing the origin and progress of the gunpowder plot. There is perhaps a relation between this piece and the equally elaborate *Locustae* of Phineas Fletcher, but the idea of a demoniac origin of the plot was a commonplace and the anti-catholic bitterness of Milton's poem represents the prevailing and appropriate sentiment for the occasion. Thus early does the gentle and humane spirit of the youthful artist

---

deadly plague which Libitina spread on English soil, when dire Death, fearful with his sepulchral torch, entered the glorious marble towers of the great, shook the walls heavy with jasper and gold, and feared not to lay low with his scythe the host of princes. Then I thought on that illustrious duke [Duke Christian of Brunswick, a victim of the War of the Palatinate] and his worshipped brother-in-arms, whose bones were consumed on untimely pyres; and I thought on those heroes whom all Belgia saw snatched away to the skies, — saw, and wept her lost leaders. But for you chiefly I grieved, good Bishop, once the great glory of your Winchester.

[12] Loved master, I pray that your limbs may rest quiet beneath the gentle sod, and that from your grave roses may spring, and marigold, and the purple-mouthed hyacinth. May Aeacus pronounce judgment mildly on you, and Proserpina, maid of Aetna, give you a smile, and may you walk forever in the Elysian fields among the blessed.

who could already invest the pain of death with beauty and send his Muse beyond the " flaming walls of space and time " receive his schooling in the harsh animosities which were for his day a necessary ingredient of patriotism and Protestant zeal. The remarkable thing is that he can throw himself so fully into the spirit of his alien theme. It is another evidence of the protean responsiveness of his genius to the divers and even contradictory influences of the various literary traditions in which he happens from time to time to be writing. The range and character of these influences I have barely indicated. To trace them in detail would be beyond my purpose. The point to observe is that Milton's poetry, as we have thus far surveyed it, is essentially imitation, though imitation of a peculiarly generous and dynamic kind. The process of literary composition is with him in each case the result of a cultural enthusiasm which enables the poet to identify himself so completely with a literary mode that he can express himself in it freely and spontaneously without having to resort to a particular model. In the act of reproducing such a tradition Milton makes it permanently his own. The successive contacts open to him new ranges of poetic thought and expression and their influence is, as we have seen, definitely traceable in his maturest work.

It remains to consider a set of reactions of a more positive nature, reactions which belong peculiarly to the period of Milton's adolescence and which have a very different bearing on the problem of the development of his poetic personality. The first evidence of the dawn in him of an emotional experience more inwardly disturbing than the artistic melancholy which he has elaborated out of the incidents of the plague is to be found in the poem which he afterwards printed as the first of his Latin elegies. This poem, written presumably in the same spring which saw the composition of the lament for the Fair Infant, is significantly addressed to Charles Diodati, the friend who for many years served Milton as the confidant of his deepest experiences and most cherished dreams. The occasion is the incident of the poet's rustication in consequence of a quarrel with his University tutor, and *Elegy I* teaches us to look to that event as marking an important moment in the breaking down of the carefully schooled docility of Milton's boyhood. The fact of a real and fundamental change in the poet's experience is confirmed by all that we know of his relations to the University. Our fullest information comes from Christopher Milton through the biographer Aubrey, as follows: " He was a very hard student in the University and performed all his exercises there with very good applause. His first tutor there was Mr. Chapell, from whom receiving some unkindness (whipped him), he was afterwards (though it seemed opposite to the rules of the college), transferred to the tuition of one Mr. Tovell, who died parson of Lutterworth." [13] The other early biographers say nothing of any trouble, though Wood, after repeating from his authorities the statement that Milton won the admiration of all by his exercises and was esteemed to be a virtuous and sober person, adds the qualification "yet not to be ignorant of his own parts." [14] The fact and date of the rustication are established by the elegy and Aubrey's parenthetical explanation of its cause apparently confirmed by the poet's mention of a " harsh master's threats " and " other things not to be endured by my nature." The circumstances are not difficult to reconstruct if we bear in mind the liberal environment from which Milton had just come and the atmosphere of intelligent appreciation which so evidently surrounded him at home and at school. The letters written from the University to Young and Gill [15] are evidence of the friendly relations in which he stood to these admired mentors of his boyhood. In Chapell he doubtless encountered an individual of smaller mould whose methods and attitude he resented.

Much light is thrown on Milton's situation at the University by later utterances in which he expresses a hostile point of view toward the discipline and ideals in vogue there in his time. There is contemporary evidence of still greater value. It is quite clear that he allied himself almost from the first with the group of intellectual liberals who carried on into the seventeenth

[13] Lockwood, p. xl.
[14] Lockwood, p. xlv.
[15] *The Works of John Milton in Prose and Verse,* ed. John Mitford, VII. 368–371.

century the old battle of humanistic culture against the narrow and jejune scholasticism which had taken its last refuge in the universities and which still dominated the thought and practice of the academic body as a whole. This is the basis of Milton's disparaging remarks about the students themselves in the letter already referred to. (*Alexander Gillio,* Cantabrigia, Julii 2, 1628): "Sane apud nos, quod sciam, vix unus atque alter est, qui non Philologiae, pariter et Philosophiae, prope rudis et profanus, ad Theologiam devolet implumis."[16] In the same letter he refers to certain Latin verses which he had just been writing for a friend who was Respondent in the philosophical disputation at the commencement of that year. These verses have been very plausibly identified with the poem "*Naturam non pati senium,*" which Milton included in the edition of 1645, and Masson assumes that the general subject of the disputation must have been suggested by the publication in the preceding year of George Hakewill's *Apologie or Declaration of the Power of God in the Government of the World, Consisting in an examination and Censure of the Common Errour Touching Nature's Perpetual and Universal Decay.*

The importance of Hakewill's point of view in the campaign against the vestiges of medievalism in the philosophy of the time is well recognized by the historians of thought. In championing the idea of progress against the fatalistic conception of a decline of human achievement Hakewill joins forces, as Mr. Richard Jones has recently pointed out,[17] with Francis Bacon and with the whole intellectual movement of which he was the prophet. Particularly important is his exaltation of the attainments of the moderns in such fields as mathematics, geography, and astronomy. The opposite theory of a necessary decay of nature Hakewill recognizes to be fundamentally disheartening to human endeavor: "For being once thoroughly persuaded in

[16] "Among us, as far as I know, there are only two or three, who without any acquaintance with criticism or philosophy, do not instantly engage with raw and untutored judgments in the study of theology.—*Milton's Prose Works,* Bohn Library edition. So throughout for the translations from the *Familiar Letters.*

[17] *The Background of the "Battle of the Books," Washington University Studies, Humanistic Series,* vol. VII (1920), No. 2, pp. 107 ff.

themselves," he writes of the maintainers of the more orthodox point of view, "that by a fatall kinde of necessitie and course of times, they are cast into those straights that notwithstanding all their striving and industrie, it is impossible they should rise to the pitch of their noble and renowned Predecessors, they begin to yield to times and to necessity, being resolved that their endeavours are all in vaine, and that they strive against the streame."

These broader issues are untouched in Milton's verses, which deal only, in highly imaginative strains, with the alleged physical decrepitude of nature, the less fruitful theme of Hakewill's first book, and are designed as a moment of poetic ornament in a serious discussion. Even so, however, his juvenile participation in this debate on the side of the moderns, is significant in its consistency both with his humanistic inheritance and with his later attitude in theology, politics, and education. The inferences thus suggested regarding Milton's intellectual attitude are confirmed, moreover, by the position which he consistently adopts in his own academic orations, whenever the subject affords the least opportunity for the expression of his real convictions on vital issues.

In the first Prolusion,[18] dated by Masson in 1628–9, though the subject is a trifling one, Milton plainly alludes to differences in point of view which have thrown him into opposition with the majority of students and tutors. "Etenim qui possim ego vestram sperare benevolentiam, cum in hoc tanto concursu, quot oculis intueor tot ferme aspiciam infesta in me capita; adeo ut Orator venisse videor ad non exorabiles. Tantum potest ad simultates etiam in Scholis aemulatio, vel diversa Studia, vel in eisdem studiis diversa judicia sequentium."[19] The second exercise,[20] presumably somewhat later, embodies a

[18] *Utrum Dies an Nox praestantior sit?,* Mitford, VII. 411 ff.

[19] "For how can I hope for your good will, when, in this so great concourse, as many heads as I behold with my eyes, almost the same number do I see of visages bearing malice against me; so that I seem to have come as an *orator* to persons not *exorable?* Of so much efficacy in producing private grudges is the rivalry even in schools of those who follow different studies, or different methods in the same studies." — Masson, vol. I. 276.

[20] *De Sphaerarum Concentu,* Mitford, VII. 421 ff.

disparagement of Aristotle in comparison with Plato, and the same point of view is represented in the undated Latin verses *De Idea Platonica quemadmodum Aristoteles intellexit.* Here Milton speaks in scorn of the unimaginative mind which cannot conceive the archetypal idea because he cannot see and touch it. With fine irony at the close he declares that if Plato expects his philosophic fancy to be received as truth he must call back the poets whom he has banished from his Republic. The third Prolusion [21] is an argument against scholasticism and a broad defense of the humanistic attitude and of the study of science. In the spirit of Bacon's *Novum Organum,* Milton condemns the perpetual wrangling of the schools as unfruitful either for virtue or true knowledge, and he invites the student to turn his eyes abroad upon the rich world of man and nature, ascending by degrees to the knowledge of himself and of God. His statement shows perfect comprehension of the case against the very debates in which he was himself called on to participate, and it establishes the groundwork for his entire program of future intellectual activity. The *Tractate of Education* is but an application of the method of approach advocated in this early exercise and much of *Paradise Lost* an embodiment of its results. The emphasis on physical science is particularly noteworthy. Milton can hardly be said to have possessed the true Baconian vision of man's mastery of nature by experiment and observation, but he certainly maintained throughout his life a more than ordinary interest in all branches of scientific knowledge, his deepest enthusiasm being naturally reserved for astronomy, with the most modern conceptions in which field he was, as has often been noted, thoroughly familiar.

The documents at which we have been glancing are proof, then, of the early confirmation of Milton's general intellectual point of view. They reveal the true source of all his later radicalism in humanistic culture rather than in the more specific and practical traditions of politics and religion, pointing to Erasmus and not to Luther as his progenitor. They show also the untimely establishment in him of the propagandist attitude.

[21] *Contra Philosophiam Scholasticam, op. cit.,* pp. 425 ff.

He consciously assumes the rôle of spokesman for a cause, playing in the little world of the University a part strikingly analogous with that which he was afterwards to adopt in public affairs. Such activities lie, of course, outside the sphere of poetry. They spring, however, from kindred sources in Milton's consciousness. No student of the poet need be told how impossible it is to separate his general opinions and purposes from his more intimate emotions, or his propagandist utterances now and later from his dominant instinct for self-portraiture and self-justification. The Latin exercises are rich in indications of Milton's early absorption in his own career, and they contain the germs of many elements in his later conception of himself as a being set apart from others and bound to cultivate himself for special uses. In the Latin portion of the exercise composed for the vacation celebration of 1628 [22] he alludes as follows to his college nickname, "the Lady," converting what was intended or thought to be intended as a disparagement into an argument of superiority." A quibusdam audivi nuper Domina. At cur videor illis parum masculus? . . . scilicet qui Scyphos capacissimos nunquam valui pancratice haurire; aut quia manus tenenda stiva non occaluit, aut quia nunquam ad meridianum Solem supinus jacui septennis bubulcus; fortasse demum quod me virum praestiti, eo modo quo illi Ganeones: . . . at videte quam insubide, quam incogitate mihi objecerint id, quod ego jure optimo mihi vertam gloriae. Namque et ipse Demosthenes ab aemulis adversariisque parum vir dictus est. Q. itidem Hortensius omnium Oratorum post M. Tullium, clarissimus, Dionysia Psaltria appellatus est a L. Torquato." [23] That he had already begun to meditate on fame, on the kind of audience,

[22] *In Feriis aestivis Collegii* etc., Mitford, VII. 441 ff.

[23] "By some of you I used lately to be nick-named 'The Lady.' Why seem I to them too little of a man? . . . Is it because I have never been able to quaff huge tankards lustily, or because my hands never grew hard by holding the plough, or because I never, like a seven years' herdsman, laid myself down and snored at midday; in fine, perchance, because I never proved my manhood in the same way as those debauched blackguards? . . . But see how absurdly and unreflectively they have unbraided me with that with which I on the best of grounds will turn to my glory. For Demosthenes himself was also called too little of a man by his rivals

fit though few, to which it was worth while to address himself, and on the need of long preparation for the high tasks to which he felt himself called, is evidenced in the same exercise and elsewhere in the Prolusions.

These thoughts are the materials out of which Milton is to build the ideal structure of his personality, as we have it displayed in self-sufficient grandeur in his later works. As yet the conception is too new and fragmentary to be manageable as a theme of art, but we may find in *Elegy I* an echo, however softened, of the psychological processes which manifest themselves more rawly in the prose. It is thus that he refers to the incident of his banishment from Cambridge:

> Me tenet urbs reflua quam Thamesis alluit unda,
> Meque nec invitum patria dulcis habet.
> Iam nec arundiferum mihi cura revisere Camum,
> Nec dudum vetiti me laris angit amor.
> Nuda nec arva placent, umbrasque negantia molles;
> Quam male Phoebicolis convenit ille locus!
> Nec duri libet usque minas perferre Magistri,
> Caeteraque ingenio non subeunda meo.
> Si sit hoc exilium, patrios adiisse penates,
> Et vacuum curis otia grata sequi,
> Non ego vel profugi nomen sortemve recuso,
> Laetus et exilii conditione fruor.
> O utinam vates nunquam graviora tulisset
> Ille Tomitano flebilis exul agro;
> Non tunc Ionio quicquam cessisset Homero,
> Neve foret victo laus tibi prima, Maro.[24]

---

and adversaries. Quintus Hortensius, too, the most renowned of all orators after M. Tullius, was nicknamed 'a Dionysiac singing woman' by Lucius Torquatus." — Masson, I. 292. Milton's tone here is bantering, but one can read between the lines.

[24] "That city which Thames washes with her tidal wave keeps me fast, nor does my pleasant birth-place detain me against my will. I have no wish to go back to reedy Cam; I feel no homesickness for that forbidden college room of mine. The bare fields there, niggard of pleasant shade, do not please me. How ill does that place suit with poets! I have no fancy to endure forever my stern master's threats or those other actions at which my nature rebelled. If this is "exile," to live under my father's roof and be free to use my leisure pleasantly, I will not repudiate either the outcast's name or lot, but will in all happiness enjoy this state of exile. Oh would that Ovid, sad exile in the fields of Thrace, had never suffered

One catches in these lines, in spite of the assumed lightness and well-bred indifference which the cultured but naïve youth wears like a borrowed garment, more than a hint of his real mood of resentment and hurt pride. Any touch of disgrace he may have felt is promptly converted to a judgment of the University as no fit place for poets and to a consciousness of satisfaction in his superior surroundings and pursuits at home. Very interesting as evidence of the kind of mental activity prompted in Milton by such an experience is the allusion to Ovid. There is obviously something here which goes beyond ordinary Renaissance practice of classical illustration. Milton has been meditating on the analogy between his own little exile and the fate of Ovid until he has made a kind of imaginative identification of himself with his Roman predecessor, as later, when the assault was intended to the city he fancied himself a Pindar, striking reverence into the heart of the military conqueror, and, finally, in blindness, found a solace for affliction and an answer to his enemies by remembering:

> Those other two equall'd with me in fate,
> So were I equall'd with them in renown,
> Blind Thamyris and blind Maeonides,
> And Tiresias and Phineus, prophets old.

For Milton the fellowship of the great is at once a refuge and a vindication. The passage in *Elegy I* is the transmutation into poetry of the personal references in the prose oration, the passages in *Paradise Lost* on his blindness are the verse renderings of the replies which he made to Salmasius' tauntings in the *Second Defence.*

But these considerations by no means exhaust the importance of the first elegy as an index to Milton's awakening emotional and imaginative life. In his defensive retreat from the hostility of the real world he takes refuge not alone in his reverence for the past but in a conscious devotion to beauty in all its forms. The disfavour into which he has momentarily fallen, while not

---

a worse lot! Then he would have yielded not a whit even to Ionian Homer, nor would the first praise be thine, Virgil, for he would have vanquished thee."

taken too seriously, has had the effect of throwing him back upon himself and has prompted him to reveal sensations which have hitherto found no place in his poetry. Thus, after greeting Diodati and alluding to the cause of his sojourn in London, he launches into a description of the enjoyments which his leisure affords him. The poem is a less mature and more personal *L'Allegro* and *Il Penseroso* in one. He speaks briefly of his reading, then, at greater length of attendance at the theater. Finally he turns to nature and the spring, reserving for chief place among the objects of his enthusiasm "the maiden bands who go by like flaming stars." On this theme he expatiates with an ardor which belies the artificial medium in which he writes. The lines abound in images full of enticement to the sense of youth.

> Et decus eximium frontis, tremulosque capillos,
> Aurea quae fallax retia tendit Amor;
> Pellacesque genas, ad quas hyacinthina sordet
> Purpura et ipse tui floris, Adoni, rubor! . . .
> Creditur huc geminis venisse invecta columbis
> Alma pharetrigero milite cincta Venus,
> Huic Cnidon, et riguas Simoentis flumine valles,
> Huic Paphon, et roseam posthabitura Cypron.[25]

It was, of course, to be expected that Milton should express himself with decorum and in an established academic mode. Sensuous desire is never with him a simple lyric force. It is from the beginning complicated by ethical and ideal influences and moulded in its expression by literary traditions. As, before, the poets have been Milton's guides in the milder affections of his youth, so now they are his tutors in the more compelling ones. For the present his guide is clearly Ovid, to whom he twice refers in *Elegy I* and whose stylistic example he mainly follows throughout the poems of this group. We might infer from the elegies alone the intense delight with which he has given himself to the study of the *Heroïdes* and the *Amores,* and the stimulating effect

[25] "And exquisite grace of brow, and floating locks,—golden nets which Love casts deceivingly,—inviting cheeks, to which the purple of the hyacinth, yea, even the blush of thy flower, Adonis, is dull! Men say that hither blessed Venus came, escorted by her quivered soldier-boy, drawn by twin doves, willing to love London more than Cnidos, or the vales watered by the stream of Simöis, or Paphos, or rosy Cyprus."

which this study has had on his awakening imagination. Fortunately, however, there is other evidence, for Milton has given in one of his prose works an account of his Ovidian enthusiasm, and indeed of the whole phase of his experience which this enthusiasm initiates, an account at once so coherent and so minutely faithful as to make it an outstanding document in the study of his early literary development.

The passage consists of an elaborate analysis in the *Apology for Smectymnuus* of the formation of his youthful ideals of chastity, written in 1642 in reply to certain defamatory statements of Bishop Hall. Although provoked by a stinging accusation and taking the form of a piece of special pleading, Milton's utterance is obviously much more than a merely improvised defense. It is rather the result of a long process of introspective meditation, now summarized in a review of that part of his early creative work which he recognizes as most essentially individual in its inspiration, and serving, for those who cared more for the writer than for the controversial issue, as a kind of biographia literaria or " Growth of the Poet's Mind." The opening sentences go far toward interpreting the emotional reactions which, as we have seen, find partial expression in *Elegy I*.

> I had my time, readers, as others have, who have good learning bestowed upon them, to be sent to those places where, the opinion was, it might soonest be obtained; and as the manner is, was not unstudied in those authors which are most commended. Whereof some were grave orators and historians, whose matter methought I loved indeed, but as my age then was, so I understood them; others were the smooth elegiac poets, whereof the schools are not scarce, whom both for the pleasing sound of their numerous writing, which in imitation I found most easy, and most agreeable to nature's part in me, and for their matter, which what it is there be few who know not, I was so allured to read, that no recreation came to me better welcome. For that it was then those years with me which are excused, though they be least severe, I may be saved the labour to remember ye. Whence having observed them to account it the chief glory of their wit, in that they were able to judge, to praise, and by that could esteem themselves worthiest to love those high perfections, which under one or other name they took to celebrate; I thought to myself by every instinct and presage of nature, which is not wont to be false, that what emboldened them to this task, might with such diligence as they used embolden me; and that what judgment, wit, or elegance was my share, would herein best appear, and best value itself, by how much more

wisely, and with more love of virtue I should choose (let rude ears be absent) the object of not unlike praises. For albeit these thoughts to some will seem virtuous and commendable, to others only pardonable, to a third sort perhaps idle; yet the mentioning of them now will end in serious.

Nor blame it, readers, in those years to propose to themselves such a reward, as the noblest dispositions above other things in this life have sometimes preferred: whereof not to be sensible when good and fair in one person meet, argues both a gross and shallow judgment, and withal an ungentle and swainish breast.[26]

We have here indicated a highly important moment in Milton's responsiveness to the stimulus of reading. The grave historians and orators, imperfectly apprehended, have left him moved by a cool and detached enthusiasm only; the smooth and glowing love poetry of the Roman elegists has spoken powerfully to his emotions and has roused in him the desire to exercise on similar themes the poetic talent which he is already conscious of possessing.[27] In a youth nursed in the literary traditions of the Renaissance, and, indeed, in any youth of Milton's temperament, this was entirely natural. The pagan sensuousness and romantic tone of Ovid and his fellows have put them in a quite different category from other classic writers, giving to their appeal an immediacy and force like that of contemporary poetry. It is characteristic of Milton that he should represent his enjoyment of these authors as accompanied by reflection and his creative impulse as guided by a conscious purpose and ideal. The elegists must, he thinks, have accounted it the first glory of their genius that they were able to judge of the excellence which they celebrated in verse. Their ability adequately to judge and praise these excellences was, moreover, the proof of their worthiness to love them. True glory, Milton implies (and

[26] *Prose Works,* Bohn edition, III. 116–117.

[27] Did Milton make his excursions into the seductive region of Ovidian elegy in the regular course of school reading, as he seems to imply, or on his own initiative and privately? The *Metamorphoses* appears in all the school curricula of the time, but I find no mention of any other work of Ovid. Presumably the amatory poems would be ruled out of St. Paul's on moral grounds, and one hardly imagines even a university tutor directing a boy of sixteen to them. Milton does not mention Ovid at all among the authors to be read in his own model school. Probably he takes the *Metamorphoses* for granted.

the idea is one to which he clung throughout his life) comes not from the praises of men but from the well-grounded consciousness of inner worth. This satisfaction he will be able to enjoy in higher degree than the elegists in proportion to the superior wisdom and virtue with which he will make choice of the object of his praise.

Something of all this is clearly matter of later interpretation. In the first elegy there is little, if any, of the devotion to an ideal object implied in the prose statement. The moral reaction is negative rather than dynamic. It is evidenced in the fact that the poet allows himself no indecencies of expression and that he checks himself in his praise of the starry maidens, by announcing that, while Cupid grants him immunity, he will make haste to quit their presence:

> Et vitare procul malefidae infamia Circes
> Atria, divini Molyos usus ope.

The herb moly, again employed in Milton's elaboration of the Circe myth in *Comus,* may be taken to represent the sure guidance of Christian ethics, to which he has hitherto owed his safety amid the strongly felt allurements of the senses. Aside from this Puritan touch (and even this has a kind of precedent in Ovid's declaration that though his verse is corrupt his life is chaste) there is nothing in the poem to suggest that Milton was as yet anything but the enthusiastic though somewhat timid disciple of his Roman predecessor in matter as in manner. The one passage in which he explicitly challenges comparison with Ovid is prompted by patriotism rather than by any philosophically based consciousness of superiority:

> Nec Pompeianas Tarpeia Musa columnas
> Iactet, et Ausoniis plena theatra stolis.
> Gloria virginibus debetur prima Britannis;
> Extera sat tibi foemina posse sequi.[28]

In general, then, *Elegy I* is an expression, on the one hand, of Milton's sensitive self-love, on the other of a new and intense

[28] "Let not the poet who lived by the Tarpeian rock [Ovid] boast the dames of Pompey's porch, nor the theatre full of Roman stoles. To the virgins of Britain first glory is due; suffice it, foreign woman, that thou canst follow them."

delight in beauty, nourished by contact with the most sensuous and romantic of ancient poets and given artistic direction by the typical Renaissance ambition to "overgo" some reputed classic name in his own tongue and upon a kindred theme. These related motives are the basis of an enduring inspiration. We may trace the first of them in a poem of the succeeding year, the epistle to Thomas Young, where warm personal affection, more strongly felt no doubt in the partly hostile environment of the University, is combined with indignation at the harshness of the English church which has compelled so excellent a man to seek his sustenance abroad. Milton's sympathy for Young is a kind of extension of the mood of defensive self-pity which we have seen implied in *Elegy I.* He reminds him that other preachers of the word — Elijah, Paul, Jesus — have been victims of persecution, as he had earlier reminded himself that Ovid, a poet, was driven into exile. Finally he gives a personal application to the motive of Psalm CXXXVI, assuring his friend that the Lord of Hosts who defended Zion will stand at his side amid the clash of battle which surrounds him. Milton writes with an accent of sincerity which leaves no doubt of the hold which the subject has taken on his emotions, but he indulges in no such aesthetic dreaming as in the first elegy and the suppressed excitement which underlies the erotic imagery of the earlier poem is entirely lacking.

It emerges again, however, in *Elegy VII,* Milton's next work, which belongs apparently to the year 1628. Here the poet picks up the theme of *Elegy I* and carries the amatory experience therein initiated to a second stage. In the first poem, as we have seen, he had made declaration of a general susceptibility to the attraction of sex and implied a fear lest, if he remained in London, Cupid might not long grant him immunity. In *Elegy VII* he represents himself as having at length enrolled perforce in the ranks of actual lovers. The deity appears to the poet in the early dawn of a spring morning, boasts of his power over men and gods, and warns him that he too shall feel it. His Muse shall not succor him, nor the serpent of healing Apollo give him aid. There follows the description of an amatory encounter — the mere exchange of glances with one among the maidens toward whom in his suburban walk he rashly allowed his eyes to rove. Her beauty pierces to the heart and the poet becomes a hopeless servant of the God whose power he has defied. In elaborating the episode Milton draws heavily upon the phraseology of ancient erotic verse, and in particular upon the allegorical and mythological love machinery of Ovid. His more immediate model is the *De Neaera* of Buchanan.[29] The Scotch poet, like Milton, represents himself as a rebel against love. The blind boy, in anger, empties his quiver against him and fills his breast with arrows. Finding even this in vain he binds him with the tangles of Neaera's hair and leads him captive as a warning trophy for all scorners of his might. Strongly, however, as Milton's poem smells of the oil of humanism, there can be no mistaking the eager delight with which he gives himself to the spirit of his theme, importing into his verses an enthusiastic glow which is entirely absent from the elegant and pointed couplets of his original. The opening allegory of Cupid and the subsequent description of the poet's woe are academic enough and effectively conceal emotion; the lines, on the other hand, in which he narrates his springtime encounter with a nameless love sound wholly real and individual:

Et modo qua nostri spatiantur in urbe Quirites,
  Et modo villarum proxima rura placent.
Turba frequens, facieque simillima turba dearum,
  Splendida per medias itque reditque vias;
Auctaque luce dies gemino fulgore coruscat.
  Fallor? an et radios hinc quoque Phoebus habet?
Haec ego non fugi spectacula grata severus,
  Impetus et quo me fert iuvenilis agor;
Lumina luminibus male providus obvia misi,
  Neve oculos potui continuisse meos.
Unam forte aliis supereminuisse notabam;
  Principium nostri lux erat illa mali.[30]

[29] *Elegiarum Liber, Poemata,* Amstelaedami, p. 317.

[30] "And now I took my pleasure, sometimes in the city parks, where our citizens promenade, sometimes at neighboring country-places. Crowds of girls, with faces like to the faces of goddesses, came and went radiantly through the walks; the day brightened with a double splendor. Surely, the sun himself stole his beams from their faces. I was not stern

Whether or not these verses recount an actual incident they express real and acute sensations, and the poem as a whole gives evidence of an all but complete surrender to the Ovidian attitude and mood.

An even bolder abandon characterizes *Elegy V*, the next poem in this series, written in the spring of Milton's twenty-first year. The poet greets the season and describes in ecstatic language the sensation of a returning poetic impulse in his breast. The spring it is which has given him his genius and the spring shall be celebrated in his song. What follows is strikingly pagan in tone and luxuriant in imagery. Earth bares her rich breast to the love of Phoebus. Cupid wanders about the world stirring all Earth's children to follow her example. Venus rises with restored youth as from the warm sea. The youths cry " Hymen " throughout the marbled cities. Throngs of golden-girdled maidens go forth yearning for love. At nightfall Sylvanus and the Satyrs wanton in the fields; Pan riots, and Faunus pursues the Oread, who hides in order that she may be found.

In subject and general conception this piece, like *Elegy VII*, depends upon a poem of Buchanan, the *Majae Calendae*, printed in the *Elegiarum Liber*.[31] There are resemblances also in detail. Thus Buchanan as well as Milton alludes to the rejuvenation of Venus, depicts Cupid as furbishing his arrows and rekindling his torch, and describes the rout of all Earth's sons and daughters under the impulse of desire:

> Applauduntque deo pueri, innuptaeque puellae
> Queis rudis in vacuo pectore flamma calet.
> Plaudit utrique deo quicquid creat humidus aer,
> Quicquid alit tellus, aequora quicquid alunt.

In Buchanan, however, the love theme is subsidiary and there is nothing to correspond to Milton's description of the effect of the coming of spring on his own inspiration as a poet. The

---

with myself; I did not flee from the gracious spectacle, but let myself be led wherever youthful impulse directed. Rashly I sent my gaze to meet theirs; I could not control my eyes. Then by chance I noted one supreme above the others, and the light of her eyes was the beginning of my ills."

[31] *Poemata,* p. 301.

difference is essential and stamps Milton's work as a directly personal utterance, the fullest expression we have yet encountered of the motives and yearnings which dominated his imagination at this time.

We may pause at this point to consider the significance of the fact that these very intimate reactions should take place under the influence of classical rather than of English poetry and should come to expression in Latin rather than in the poet's mother tongue. It has already been noted that Milton seems in his second academic year to have abandoned for the time being his early experimentation in English verse, presumably as a result of the humanistic tendency to undervalue the vernacular as a source of serious culture. There were additional reasons why he should have employed the learned medium in the poems which we have just considered. The element of Puritanism in his early environment had bred in him a timidity and sense of shame which inhibited his open utterance of any but the most decorous and approved, or in some cases, the most trivial sentiments. To give rein to sensuousness in the vernacular was to range oneself with a group of unacceptable licentious rhymsters. To do so in Latin was to follow the tradition of the honored classics and of the eminently respectable learned moderns, like Buchanan, who had imitated them. Against this somewhat pedantic attitude stood Milton's patriotism and his natural instinct for expression in his mother tongue, and ultimately these forces triumphed over his humanistic predispositions and freed him to pour himself out in English. His feelings on the subject are recorded in the enthusiastic apostrophe to his native language from which quotation has already been made. This piece, an English digression in a Latin vacation exercise, was composed during the Easter term of 1628, a year earlier than the fifth Latin elegy, and it is natural to associate Milton's renewed consciousness of the claims of English verse with the access of creative power which he describes in the latter poem. We may connect it also with more mature and serious meditation on his vocation as a poet, clear evidence of which appears in these pieces for the first time. In *Elegy V* Milton characterizes his poetic insight in terms which manifestly anticipate his later consciousness of the kind of task to which he felt himself called:

> Iam mihi mens liquidi raptatur in ardua caeli,
>   Perque vagas nubes corpore liber eo;
> Perque umbras, perque antra feror, penetralia vatum;
>   Et mihi fana patent interiora Deum;
> Intuiturque animus toto quid agatur Olympo,
>   Nec fugiunt oculos Tartara caeca meos.
> Quid tam grande sonat distento spiritus ore?
>   Quid parit haec rabies, quid sacer iste furor? [32]

In the *Vacation Exercise* there is an expansion, in similar terms, of the same idea:

> Yet I had rather, if I were to choose,
> Thy service in some graver subject use,
> Such as may make thee search thy coffers round,
> Before thou clothe my fancy in fit sound;
> Such where the deep transported mind may soar
> Above the wheeling poles, and at Heaven's door
> Look in, and see each blissful deity
> How he before the thunderous throne doth lie,
> Listening to what unshorn Apollo sings
> To the touch of golden wires, while Hebe brings
> Immortal nectar to her kingly sire;
> Then, passing through the spheres of watchful fire,
> And misty regions of wide air next under,
> And hills of snow and lofts of piled thunder,
> May tell at length how green-eyed Neptune raves,
> In Heaven's defiance mustering all his waves;
> Then sing of secret things that came to pass
> When beldam Nature in her cradle was;
> And last of kings and queens and heroes old,
> Such as the wise Demodocus once told
> In solemn songs at King Alcinous' feast,
> While sad Ulysses' soul and all the rest
> Are held with his melodious harmony,
> In willing chains and sweet captivity.

The fruits of Milton's declared intention to return seriously to English composition were delayed for some six months after

[32] Now my spirit is rapt into the skyey steeps, and freed from the flesh I walk through the wandering clouds; through the shades I go, and the caverns, inmost prophetic sanctuaries; and the inner fanes of the gods lie open to me. My soul sees all that comes to pass in Olympus, and the darks of Hades escape not my vision. What lofty song does my soul intend, as it stands with lips apart? what does this madness bring to birth, this sacred fury?

the writing of the *Vacation Exercise.* There exist the English *Song on a May Morning* and the sonnet *To a Nightingale,* both of which I should ascribe to period of the Latin elegies, and, indeed, specifically to the spring of 1629.[33] The first is a purified lyric comment on the theme of *Elegy V,* its contrast with the latter poem in style and mood being due to Milton's momentary reversion to the spirit of Elizabethan song. In the sonnet the opening lines are a direct translation from the Latin, and the conclusion embodies a declaration of the rôle which Milton has consciously adopted in accordance with his own feelings and his devotion to his Roman models:

> Whether the Muse or Love call thee his mate,
> Both them I serve, and of their train am I.

The sonnet is not, however, itself Ovidian in tone. Neither is it, like the song, Elizabethan. It suggests rather the direct influence of Italian models and represents a transition on Milton's part to a new set of foreign poetic allegiances, responding to and helping to determine an important change in literary mood.

Such a transition is duly recorded in Milton's account of himself in the *Apology for Smectymnuus.* The significance of the passage, the first sentence of which has already been quoted, appears to have been overlooked entirely by the poet's biographers and critics:

> For blame it not, readers, in those years to propose to themselves such a reward as the noblest dispositions above other things in this life have sometimes preferred; whereof not to be sensible when good and fair in one person meet argues both a gross and shallow judgment, and withal an ungentle and swainish breast. For by the firm settling of these persuasions, I became, to by best memory, so much a proficient, that if I found those authors anywhere speaking unworthy things of themselves or unchaste of those names which before they had extolled, this effect it wrought on me, from that time forward their art I still applauded, but the men I deplored; and above them all preferred the two famous renowners of Beatrice and Laura, who never write but honor of them to whom they devote their verse, displaying sublime and pure thoughts, without transgression.

[33] The argument, so far as the sonnet is concerned, is given in detail in my article *The Arrangement and Dates of Milton's Sonnets, Modern Philology,* Jan., 1921. The position which I have assigned to the Song is made probable by its relation to *Elegy V.*

Milton associates the change in his literary point of view with his ambition and his personal idealism, making it an inevitable outcome of the resolve to be the highest that his mind perceived. He becomes an adept in rejecting the grosser enticements of the flesh, and his literary taste responds to the conscious exercise of his judgment. Dante and Petrarch are the poetic embodiments of his new aspirations. In these poets, as in the Romans, he finds illustrations of the devotion of genius to the praise of beauty, but he finds them also inflamed by a pure idealism in the light of which the limitations of their predecessors may be judged. The art of the Romans he still, like a good humanist, judges superior, the men themselves far lower in the spiritual scale. His own path is clear. He will continue to rival the pagans in their perfection of outward form, but he will follow the Christians in the purity and elevation of their conceptions. This is the formula for Milton's youthful poetic aspirations. It was later transformed to suit with a more mature idea of his true objects, but it was never abandoned. We may well question, however, whether, in viewing his early romantic yearnings and aesthetic enthusiasms as an aspect of the higher aspirations of the soul, Milton is not reading retrospectively into his experience the ideas of a later time. Such a process is a familiar one in the literary history of the Renaissance. We have its prototype in Dante's spiritual interpretations in the *Vita Nuova* of sonnets many of which were written in a purely mundane mood. The most, then, that we can infer from the passage quoted is that Dante and Petrarch came in turn to supplant Ovid as objects of Milton's literary discipleship. The results of this new allegiance are indicated in the *Sonnet to a Nightingale* and more directly in the Italian poems which immediately follow it in the edition of 1645.

The assumption that these pieces must have been composed in Italy has hitherto obscured their significance in the scheme of Milton's early work. They are to be read as documents in the history of the phase of Milton's emotional and imaginative life which begins when he first enrolls himself as a lover and which definitely ends, as we shall see, before he took up his residence at Horton. I should date them immediately after *Elegy V* and the English Sonnet, i.e., between the spring of 1629 and the winter of 1629–30.[34]

The Italian sequence is, like the first elegy, addressed to Diodati and is ostensibly devoted to the praise of a foreign lady named Emilia,[35] whom Milton has apparently met in London and whose servant he proclaims himself in language of extravagant compliment to be. These poems are manifestly Petrarchan. Milton is still more interested in himself and his verses than he is in the object of his praise. In the second sonnet and the canzone he gracefully elaborates the image of himself endeavoring to transplant the flower of Italian speech into an alien soil surrounded by the ridicule of uncomprehending English youths who bid him pluck the laurels which await him in his mother tongue. His answer is that his lady tells him "This is the language of which Love himself is boastful." In the third sonnet he confesses to Diodati his former scorn of love has yielded. In the last poem in the series he tells that his heart is bold and constant, armed in adamant, secure against the attacks of force or envy, raised above vulgar fears and hopes, eager for every excellence and devoted to the Muses; it is less firm in its susceptibility to love alone. Even such a one, it will be remembered, is Adam,

> in all enjoyments else
> Superior and unmoved, here only weak
> Against the charm of beauty's powerful glance.

Elsewhere he praises the lady's gentle spirit and dark-eyed beauty. She is possessed of more languages than one, and her song draws the moon down from its sphere. In such degree only do the poems express enthusiasm for a feminine embodiment of the good and fair. It was, of course, to be expected that this

[34] This is in accord with the consensus of recent scholarly opinion. See John Smart, *Milton's Sonnets;* also D. H. Stevens, *The Order of Milton's Sonnets, Modern Philology,* April, 1919, and my own study cited above. No error has done more to obscure Milton's early poetical development than the assumption that the Italian poems must have been written during Milton's continental journey.

[35] See Smart's work cited above.

amatory verse should contain nothing inconsistent with the standards of conduct and taste which Milton had set for himself. What we miss is such sublimation of emotional experience as might have resulted if Milton's spirit had really been enkindled at this time by the *Vita Nuova* and the lyric poetry of the *dolce stil*, as he had a little earlier been enkindled by the Roman elegies. But though he mentions Dante it is evidently only Petrarch who really avails him, and the religion of love, which glows in Dante with transcendent fervor, is pale and conventionalized in his successor. This religion in its sincerity is not for Milton. In the Italian sonnets he has, indeed, rid himself of sensuousness, but only by means of a temporary abstraction of his art from his actual emotional experience. The higher mood, when it comes to him at this stage in his development, will be born of an ethical reaction, for Milton is at heart a humanist and a Protestant and his acceptance of the point of view of courtly and romantic love is, after all, a *tour de force*.

For the first clear indication in his creative work of such an ethical reaction we are prepared by the next passage in the prose statement. The change in attitude is again connected with his purpose and ambitions as a poet. The suggestions as to the character of his thoughts on this subject which we have noted in the *Vacation Exercise* and in *Elegy V* are now explicitly confirmed.

> And long it was not after [he continues] when I was confirmed in this opinion, that he who would not be frustrate of his hope to write well hereafter in laudable things, ought himself to be a true poem; that is a composition and pattern of the best and honorablest things; not presuming to sing praises of heroic men, or famous cities, unless he have in himself the experience and practice of all that which is praiseworthy.

Milton's language suggests that the confirmation of his convictions regarding the relation between personal conduct and poetic achievement and the accompanying resolution to devote himself to something higher and more serious than amatory lyrics marks a definite stage in his inner history. We can fix the moment of this change with considerable precision, for its first fruits in his poetry are to be found in the sixth Latin elegy, written at the Christmas season of 1629, some six months later than *Elegy V*.

The poet addresses Diodati, "who, sending the author some verses from the country at Christmas time, asked him to excuse their mediocrity, on the ground that they were composed amid the distractions of the festival season." Milton expostulates at the implication that revelry is not propitious to poetry, citing to the contrary the examples of Ovid, Anacreon, Pindar, and Horace. Bacchus and Erato, Ceres and Venus, are the patrons of elegy, and feasting, wine, and love its proper sources of inspiration. With the epic poet it is different. He must live austerely like an ascetic. His life must be pure. He is like a priest who ministers at the altars of the gods. In conclusion Milton tells what he himself is writing — an ode on the Nativity as a birthday gift to Christ.

The formula here given for the discipline of the epic poet is, allowing for the more exalted language of poetry, so precisely identical with that of the statement in the *Apology* as to make it clear that Milton is in the latter statement looking back to and thinking in terms of his meditation of 1629. We may infer that the Latin utterance represents a definite resolution regarding his life work. It is natural to associate such a resolution with the poet's coming of age on December 9 of the same year. He was apparently in the habit of taking account of himself at various anniversaries of his life, witness the *Sonnet on His Being Arrived to the Age of Twenty-three* and the one to Skinner on the third anniversary of his blindness. The thought that he was now in the technical sense a man may well have prompted him to look upon his earlier performance as belonging to the past, and the coincidence of his birthday with the Christmas season explains the mood in which he took up the subject of the Nativity.

The poem itself, as all critics have recognized, strikes a new note in the poetry of Milton. Belonging in its general tradition to the sober vein to which he had already declared allegiance in the English poems and exhibiting, like them, the influence of the Spenserian school, it quite transcends the earlier poems in elevation and poetic fervor. We feel that here, for the first time, we have the genuine and characteristic reaction of Milton's personality upon a serious religious object. He contemplates the event, not at all with the loving surrender of a Catholic poet to its human sweetness, but with an austere intellectualized emotion stirred in him by the idea of its moral significance. Christ is, for him, not a babe, nor indeed a person at all, but a symbol of purity and truth, that truth which " came once into the world with her divine Master, and was a perfect shape most glorious to look on." The pagan deities are multiform ugliness of error, put to rout by the god-like simplicity of Christ as shadows by the sun. The poet completely identifies himself with his conception and this identification calls forth all his imaginative and expressive powers. However much Milton's precise theological ideas may have changed in later life and his ethical sense become enriched with the content of experience, his attitude retains to the end the form which it assumes in the *Nativity Ode*. The poem is the lyric prelude of *Paradise Lost* and in an exacter sense of *Paradise Regained*.

I have, I think, said enough to suggest that the moment in Milton's literary life represented by *Elegy VI* and the *Nativity* is something more than a passing mood. It remains to consider how consistently he maintained this lofty and severe position.

Obviously we need look for no such complete break with the past as would result from a sudden religious conversion, nor even for the kind of outward change of profession for which not a few of his seventeenth century predecessors and contemporaries in English verse gave precedent. Milton never felt the need of clothing his Muse in a mourning garment. He remains to the end what he had always been, a humanist, and his ultimate exclusive adherence to religious themes is the result of a long development. His work after 1629 is still eclectic in its inspiration and full of variety. The poem on Shakespeare, the two epitaphs on the University Carrier, and the elegy on the Marchioness of Winchester belong to the immediately succeeding years. These works exhibit a fresh range of contact with earlier English verse. Largely abandoning the manner of the Fletchers and definitely rejecting the " new-fangled toys and trimming slight " of the metaphysical school, Milton enrolls himself among the sons of Ben. *On Shakespeare* and the two Hobson poems

(1630 and 1631) are in the vein of seventeenth century epigram. The elegy for the Marchioness (1631) is his first essay in octosyllabic couplets, a measure which carries with it the pure and classic style of the Jonsonian lyric:

> Gentle Lady, may thy grave,
> Peace and quiet ever have!
> After this thy travail sore,
> Sweet rest seize thee ever more.

The spirit of the earlier elegy on a Fair Infant finds an echo in the tender delicacy with which Milton celebrates this gentle mother's death in child-bed, likening her to the biblical Rachel,

> Who, after years of barrenness,
> The highly favored Joseph bore
> To him who served for her before,
> And at her next birth, much like thee,
> Through pangs fled to felicity,

but the poetic mode has changed. A direct suggestion for the poem appears to have come from William Browne's celebrated *Epitaph on the Countess Dowager of Pembroke.*[36] Compare the two openings:

> Under this marble hearse
> Lies the subject of all verse:
> Sidney's sister, Pembroke's mother,

and Milton's

> This rich marble doth inter
> The honored wife of Winchester,
> A viscount's daughter, an earl's heir.

The last lines of Browne's lyric similarly supplied Milton with the conceit upon which he constructed the poem on Shakespeare:

> Marble piles let no man raise
> To her name: for after days
> Some kind woman born as she,
> Reading this, like Niobe
> Shall turn marble, and become
> Both her mourner and her tomb.

[36] The lines, as given in the text, had appeared in the fourth edition of Camden's *Remains* (1629), p. 336. See *Athenaeum,* Aug. 11, 1906, p. 159.

> What needs my Shakespeare for his honored bones,
> The labour of an age in piled stones. . . .
> Then thou, our fancy of itself bereaving
> Dost make us marble with too much conceiving;
> And so sepulchred in such pomp dost lie,
> As kings for such a tomb would wish to die.

These poems, then, give evidence of Milton's continued delight in the pure artistry of verse and of his willingness to give himself even after the earnest declaration of *Elegy VI* to various more or less impersonal aesthetic moods. There are, however, clear indications of a conscious change in the main direction of his literary purposes from this time on. The seven Latin elegies represent, as we have seen, the serious fruit of Milton's early ambition to enter the lists with the great names of literature, the choice of Ovid as a model being dictated by the example of Buchanan, by his own sympathetic taste, and by a sense of the appropriateness of the material to youth. Having attained his goal he promptly abandons it in favor of the higher seriousness of epic poetry. His progress, as Professor Rand points out, is strikingly parallel with that of Virgil, whose poetry passes through various stages from the atmosphere of Alexandria to that of Augustan Rome. Of this parallel Milton himself was fully aware. The idea of it must already have been present in his mind when he wrote the poem *On the Morning of Christ's Nativity,* as a true messianic eclogue, corresponding to the Roman poet's prophecy of the Golden Age which was to follow upon the birth of a son to Pollio and matching that utterance in its already half-epic exaltation. The materials of Milton's future poetry are as yet but vaguely defined, but his mind is plainly set toward the mysteries of Heaven and Hell and the deeds of "pious heroes and leaders part devine." The spell of Petrarch allures him only momentarily from his true path. In taking formal farewell of the elegiac mood he takes farewell of all amatory trifling. At any rate he no longer appears in the rôle of a romantic lover, and a postscript appended to the Latin poems dismisses the whole experience as belonging to a bygone phase.

Haec ego mente olim laeva, studioque supino,
  Nequitiae posui vana trophaea meae.
Scilicet abreptum sic me malus impulit error,
  Indocilisque aetas prava magistra fuit;
Donec Socraticos umbrosa Academia rivos
  Praebuit, admissum dedocuitque iugum.
Protinus, extinctis ex illo tempore flammis,
  Cincta rigent multo pectora nostra gelu;
Unde suis frigus metuit puer ipse sagittis,
  Et Diomedeam vim timet ipsa Venus.[37]

That we do not find Milton turning at once to epic verse is not surprising. For a work designed to rank his name with greater ones than Ovid he naturally felt himself, at the age of twenty-one, unready. Instead, he proposes, apparently, a series of lofty religious poems celebrating the successive events in the life of Christ and the festivals of the Christian calendar. Of these the *Nativity* was triumphantly completed, and a poem *On the Passion* earnestly begun at the Easter season of the following year. His failure to complete this piece illustrates the breakdown of his higher inspiration when the theme found no responsive echo in his own experience. The crucifixion, neither now nor later, had the slightest hold on his emotions. That Milton did not fully recognize the conditions of the successful exercise of his poetic faculty is suggested by the character of the note appended to the *Passion*,[38] and also, perhaps, by the fact that he appears still to have cherished the plan of a series of poems on the events as late as the Horton period, when he wrote the complete but uninspired piece *On the Circumcision* (see below).

[37] These vain trophies of my idleness I set up in time past, in unbalanced mood and with lax endeavor. Vicious error hurried me astray, and my untaught years were an ill mistress to me; until the shady Academe [*i.e., Plato's philosophy*] offered me its Socratic streams, and loosened from my neck the yoke to which I had submitted. At once all these youthful flames became extinct, and since then my breast is rigid with accumulated ice; whence Cupid himself fears freezing for his arrows, and Venus dreads my Diomedean strength.

[38] "This Subject the Author finding to be above the years he had when he wrote it, and nothing satisfied with what was begun, left it unfinished."

We have, I think, in Milton's inability to satisfy with anything like the fullness of success which he had attained in the elegies the ideal which he had set for himself in 1629 the true explanation of his feeling of immaturity and failure confessed in the noble sonnet *On His Being Arrived to the Age of Twenty-three.* Milton did not, when he wrote these lines, " forget the Latin poems," as Moody suggests. He remembered them all too well. Nor could he have been dissatisfied with anything in the mere technique of his achievement in English verse. The idea that he was thinking of Thomas Randolph as one of the spirits more timely happy than himself is patently absurd, for there was nothing in the work of Randolph or any contemporary poet that Milton could have envied. The Roman epic poet Lucan or even Sir Philip Sidney would be a more plausible suggestion, if we must assume that Milton had any particular person in mind. But his sense of a lack of inward ripeness was primarily with reference to his own ideals and it could have been dissipated only by a successful beginning at epic poetry, which he had not, so far as we know, attempted, or by the maintenance through a number of similar works of the level of high seriousness which he had momentarily attained in the poem on the Nativity. The result of his dissatisfaction appears to have been the resolution to wait patiently for his time, withdrawing his energies for the present from serious composition and devoting himself to intellectual, moral, and aesthetic self-cultivation. Not until after his Italian journey, i.e. in 1639–40, did Milton deliberately set forth to vindicate his " inward ripeness " by attempting to realize the next stage in his literary plans.

The intervening years of his residence at Horton I am disposed to regard as scarcely less epochal than the earlier period at the University. Though the foundations of his culture were firmly established and the controlling ideas and motives of his life already operative, his transition to full intellectual maturity had not yet taken place; and the divergent or contradictory elements in his consciousness remained to be fused by the tremendous energy of Milton's mind into philosophic and aesthetic wholeness. Among the all too scanty documents which enable us to trace Milton's spiritual development in the years under discussion the manuscript letter to an unknown friend, written apparently near the beginning of the Horton period, bears emphatic testimony to the strain of moral earnestness which found expression in *Elegy VI* and the sonnet *On His Being Arrived to the Age of Twenty-three.* This elaborate piece of self-analysis in the more explicit medium of prose represents, like Milton's earlier and later vindicatory utterances, the fruits of a process of serious self-examination regarding his way of life. It was his habit, as we have observed, to call upon his powers of expression as a means of confirming himself in a course of action to which his nature and his reason counselled him. The tone of confident assurance which this letter shares with other similar pronouncements is, I am inclined to believe, primarily a form of utterance and may cover real uncertainty and debate.

Such a debate would naturally have preceded Milton's decision to postpone or abandon his proposed entry into the church and settle down for a period of independent study on his father's country estate. The actual literary expression of his purposes and meditations was apparently occasioned by the expostulation of a serious-minded friend, who took it upon himself to be the prompter of the youthful poet's conscience. This friend (whom we may assume to have been a divine) had evidently warned Milton that the hours of the day were passing and had suggested that he was allowing his love of study to become a form of idleness and self-indulgence. In reply, Milton admits that study as a mere gratification of curiosity is not praiseworthy, but he feels assured that this weakness cannot be ascribed to him. The love of learning alone, he says, would not suffice to weigh against the motives which would naturally urge him toward an active life. These motives he analyzes with characteristic thoroughness: they are the need of providing for a family and home; the desire of fame; the consciousness that God demands our employment of the talent which is lodged in us. His real reason, he concludes, viewing the matter quite objectively, is precisely that he may more thoroughly prepare himself to render up a true account. He is, he adds, the more inclined to this course because he has noted a certain belatedness in himself, as recorded in the sonnet written on the occasion of this twenty-third birthday. The sonnet is included in the letter and indeed the prose composition has somewhat the air of an artistic setting for the poetical gem. It is even possible that the expostulating friend is a figment of Milton's imagination. At any rate, what he is primarily doing is giving expression to the recurrent mood of earnestness which had already come to constitute a profound and essential element in his emotional experience.

It is odd but characteristic that Milton should, in this statement, say nothing whatever regarding his literary purposes and ambitions. No reader previously unacquainted with his thoughts on this subject could possibly infer them from the letter, the plain implication of the language being that he intends, when he is ready, to labor in the vineyard as a minister. It is possible, of course, that in the suggestion about a congregation and preaching Milton was maintaining a mental reservation, having already determined to interpret his ministry in terms of the poetic enunciation of divine truth. More probably he had not yet altogether abandoned the plan of entering the church. In any case there is a misleading suppression of a part of his full mind, which we may regard as a characteristic manifestation of Miltonic strategy. The friend is representative of the normal judgment of the world. He is not, therefore, an intimate of the inner shrine of Milton's purposes and, since he presumably holds the common inadequate view of art, would misunderstand and condemn a confession of the important place which poetry occupied in his thought. In his undergraduate days Milton had freely enough proclaimed his interest to the circle of his academic contemporaries. Since he had come to take a more serious view of himself he had reserved his confidences, communicating them privately to the entirely sympathetic Diodati, and now, with an apologia based on the true and elevated conception of poetry, to his father.

The charming Latin epistle *Ad Patrem* was probably written

contemporaneously with the English letter at the beginning of the Horton period, and it should be set beside the latter statement as completing the representation of Milton's point of view at this time. The contrast between the two is striking. In the Latin epistle Milton surrenders himself entirely to his enthusiasm for self-cultivation and creative art. We hear nothing of his intention to enter the church, nothing of the need of rendering account of the "one talent which 'tis death to hide." Milton extolls poetry as a worthy object of highest endeavor, drawing his arguments from the tradition of Renaissance criticism so nobly embodied in Sidney's *Apology for Poetry,* and he appeals to his father on the strength of his own devotion to a sister art to continue to indulge the son in his pursuit of knowledge and in his conception of himself as "a part though the humblest of the gifted throng." That Milton does not directly give expression to his dominant ethical motive while he is hymning his delight in the Muses for their own sakes is an illustration of the characteristic zeal which leads him to suppress one part of his consciousness while another is momentarily engaging his attention. But even here the implications of his idealism are present. He will not mix obscurely with the dull rabble or join forces with the profane. The poetry which he praises is that which chants the exploits of heroes, and chaos, and the broad-laid foundations of the world. The viewpoint is essentially that of *Elegy VI,* though the emphasis has changed with the occasion.

We are now prepared to consider in detail the poetic fruitage of the Horton era. It was probably at the very beginning of the period, before the date of the English letter to a friend, that he composed the famous pair of lyrics, *L'Allegro* and *Il Penseroso.* Indeed, it is quite possible that they go back to some vacation interval in his university life. The uncertainty somewhat disturbs the precision of our study of Milton's early literary career. In any case, however, the poems can hardly belong to the period of the fifth elegy and the *Song on a May Morning.* They resemble these pieces, to be sure, in their enthusiastic expression of Milton's joy in beauty, but they exhibit a conscious particularity in the development of the aesthetic motive which may be taken to imply a later and more complex attitude. It is as if Milton had deliberately set out to imprison the essence of his literary culture without admixture of more personal ideals and to survey systematically the whole range of his aesthetic pleasures. Whether this was done in his last years at the University, along with the poem on Shakespeare and the elegy on the Marchioness of Winchester, or in the first exhilaration of his release from the academic environment, among the fresh delights of Horton, does not much matter.

The true bearing of the companion pieces is best understood by comparison with *Elegy I*. In the Latin poem, as we have seen, Milton combines the recitation of his intellectual and artistic delights with an account of his reaction against the University and a confession of his susceptibility to love. The passage on the theater does not separate comedy from tragedy; the expression of his enthusiasm for nature is not elaborated and passes quickly into a rhapsody on the English maidens. In *L'Allegro* and *Il Penseroso,* taking rather more than a hint from Burton, Milton amuses himself by analyzing his aesthetic reactions and classifying them in two contrasting modes. There is, of course, no question of two individuals. *L'Allegro* and *Il Penseroso* are equally Milton. To interpret the fiction otherwise is to assume that a cultivated lover of music may care only for the scherzo movement of symphonies, or that a nature enthusiast takes pleasure in sombre but not in cheerful landscapes or a trained play-goer in tragedy to the exclusion of comedy. It is to deny, in short, the catholicity of Milton's taste, the very thing that the poems are designed to illustrate and do illustrate.

Equally absurd is Moody's description of the poems as a kind of summing up of two possible attitudes toward life, which Milton, while feeling the appeal of each, must have recognized the practical impossibility of combining, or his suggestion that *Il Penseroso* reflects the advancing shades of Puritanism and, in Milton, the giving way of the exuberance of youth to the sobriety of manhood. In point of fact *Il Penseroso* is quite as much Elizabethan in mood as *L'Allegro* and as little touched with

Puritanism, while the cheerfulness of the latter poem is anything but the exuberance of youth. The two pieces taken together are, indeed, the evidence of a carefully disciplined and completely self-possessed maturity of aesthetic cultivation and of a mind free for the moment from temperamental bias of any sort. The poems are studiously objective, even the effects of his reading being represented as elements in an impersonal experience. The element of sex, moreover, is carefully excluded. The choirs of maidens who usurped the landscape in *Elegy I* are here kept at a becoming distance. The passing reference to neat-handed Phillis, and the "store of ladies whose bright eyes rain influence," with the vaguer surmise of a possibly beauty in a distant tower, are but pleasurable additions to an undisturbed sense of visible and meditated loveliness.

But Milton's sojourn in the realm of purely idyllic beauty could not, given his nature and education, be very long. For him the writing of poems like *L'Allegro* and *Il Penseroso,* however exquisite the result, was in a sense a *tour de force.* We may assume that after a year or so, at most, of aesthetic leisure on his father's estate he would have felt the need of a return to more serious and purposeful endeavor. The English letter, which I have already analyzed and which we may now fit more exactly into its place in the Horton era, reflects such a moment in his thought. The fact that Milton at this time began to set down his compositions in the Cambridge manuscript may also be significant. A little later (c. 1636), as we shall see, he embarked on a more consistent course of study than the discursive and dilletante readings recorded in *L'Allegro* and *Il Penseroso,* and started to accumulate notes toward a philosophy of life in the *Commonplace Book.* In poetry he returns for a brief interval to the sober vein of the *Nativity.*

I have already noted his attempt to continue the devotional strain of that poem in the odes on the Passion and the Circumcision. Both these pieces are undated. The first of them most probably succeeded the *Nativity* at the following Easter season. It is tempting to assume that the poem on the Circumcision came between them on the appropriate occasion in

January, 1629–30. But this is almost certainly not the case. For though the piece is allied in theme to the *Nativity,* in form and style it is closely associated with the verses *At a Solemn Music* and *On Time,* and all three belong to a later date in Milton's literary career. The evidence of the Cambridge manuscript is, I believe, decisive on this point. In that document, *At a Solemn Music,* in three drafts, immediately precedes the *Letter to a Friend,* and the poems *On Time* and *On the Circumcision* follow it. Then comes *Comus,* establishing a *terminus ad quem* in 1634. The letter and the three companion odes are not much earlier; they would, indeed, belong to the same year if Masson's date for *Arcades,* which precedes them in the manuscript, is to be trusted. The poems represent a new experiment in English verse of the more solemn sort. *On Time* has its kinship in idea with the English letter and the sonnet *On His Being Arrived to the Age of Twenty-three,* but in place of the mood of disturbed self-searching reflected in those utterances, it is expressive of deep religious and contemplative joy, the chords of which Milton had already touched in the *Nativity:*

> Then long Eternity shall greet our bliss
> With an individual kiss,
> And joy shall overtake us in a flood;
> When everything that is divinely good,
> And perfectly divine,
> With Truth, and Peace, and Love shall ever shine
> About the supreme throne
> Of him to whose happy-making sight alone
> When once our heavenly-guided soul shall climb,
> Then, all this earthly grossness quit,
> Attired with stars we shall for ever sit,
> Triumphing over Death, and Chance, and Thee, O Time.

Similar imagery and an identical emotion pervade the poem *At a Solemn Music.* Both works are dignified and noble compositions, deeply felt and phrased in beauty. They are more mature in style than the *Nativity,* but come short of it in metrical felicity and in poetic fervor. The more vital forces of Milton's personality are not engaged in them. *Upon the Circumcision* is less fortunate. Milton strives to frame his thoughts to sadness in remembrance of Christ's sacrifice, symbolically suggested according to religious convention by the event which he commemorates, but the Muse withholds her wonted blessing on his endeavor. Only in the opening, where the poet is dealing momentarily with his native theme of the celestial song which attended the birth of Christ, does he achieve real beauty of feeling and expression:

> Ye flaming powers, and winged Warriors bright,
> That erst with music and triumphant song,
> First heard by happy watchful shepherds' ear,
> So sweetly sung your joy the clouds along,
> Through the soft silence of the listening night. . . .

The succeeding lines show, to my judgment, a falling off of inspiration.

With these comparatively slight and experimental pieces Milton apparently abandons any further attempt to express the religious mood in verse. But two poems of any sort, *Comus* and *Lycidas,* were written during the remaining four or more years of the Horton period and both of these were composed for definite occasions at the request of others. At the opening of *Lycidas* Milton alludes to his feeling of unreadiness and to the resolution which he had apparently cherished of waiting for his ultimate inspiration before writing again at all:

> Yet once more, O ye Laurels, and once more,
> Ye Myrtles brown, with ivy never sere,
> I come to pluck your berries harsh and crude,
> And with forced fingers rude
> Shatter your leaves before the mellowing year.
> Bitter constraint and sad occasion dear
> Compels me to disturb your season due.

The occasional character of these poems does not, however, diminish their significance. They are, indeed, the great masterpieces of Milton's youth, springing from the deepest sources of his inspiration. They reveal, moreover, new influences of more far-reaching importance in the moulding of his inner life than the delightful but unserious children of the Muse who had dominated his art in the composition of *L'Allegro, Il Penseroso,* and *Arcades.* The key is again provided by Milton's autobiographical statement in the *Apology for Smectymnuus:*

> Next (for hear me out now readers, that I may tel ye whither my younger feet wandered), I betook me to those fables and romances, which recount in solemn cantos the deeds of knighthood founded by our victorious kings, and from hence in renown all over Christendom. There I read it in the oath of every knight that he should defend to the expense of his best blood, if so befell him, the honour and chastity of virgin or matron; from whence even then I learned what a noble virtue chastity must be, to the defence of which so many worthies, by such a dear adventure of themselves, had sworn. And if I found in the story afterward, any of them, by word or deed, breaking that oath, I judged it the same fault of the poet, as that which is attributed to Homer, to have written indecent things of the gods. Only this my mind gave me, that every free and gentle spirit, without that oath, ought to be born a knight, nor needed to expect the gilt spur, or the laying of a sword upon his shoulder to stir him both by his counsel and his arms, to secure and protect the weakness of any attempted chastity. So that even these books, which to many others have been the fuel of wantonness and loose living, I cannot think how, unless by divine indulgence, proved to me so many incitements, as you have heard, to the love and steadfast observation of that virtue which abhors the society of the bordellos.

The interest of this passage as an index to Milton's enthusiasm for the literature of romance and as a revelation of the intense subjective passion with which he read, is obvious. One is reminded of the phrase about "dinging a book a quoit's distance from him" in *Areopagitica*. Considered from the point of view of our detailed analysis of the poet's early literary development the statement bears a more particular significance. The plain implication of the context is that these imaginative wanderings of his youthful feet belong not to an indefinite period, and certainly not to his boyhood, but to the epoch which immediately succeeded his devotion to Dante and Petrarch and his resolution to shape his career toward the highest forms of poetry. In view of the reliability of Milton's account thus far the presumption is in favor of an equal precision in his statement at this point. Let us consider the passage more closely with a view to determining the exact character of the literary reference.

The general terms of the description apply well enough to the *Morte d'Arthur,* a book, certainly, in which the high vows of knighthood are both taken and broken and which has often enough been "fuel of wantonness," but it is not Malory who would have inflamed a young idealist with the love of chastity and it is not his work of which Milton is thinking as marking an epoch in his development as a poet. Much more plausibly it is the romantic poets of the Renaissance — Boiardo and Ariosto among the Italians, and particularly Spenser who would first have come to his attention and first aroused his enthusiasm for their subject matter, leading to a subsequent exploration of the more authentic legends in medieval romance and chronicle. The single phrase " solemn cantos " is sufficient to determine the fact that Milton had the *Faerie Queene* specifically in mind. We may compare the later expression in *Areopagitica,* " our sage and serious Spenser " and the reference in *Il Penseroso,*

> Or if aught else great bards beside
> In *sage and solemn* tune have sung
> Of turneys and enchantments drear
> Where more is meant than meets the ear.

Now the time at which Milton first made the acquaintance of Spenser or the Italians is uncertain. The allusions to Ariosto in the *Commonplace Book* belong between circa 1634 and 1637 and may well represent a first extensive study in this period, following upon the earlier occupation with Dante and Petrarch. The *Faerie Queene* Milton must, one would suppose, have read before. We may, however, safely infer from the quoted passage that, no matter how early he may have felt the interest and charm of Spenser, the influence of his lofty and serious cantos as a powerful stimulus to his emotions was first deeply felt at the point in his development which we have now reached. It is in consonance with such an assumption that there are in Milton no allusions to Spenser and no marked trace of his influence in anything written before the Horton period. In a poet as susceptible of literary influence as Milton has shown himself to be, this would be strange indeed if he had already been profoundly stirred by the enthusiasm which he describes. Striking too is the fact that in his first statements regarding his plans for epic he should give no hint of his later intention to deal with Arthurian material. It seems probable that his purposes were shaped in this direction by his study of the Italians and by his acceptance of Spenser as his English master.

The proof that Milton's statement does actually mark the

moment of a new allegiance and that this moment coincides with the beginning of the Horton period is to be found in the English poems themselves. His adoption at this time of the pastoral mode is in accord with the precedent of Spenser as well as with that of Virgil. The clear allusion to the *Faerie Queene* in *Il Penseroso* I have already quoted. It is, however, when we come to *Comus* that we feel for the first time the full effects of the impregnation of Milton's thought with the poetic idealism of his great Elizabethan predecessor. We are prepared by the terms of Milton's description to find the relation here dynamic and essential. The extraordinary degree to which Spenser actually affected Milton's art I shall consider in a moment. For the present the important thing to observe is that he carried to the *Faerie Queene,* by his own confession, the same highly serious and subjective attitude which he had brought to his earlier reading, finding in his exaltation of chastity something to which his own nature and mood responded with unusual power, and that this response belongs definitely to a phase of his emotional idealism for which he had not yet found a satisfactory expression. If the way of thinking and judging in the passage from the *Apology* seems rather immature for the age of twenty-two or thereabouts, this only harmonizes with our general impression of Milton's temperament and with what he appears to have felt about himself. It remains, of course, quite possible that such ascetic dreamings go back in their origin to an earlier period, for Milton is not fixing a chronology but describing the stages in a development, and we need believe only that these influences and this experience first reached their full fruition in the Horton period. This consideration applies also to Milton's further statement regarding his contact with Platonic philosophy, which it is desirable to quote before undertaking the analysis of *Comus*.

Thus from the laureate fraternity of poets [he goes on], riper years and the ceaseless round of studies led me to the shady spaces of philosophy; but chiefly to the divine volumes of Plato and his equal Xenophon: where if I should tell ye what I learned of chastity and love, I mean of that which is truly so, whose charming cup is only virtue, which she bears in her hand to those who are worthy (the rest are cheated with a thick intoxicating potion, which a certain sorceress, the abuser of love's name carries about) and how the first and chiefest office of love ends in the soul, producing those two happy twins of her divine generation, knowledge and virtue. With such abstracted sublimities as these, it might be worth your listening, readers, as I may one day hope to have ye in a still time, when there shall be no chiding.

The actual beginnings of Milton's study of Plato go back to his school days. The passionate assimilation of the doctrine of love and virtue is evidently the work of his later youth. The dialogue uppermost in his thoughts is the *Symposium*, which he has evidently been studying along with the parallel account in Xenophon's work of the same name in the Horton period, perhaps for the first time. It is significant that he makes his new interest follow and grow out of his reading of poetry. That a poet should be a poet's guide to emotional Platonism is very natural. That Spenser should have been the guide of Milton is particularly so. For the later born poet found in his predecessor not only his own serious love of virtue combined with a fine responsiveness to sensuous beauty, but the embodiment of the Platonic philosophy with which he was already acquainted, touched after the fashion of the Renaissance with the romantic charm of sex. The two influences are henceforth one. They combine in *Comus* to give a quality of poetic inspiration wholly new in Milton's work, a fusion of the ecstacies of sense and spirit which the poet has hitherto been unable to obtain.

The myth of Circe had long been established as a Platonic symbol of the degredation of the soul through sensuality [39] and as such had attracted Milton as early as the first Latin elegy. It had received imaginative transformation and adaptation to the Christian ideal of sexual purity at the hands of Spenser in the second book of the *Faerie Queene*. The reference in *Areopagitica* shows the impression which the allegory of the Bower of Bliss had left on Milton's mind.[40] It seemed to him the prime

[39] For example, in Heraclitus Ponticus, *Allegoriae in Homeri Fabulas de Diis,* a copy of which has come down to us bearing Milton's signature and the date 1637. See Sotheby, *Ramblings*, p. 125.

[40] ". . . which was the reason why our sage and serious poet Spenser, whom I dare be known to think a better teacher than Scotus or Aquinas, describing true temperance under the person of Guion, brings him in with

illustration of the superior power of poetry to enforce a moral truth, a principle on which his own subsequent practice of the art was to take its stand. The appropriateness of the material to the masque was obvious.[41] Very naturally, therefore, he chose the motive as a vehicle for the expression of those inmost thoughts and feelings which had gradually grown clear and dominant in his consciousness. The classical framework of the myth is, as might be expected, adhered to more closely by Milton than by Spenser, or rather he definitely attaches his own invention to it where Spenser transforms the original to the substance of his dream. The embodiment of Platonic thought, moreover, is specific, appearing in particular passages, very strikingly in the famous one on chastity, and in the poem as a whole. Milton has taken evident pains to point the allegory and to make his fiction wear the aspect of a Platonic myth. Take, for example, the following exposition of the symbolism of Circe's cup,

> which as they taste
> (For most do taste through fond intemperate thirst),
> Soon as the potion works, their human countenance,
> The express resemblance of the gods, is changed
> Into some brutish form of wolf or bear,
> Or ounce or tiger, hog, or bearded goat,
> All other parts remaining as they were.
> And they, so perfect is their misery,
> Not once perceive their foul disfigurement,
> But boast themselves more comely than before,
> And all their friends and native home forget.

Incidentally he moralizes, after the fashion of Plato and his followers, the stories of Diana and Minerva, and that of Cupid and Psyche, creating a genealogy analogous to that of Love in the *Symposium*.

All this is the fruit of Milton's conscious classicism. It is, however, to Spenser that *Comus* is most deeply indebted in its poetic essence. In his elaboration of the fiction, as in the quality of his emotion, Milton has been influenced by his master's

---

his palmer through the cave of Mammon and the bower of earthly bliss, that he might see and know, and yet abstain."

[41] The Circe myth had been employed in Browne's *Inner Temple Masque,* presented Jan. 13, 1614.

romantic allegory of chastity in the third book of the *Faerie Queene.* This is clearest, so far as plot incident is concerned, in the parallel between the rescue of Amoret in Book III and the freeing of the Lady at the close of *Comus.* In both works the enchanter is surprised as he stands before his enthralled victim endeavoring to subdue her will to his lust. In Spenser the rescuer (Britomart) strikes him down, but is told that only he can undo the spell which he has worked. She then forces him "his charms back to reverse." In Milton the brothers, after having put Comus to flight, are informed by Thyrsis that they should have secured him as the instrument of the Lady's release.

> Without his rod reversed
> And backward mutters of dissevering power
> We cannot free the Lady that sits here.

The identity of phrase and of idea is quite conclusive of Milton's indebtedness at this point. He undoubtedly received modifying suggestions for the plot from other sources, but nothing so essential as he derived from the *Faerie Queene.* The relationship here is one which extends to the fundamental philosophy and poetic method.

It is not by any means confined to this one episode. Britomart, the central figure in Book III, is Spenser's symbol of what Milton calls the sun-clad power of chastity. The martial conception underlies such passages as *Comus,* 440 ff. The idea that chastity draws down Heaven to its defense, which is the dominant motive in the whole of *Comus,* is set forth by Spenser in the episode of Proteus's rescue of Florimel attacked by the lustful fisherman, with the poet's comment, so much in the spirit of certain passages in *Comus,*

> See how the heavens, of voluntary grace
> And sovereign favour towards chastity
> Doe succor send to her distressed cace.
> So much high God doth innocence embrace.

A more specific suggestion came to Milton from the description of the Garden of Adonis in Canto VI. I have already alluded to his introduction of Cupid and Psyche, with the mention of their allegorical descendants, Youth and Joy, as an instance of his Platonizing mythography. The immediate pattern of Milton's description is Spenser, who introduces as symbols of the Platonic creative principle first Venus and Adonis, then Cupid and Psyche, endowing the last two with a daughter, Pleasure. To the detail of Milton's curious application of this material I shall return in another connection. Enough has been said to confirm the assumption that *Comus* was written under the dominating poetic influence of Spenser, as surely, though not as exclusively, as the Latin elegies were written under the spell of Ovid and the Italian sonnets under that of Petrarch. Imitative, on the other hand, *Comus* certainly is not, for the unique personality of Milton is stamped upon the whole composition and the accent of his poetic idiom is heard everywhere. Milton could thus acknowledge his indebtedness as to a revered and beloved teacher, without feeling that his originality had been subjugated. He evidently considered his relationship to be analogous to that which Spenser had himself maintained toward Chaucer, and as the Elizabethan poet had delighted to express his gratitude to his predecessor under the name of Tityrus, so Milton pays graceful tribute to Spenser as Meliboeus,[41a]

> The soothest shepherd that ere piped in plains.

I am not disposed to attach exaggerated importance to Milton's confession to Dryden in his old age that Spenser was his "original." If the phrase is taken to mean that Spenser, more than any other poet, enabled Milton to interpret his genius to itself and to find a medium for his emotions at a crucial moment in his development, it says no more than truth. It is true also that Milton continued in Spenser's debt throughout his career and that, as Professor Greenlaw has ably shown,[42] the poetic fabric of *Paradise Lost* owes vastly more to the *Faerie Queene* and the *Four Hymns* than is apparent on the surface. Of all this Milton was clearly mindful. His own genius was, however,

[41a] In support of this identification see J. F. Bense, "'Meliboeus old' in Milton's 'Comus,'" *Neophilologus,* I. 62–64.
[42] *Studies in Philology,* XIV. 196–218.

after all, radically different from Spenser's and his culture was too wide and the influences under which it operated too complex to allow him to remain, like the Fletchers, a Spenserian. The idea of poetical sonship, which Milton possibly suggested to Dryden in the conversation about his own poetic origins, was a fiction prompted by gratitude and by the precedent of Spenser's own adoption of the only earlier English poet who was in any sense his equal as the one from whom he had derived his lineage.

With the principle of chastity Milton in *Comus* largely settled his account. The intensity with which he seized upon this virtue as the center and test of his ethical idealism is explained by the strength of his own romantic passion, a passion which is still the chief motive force of his imaginative life. Occasional passages give direct and moving expression to Milton's wider ethical convictions, but it is " the sage and serious doctrine of virginity " that holds the center of his thought and the mood of the poem contrasts strikingly with the glowing but mature enthusiasm of *Paradise Lost*. As a matter of fact *Comus* appears to reflect a partial suppression of the poet's sensuous excitement rather than its supersedence or complete conversion. For Milton this could be no resting-place, however happy the immediate poetic product.

I have said that the poem settled Milton's account with chastity. The subject, indeed, continued to occupy him as late as 1642 when he penned the passage in the *Apology* and, as I believe, until his marriage, but it no longer forced itself upon his creative art. What *Comus* did not do was to end the mood of youthful excitement by giving full imaginative expression to Milton's emotional life. Such an expression demanded not the exaltation of a negative virtue, but some more fervid celebration of the mystery of love, such as he apparently still had in mind when he promised to edify his readers with a representation of these abstracted sublimities at a time when there should be no chiding. A sort of fulfillment of this vague promise is, as we shall see, contained in *Paradise Lost,* but when Milton ultimately came to gather up in the epic the ripe fruit of his experience his attitude had undergone great changes, and the form in which he embodied the mystery of love bore a much modified relation to these promptings of his youth. It is rather to the documents of the later Horton period itself that we should look for the more immediate traces of Milton's idealized passion.

There needs no resort to psychological theory to show that the very restraints which Milton imposed upon himself intensified the sensuous impulses of his nature or to make clear the influence of these impulses on his reflective and imaginative processes. The very fervor with which he seizes upon the doctrines and imagery of the *Symposium* is evidence of his intoxication with something more glowing than purity as an abstract and negative ideal. He is compelled in the revelation of his new experience to repudiate the amatory phase recorded in the elegies, and he does so, not by destroying these children of his more sensuous Muse, but by carefully dating the elegies and appending to them the engaging postscript already quoted.[42a]

But the banishment of the earthly Aphrodite is only one phase of Milton's new philosophical discipleship. In the teaching of his master, friendship, the friendship of the good, is the human motive force and basis of the devotion of the soul to its ultimate divine object. With Platonic love in its romantic form Milton had, as we have seen, already experimented immaturely and unsuccessfully in the Italian sonnets. The tradition, while not without its appeal to him, was essentially foreign to his temperament. It was associated, too, in his own day with things and persons that he condemned, for the doctrine of Platonic love had received a new lease of life at the court of Henrietta Maria, where it had become more than ever a mask of triviality and corruption.[43] In contact now with the pure source which these vagaries had perverted Milton needed no longer dally with a false ideal. He substituted consciously and deliberately the principle of friendship, attaching new meaning to a sentiment which had already played a part in the experience of his boyhood and youth. It is not without significance that the first prose letters to his early acquaintance, Charles Diodati, which Milton cared to preserve and publish, should date from the year 1637

[42a] Above, p. 127.

[43] See Jefferson Fletcher, *The Religion of Beauty in Woman*, pp. 166 ff.

or that the only important poems to be composed between that year and 1641, *Lycidas* and the *Epitaphium Damonis*, should be elegies to the memory of dead friends. The earlier exchange of verse epistles with Diodati had apparently ceased some eight years before, and Milton seems to imply that letters of any sort and even meetings had recently become infrequent. The renewal of the old intimacy was evidently initiated by Milton. "Jam istuc demum plane video te agere," he writes on September 2, 1637, "ut obstinato silentio nos aliquando pervincas; quod si ita est, euga habe tibi istam gloriolam, en scribimus priores." [44] He has, he continues, taken pains to inquire after Diodati's welfare from his brother, and, having been accidentally informed that his friend was in town, he had hastened to his lodgings only to find them vacant. The letter is one of warm importunity, prompted by a desire of closer community of understanding and affection. "Quare," he concludes, "quod sine tuo incommodo fiat, advola ocyus et aliquo in loco te siste, qui locus mitiorem spem praebeat, posse quoquo modo fieri ut aliquoties inter nos saltem visamus, quod utinam nobis non aliter esses vicinus, rusticanus atque es urbicus." [44] Diodati evidently replied to this appeal by a letter in which he wished Milton health six hundred times. The poet in turn, on September 23 of the same year, writes a long letter in which he opens himself without reserve. The document is as remarkable a Miltonic revelation as we have met. It reflects as in a mirror a whole phase of the Renaissance—the attempt of high souls to make the spiritual discipline of Platonic philosophy a reality, to relive an imagined antiquity in a finer way than any humanist who was not also a poet could comprehend. It is the more heroic in that Milton in his generation stands alone as the last of a giant race. His idealism harks back to the days of Ficino and Pico and the Platonic academy of Lorenzo dei Medici.

[44] "I clearly see that you are determined not to be overcome in silence; if this be so, you shall have the palm of victory, for I will write first. . . . Wherefore as soon as you can do it without inconvenience to yourself, I beseech you to take up your quarters where we may at least be able to visit one another; for I hope you would not be a different neighbor to us in the country from what you are in town."

There can be no mistaking the change which has come over his attitude since his earlier verse epistles. His former pleasant companionship, brooded upon in absence, has taken on the character, on his side at least, of a fully developed Platonic relationship. He has, apparently, not had the many letters for which he hoped, but his old regard has suffered not the slightest diminution. "Non enim in Epistolarum ac Salutationum momentis veram amicitiam volo, quae omnia ficta esse possunt; sed altis animi radicibus niti utrinque et sustinere se; coeptamque sinceris, et sanctis rationibus, etiamsi mutua cessarent officia, per omnem tamen vitam suspicione et culpa vacare: ad quem fovendam non tam scripto sit opus, quam viva invicem virtutum recordatione. Nec continuo, ut tu non scripseris, non erit quo illud suppleri officium possit, scribit vicem tuam apud me tua probitas verasque literas intimis sensibus meis exarat, scribit morum simplicitas, et recti amor; scribit ingenium etiam tuum, haudquaquam quotidianum, et majorem in modum te mihi commendat."[45] The contrast between these and earlier expressions

[45] "For I do not think that true friendship consists in the frequency of letters or in professions of regard, which may be counterfeited; but it is so deeply rooted in the heart and affections, as to support itself against the rudest blast; and when it originates in sincerity and virtue, it may remain through life without suspicion and without blame, even when there is no longer any reciprocal interchange of kindness. For the cherishing aliment of such a friendship as this there is not so much need of letters as of a lively recollection of each other's virtues. And though you may not have written there is something that may supply the omission: your probity writes to me in your stead; it is a letter written on the innermost membrane of your heart; the simplicity of your manners, and the rectitude of your principles, serve as correspondents in your place; your genius, which is above the common level, writes, and serves in a still greater degree to endear you to me." . . . But, lest you indulge in an excess of menace, I must inform you, that I cannot help loving those who are like you; for whatever the deity may have bestowed on me in other respects he has certainly inspired me, if any ever were inspired, with a passion for the good and fair. Nor did Ceres, according to the fable, ever seek her daughter Proserpine with such unceasing solicitude, as I have sought this idea of the beautiful in all the forms and appearances of things (for many are the forms of the divine). I am wont day and night to continue my search; and I follow in the way in which you go before. Hence, I feel an irresistible impulse to cultivate the friendship of him who, despising the prejudices and false conceptions of the vulgar, dares to think, to speak, and to be that which the highest wisdom has in every age taught to be

of Milton's regard for Diodati is striking. In 1629 he had addressed him as a pleasant reveller from whose way of life his own more serious aspirations were beginning to withdraw him. Now he hails him as the embodiment of the Platonic good and fair, making their friendship a part of the loftiest meditations of his soul. "Ego enim," he continues, "ne nimis minitere, tui similes impossible est quin amem, nam de caetero quidem quid de me statuerit Deus nescio, illud certe; δεινόν μοι ἔρωτα, εἴπερ τῷ ἄλλῳ τοῦ καλοῦ ἐνέσταξε. Nec tanto Ceres labore, ut in fabulis est, Liberam fertur quaesivisse filiam, quanto ego hanc τοῦ καλοῦ ἰδέαν, veluti pulcherrimam quandam imaginem, per omnes rerum formas et facies: (πολλαὶ γὰρ μορφαὶ τῶν Δαιμονίων) dies noctesque indagare soleo, et quasi certis quibusdam vestigiis ducentem sector Unde fit, ut qui, spretis quae vulgus prava rerum aestimatione opinatur, id sentire et loqui et esse audet; quod summa per omne aevum sapientia optimum esse docuit, illi me protinus, sicubi reperiam, necessitate quadam adjungam." [45] As of old he rounds out his flight with a communication of his own poetic aspirations: "Quid cogitem quaeris; ita me bonus Deus, immortalitatem. Quid agam vero? πτεροφυῶ, et volare meditor: sed tenellis admodum adhuc pennis evehit se noster Pegasus, humile sapiamus." [45]

This letter, then, is Milton's fullest and most direct expression of the philosophic aspect of the Platonic enthusiasm which reached its height toward the close of the Horton period. Such an expression was appropriate to the cooler element of prose. In the exactly contemporary elegy *Lycidas* (it is dated November, 1637, in the Cambridge manuscript) and the somewhat later *Epitaphium Damonis*, where Milton is again the poet, with his singing robes about him, his rapture is loftier and more intense. It is commonly and I think rightly assumed concerning the first of these works that Milton had enjoyed no par-

---

the best. . . . Do you ask what I am meditating. By the help of Heaven an immortality of fame. But what am I doing? I am letting my wings grow, and preparing to fly; but my Pegasus has not yet feathers enough to soar aloft in the fields of air." — Bohn translation, with modifications.

ticularly close intimacy with Edward King, its subject. The mood is one of reflective melancholy and tender pathos rather than of poignant sorrow, though the latter note is not altogether lacking. There is no direct statement of Platonic doctrine, but the idea of a pure and inspiring friendship, founded in virtue and associating itself with the most elevated self-communion, underlies the whole poem and is in conformity with the present aspect of Milton's experience. The digressions on fame and the clergy, which are really not digressions at all, together with the concluding utterances regarding immortality, are expressions of Milton's deepest thoughts upon the central topic of the aspirations, ideals, and destiny of the poet.

In the *Epitaphium* the accent of personal grief is keener and the reflective element less pronounced. The immediacy of his sense of loss throws Milton back upon the mood of intimacy and affection which had characterized his early association with Diodati and had survived the process of Platonic idealization. The old habit of communicating his poetic plans in Latin to the sympathetic ear of Diodati is pathetically continued in the passage in which Milton describes his attempt at an Arthurian epic. The external conventions of the pastoral are adhered to even more rigidly than in *Lycidas,* but the deep emotion which inspired the poem burns through them at every point.

The culmination of this emotion in the close of the *Epitaphium* involves a moment in Milton's imaginative life which has not yet been introduced into this discussion, the result of an infusion into his consciousness of one element of Christian mysticism. The subject may best be introduced by quoting the final paragraph of Milton's prose apologia:

> Last of all, not in time, but as perfection is last, that care was ever had of me, with my earliest capacity, not to be negligently trained in the precepts of the Christian religion: this that I have hitherto related, hath been to shew, that though Christianity had been but slightly taught me, yet a certain reservedness of natural disposition, and moral discipline, learnt out of the noblest philosophy, was enough to keep me in disdain of far less incontinence than this of the bordello. But having had the doctrine of holy scripture unfolding those chaste and high mysteries, with timeliest care infused, that "the body is for the Lord and the Lord for the body;" thus also I argued to myself, that if unchastity in a woman,

whom St. Paul terms the glory of man, be such a scandal and dishonour, then certainly in a man, who is both the image and glory of God, it must, though commonly not so thought, be much more deflowering and dishonourable; in that he sins both against his own body, which is the perfecter sex, and his own glory, which is in the woman; and, that which is worst, against the image and glory of God, which is in himself. Nor did I slumber over that place expressing such high rewards of ever accompanying the Lamb, with those celestial songs to others inapprehensible, but not to those who were not defiled with women, which doubtless means fornication; for marriage must not be called a defilement.

It is, then, in the precepts of religion that Milton finally grounds his habit of restraint in matters of sex. The careful Christian discipline of his childhood and its fundamental importance in determining his actual conduct might, of course, even without his declaration, have been taken for granted. What primarily interests us in the foregoing passage, however, is its revelation of the intensity with which he seized upon certain New Testament passages and assimilated their doctrine and still more their imagery to the substance of his own poetic thought. We have here a new source of inspiration the results of which may be clearly traced in his creative work. The teaching of St. Paul is for him a "chaste and high mystery" of divine authority, which supersedes, though it is not discordant with, the inspired utterances of Diotima. The Platonic principle of the supremacy of soul has its religious counterpart and intelligible fulfillment in the pronouncement "the body is for the Lord and the Lord for the body." Thus in the passage from *Comus,* "So dear to Heaven is saintly chastity," the framework of Platonic idealism is fitted with a specific ethical and Christian content. The second scriptural passage which Milton "did not slumber over" and which he here adduces as the climax of his meditation, carries us still further. The "place" is Revelation, xiv. 1 ff.: "And I looked, and, lo, a Lamb stood on the mount Sion, and with him an hundred forty and four thousand, having his father's name written in their foreheads. . . . And I heard a voice from Heaven as the voice of many waters and as the voice of a great thunder: and I heard the voice of harpers harping with their harps: And they sung as it were a new song before the throne, and before the four beasts and the elders:

and no man could learn that song but the hundred and forty and four thousand which were redeemed from the earth. These are they which were not defiled with women; for they are virgins. These are they which follow the Lamb whithersoever he goeth."

It would be a great mistake to dismiss Milton's reference as a merely casual employment of Scripture in the usual manner of the seventeenth century controversialist. His avowal of special interest in it falls in with too much that we know to be characteristic of his state of mind in the period now under discussion. We have, for example, indications from other sources that Milton shared, in some degree at least, the predilection of his time for the shadowy semi-religious borderland between philosophy and occultism represented by the Cabala and the Hermetic books.[46] His contact with materials of this sort certainly dates from the Horton period and it is naturally associated with his Platonic studies. Thus the passage in *Il Penseroso* in which he describes his nightly readings is true to the practice of his time in its emphasis on the more dubious Neoplatonic speculations. It is not the authentic spirit of Plato which must be unsphered to reveal

> What worlds or what vast regions hold
> The mortal mind that hath forsook
> Her mansion in this fleshly nook;

and to tell

> Of those demons that are found
> In fire, air, flood, or under ground,
> Whose power hath a true consent
> With planet, or with element,

but the spirits of Hermes, Iamblichus, and Michael Psellus. It was evidently not for nothing that the poet was a coeval of Henry More. There is, to be sure, no reason to suppose that he ever committed himself seriously to the intellectual extravagance of his fellow alumnus and the little group of inspired fanatics who surrounded him. And so often in his experience the imaginative impulses which fundamentally made him a poet encountered in Milton intellectual inhibitions which prevented him from

[46] " thrice-great Hermes," *Il Penseroso*, v. 88.

surrendering himself to them without reserve. Though for that separate and limited part of Milton represented by *Il Penseroso* the speculations of Hermes might join with the translunary dreams of Plato and the enchantments drear of Spenser in affording a fascinating realm for curiosity to explore, he could hardly allow in these fantastic writings more than a small residuum of truth to challenge his more sober thought.

With the apocalyptic parts of Scripture the case was different. Even Plato and Spenser must yield precedence to inspired authority, in whose prophetic rapture a more daring and untrammeled expression was the garment of a profounder and more authentic truth. There is evidence enough of the position of importance occupied by the Book of Revelation in his thought. He adduces it in the introduction to *Samson Agonistes* in support of his thesis as to the dignity of drama, referring to the commentary of Paraeus, where the work is analyzed into scenes and choruses. The same point had been made by him over twenty years before in *Reason of Church Government*. We must remember also that it was in Revelation that Milton found the chief scriptural authority for the war of the angels,[47] with mystic and philosophic implications of which he shows himself to be conscious in his own treatment of the theme. Doubtless he was already meditating on those passages during the Horton period and glorying in their majesty and strangeness. His sense of their significance would have deepened with the years, and, in the end, enriched and elaborated by far-brought associations, they became the center of his imaginative activity. The appeal of the symbolic image of the Lamb and the throng of virgins was more immediate and intense. It clearly belongs to the passing phase of emotion which we have associated with Milton's adolescence, now drawing to a close.

The passage did not, of course, stand alone in his thought. It was connected with the general idea of Heavenly love and the mystic marriage of the soul with God, an idea which was deeply interfused with Christian tradition and appears to have enjoyed a special popularity in the religious writing of Milton's

[47] Rev., xii. 3–17.

own day. How profoundly this conception, with its ecstatic biblical expressions, impressed itself on Milton's imagination and how intricately it associated itself with Platonic forms and their Spenserian embodiments may best be understood by a comparative consideration of the three outstanding poems already mentioned as the sole fruit of Milton's creative powers between the years 1634 and 1640, namely, *Comus, Lycidas,* and the *Epitaphium Damonis.*

In the Spirit's Epilogue in *Comus* Milton sings of Paradise. The language is highly esoteric as well as exquisitely poetic, and Milton expressly calls attention in the parenthesis, " List mortals, if your ears be true," to the hidden spiritual meaning. The bliss proposed is that of Heavenly love as the ineffable compensation for a life devoted to the ideal of chastity, the representative and touchstone of all the virtues. In adopting Spenser's image of the Garden of Adonis Milton entirely changes its application, adapting it to his allegory of virtue and its reward, and impregnating the whole with mystical emotion, the rapt ecstacy of apocalyptic vision. The pagan image of the love of a mortal youth for a goddess draws insensibly nearer to the truth in the reversed symbol of the union of the God of love himself with Psyche, the human soul, and if Milton's classic taste prevents him from concluding with an allusion to the Lamb and his eternal bride it is because there is no need.

In the last lines of *Lycidas,* written three years later, the imagery is explicitly Christian:

> So Lycidas sunk low, but mounted high,
> Through the dear might of Him that walked the waves,
> Where, other groves and other streams along,
> With nectar pure his oozy locks he laves,
> And hears the unexpressive nuptial song,
> In the blest kingdoms meek of joy and love.

The nuptial music heard by Lycidas is the new song before the throne of the one hundred and forty and four thousand virgins of Revelation, the " celestial song to others inapprehensible but not to those who were not defiled with women " of Milton's own description.

Finally in the conclusion of the *Epitaphium,* again after an interval of three years, Milton throws off all restraint and concealment of expression (the mask of Latin being in itself a sufficient drapery) and indulges his imagination in a description of the joys of Heavenly love which reaches a point of sensuous intensity far beyond anything we have hitherto encountered in his verse. The first part of the passage is an elaboration of the description in *Comus:*

> Parte alia polus omnipatens, et magnus Olympus:
> Quis putet? hic quoque Amor, pictaeque in nube pharetrae
> Arma corusca, faces, et spicula tincta pyropo;
> Nec tenues animas, pectusque ignobile vulgi,
> Hinc ferit; at circum flammantia lumina torquens,
> Semper in erectum spargit sua tela per orbes
> Impiger, et pronos nunquam collimat ad ictus:
> Hinc mentes ardere sacrae, formaeque deorum.[48]

What follows has its parallel rather in the quoted lines from *Lycidas;* almost every motive, indeed, in the consolation with which Milton brings his lament for Edward King to a close being represented with a greater fervor in the account of the apotheosis of Diodati. It is necessary to give here only the final explicit description of the mystic marriage:

> Quod tibi purpureus pudor, et sine labe iuventus
> Grata fuit, quod nulla tori libata voluptas,
> En! etiam tibi virginei servantur honores!
> Ipse, caput nitidum cinctus rutilante corona,
> Laetaque frondentis gestans umbracula palmae
> Aeternum perages immortales hymenaeos,
> Cantus ubi, choreisque furit lyra mista beatis,
> Festa Sionaeo bacchantur et Orgia thyrso.[49]

[48] " In another place is the mighty stretch of sky where Olympus lies open to view. Yes, and Love is there, too; in clouds his quiver is pictured, his shining arms, his torch, his arrows tipped with fiery bronze. But he does not aim upon our earth at light minds, at the herd of vulgar souls. No; he rolls his flaming eyes and steadfastly sends his arrows upward through the orbs of heaven, never aiming a downward stroke. Under his fire the souls of the blessed burn, and the bodies of the gods."

[49] " Because thy cheek kept its rosy blush and thy youth its stainlessness, because thou knewest not the joy of marriage, lo, for thy virginal spirit virginal honors are reserved. Thy bright head crowned with light, and glad palms in thy hand, thou dost ever act and act again the immortal nuptials, there where singing is, and the lyre mixes madly with the chorals beatific, and the wild orgies rage under the thyrsus of Sion."

It is evident in this astonishing passage that the native sense impulses which first awakened Milton to the beauty of the spring and woman have lost nothing of their power. A part only of his passion has been absorbed in the real experience of friendship; the rest is transmuted into an imaginative and religious rapture which allies him for the moment with the tradition of Catholic Christianity. It does so, to be sure, only outwardly, for there is fundamental disparity between his essentially humanistic attitude and the devout asceticism of the Middle Ages. He belongs by temper and inheritance to the Renaissance. Symbolism in his hands becomes concrete and glowing imagery and the Christian meaning is transfused with the spirit as it is assimilated to the language of Pagan poetry.

With the *Epitaphium Damonis* Milton's early poetic productivity comes to an end. In its last phase it has been the product of the cloistral and contemplative period at Horton, though the mood itself has survived the Italian journey and, as the passage in the *Apology for Smectymnuus* indicates, the beginnings of his active life as a teacher and controversialist. What further fruitage it might have had we cannot tell, but there is little likelihood that the peculiar form of emotional excitement embodied in the *Epitaphium* would have continued long. The whole phase of his experience recapitulated in the *Apology* was essentially youthful and transitory, though Milton's intellectual precocity, his aesthetic discipline, and his almost infallible good taste made its expressions wear a certain deceptive air of maturity. Having served their purpose as the chief inspiration of his Muse when he was still in the main unable to give utterance to his profounder moral and intellectual consciousness, these emotions yielded to time, though not without leaving a permanent impress upon his genius.

Meanwhile Milton's cultural interests were broadening and his purposes in art and life defining themselves more sharply. In abandoning his intention to enter the church he had envisaged another form of public service more congenial to his taste and more consonant with his thirst for an immortality of fame. To fulfill this purpose it was necessary for him to equip himself with understanding of the world of men and affairs, and in particular to gain a sound basis for the formulation of his views on the great issues which were beginning to agitate the public mind of his time. Accordingly we find him embarking about the year 1635 on a course of modern historical study, beginning with the authorities on the later Roman empire, and progressing through the Byzantine writers, the Greek and Latin fathers, the medieval chroniclers of Italy, France, and England, down to the historians of the Reformation and contemporary affairs. Books of public policy and law were included in the program, as were also biography, memoirs, and treatises, ancient and modern, on the art of war. The detail of this reading is recorded in the *Commonplace Book,* where Milton made references to individual passages in his authors and copied out under appropriate headings many excerpts and observations. It is fortunately possible, as I have shown elsewhere,[50] to date many of the entries with considerable exactness, and, in particular, to set apart from the rest the entire body of materials which belong to the Horton period.

This latter group is of the greatest importance as an index to the interests and tendencies which find only scanty echoes in his earlier poetry. A considerable number of the entries reflect the contemporary interest in questions of ecclesiastical custom and in the precedents and authorities regarding them, with a marked predilection for evidence in support of the more liberal Reformation practice. The Puritanism, or more properly the liberalism, of Milton was evidently of very early growth. A note on Constantine's giving the clergy immunity from civil office and one praising the modesty of princes who refuse to meddle in matters of religion show his fundamental convictions regarding the relations of church and state to have been already in process of formation. Even more striking are the political entries, which contain the gist of Milton's whole republicanism. In the earliest stratum a broad interest is manifested in the relation of prince and subject, as in the following: "Ad subditos

[50] See *The Chronology of Milton's Private Studies,* in the *Publications of the Modern Language Association,* XXXVI. 251–313.

suos scribens Constantinus magnus nec alio nomine quam fratres appellat." In a slightly later group of entries (still within the Horton period) the political materials are more obviously related to the issues of the day. Thus the title "Rex" is begun, with entries relative to the deification of the Roman emperors, and that of "Subditus," with two notes giving instances of Papal release of subjects from allegiance to a sovereign. The setting down of the title "Census et Vectigal" is evidently connected with interest in the illegal exactions of Charles. And finally one note is definitely republican: "Severus Sulpitius ait regium nomen semper liberis gentibus fere invisum." Were it not for the unquestionable evidence of the manuscript we should have been inclined, I think, to ascribe this last citation rather to the period of the tract *Of the Tenure of Kings and Magistrates* (1649) than to that of *Lycidas*. To the earlier period, however, it certainly belongs and it is, with the rest, conclusive evidence of the degree to which Milton had matured his thought on public questions before he found himself actually surrounded by the influences which determined his public career. The Horton entries as a whole give definition to Milton's subsequent mention of "many studious and contemplative years altogether spent in the search for civil and religious knowledge" and to his description of himself as having from his youth "studied the distinctions between civil and religious rights."

The convictions thus formed came ultimately to be as intimate an element in Milton's consciousness and as available to him for poetic expression as the introspective activities of which we have been tracing the effects on his creative work. They did so in the degree to which they became associated with his personal life and ideals and with his conception of his function as a poet. Thus the outburst against the clergy in *Lycidas*, the first great passage in which he voices his convictions on an issue of the day, owes its emotional intensity to the fact that it is, in reality, a justification of his decision not to enter the church and a vindication of his idea that he could fulfill an analogous function more effectively in his own way. It is significant that neither in this passage nor in anything else written during his early years does Milton give utterance to the passion for political and intellectual freedom which became one of the supreme inspiring motives of his eloquence. His opinions on the subject were, as we have seen, already fixed, but nothing had yet happened to bring it home to him in the form of personal desire. Later, when he found himself hampered in his own activities by the restraint of a narrow authority and a narrow law, his impersonal convictions were converted into passion and achieved memorable expression in prose and verse. It is not surprising that, looking back from that later viewpoint, he should have forgotten that his feelings had not always been the same, and should have substituted for the mixed motives which kept him out of the church the single determination not to subscribe himself slave.

To say this much is not, of course, to say that the issues to which Milton devoted his life meant nothing to him until they became personal; it is simply to affirm the principle that the gap between mere intellectual and moral sincerity and poetic sincerity is a wide one and that Milton came only gradually into his full imaginative inheritance. The processes by which the infusion of his ethical and political ideals with personal emotion is accomplished, and, conversely, the process by which the promptings of desire are converted into universal truth — these processes are the fundamental facts of Milton's development. The difference between his earlier and later work is due simply to a shift in the center of his experience and to a consequent widening of his grasp of the moral issues which confront mankind. The increasing maturity of his ideas is reflected in the richer and more harmonious conception which he now adopts of his work as a poet — a conception which at length completely reconciles his need of ministering to men as a teacher of the truth with his desire to create beauty and with his passion for fame. Speaking again in the *Reason of Church Government* (1641) of his plans for epic and dramatic poetry, he concludes with the following analysis of the function of the poet-teacher:

> These abilities, wheresoever they be found, are the inspired gift of God, rarely bestowed, but yet to some (though most abuse) in every nation; and

are of power, beside the office of a pulpit, to inbreed and cherish in a great people the seeds of virtue and public civility, to allay the perturbations of the mind, and set the affections in right tune; to celebrate in glorious and lofty hymns the throne and equipage of God's almightiness, and what he works, and what he suffers to be wrought with high providence in his church; to sing victorious agonies of martyrs and saints, the deeds and triumphs of just and pious nations, doing valiantly through faith against the enemies of Christ; to deplore the general relapse of kingdoms and states from justice and God's true worship. Lastly, whatsoever in religion is holy and sublime, in virtue amiable and grave, whatsoever hath passion or admiration in all the changes of that which is called fortune from without, or the wily subtleties and refluxes of man's thoughts from within; all these things with a solid and treatable smoothness to paint out and describe, teaching over the whole book of sanctity and virtue, through all the instances of example, with such delight to those especially of soft and delicious temper, who will not look upon truth herself, unless they see her elegantly dressed; that whereas the paths of honesty and good life appear now rugged and difficult, though they be indeed easy and pleasant, they will then appear easy and pleasant, though they were rugged and difficult indeed.

Though this passage was written a year before the retrospective discussion in the *Apology,* it better represents Milton's mature aims at the outset of his career of public service, and the form of the ideal which was actually to dominate his creative activity henceforth. The poet no longer speaks privately to the aspirations of the individual, but to the public conscience of mankind. While he still cherishes for himself and for the few who can receive it the esoteric doctrine of chastity and true love, his immediate attention is bent, with all the tremendous energy of his spirit, upon the broader theme of "virtue and public civility," "justice and God's true worship," "the rugged and difficult paths of honesty and true life." He advocates public festivals, "as in those famous governments of old," where, not only in pulpits but at set and solemn panurgies, in theaters and porches, the people may be led, by wise and artful recitations, combining recreation with instruction, to the practice of justice, temperance and fortitude. The function which he here proposes to himself is thus essentially a public one, analogous, on the one hand, to that of the prophets of Israel and on the other to that of the orators of Greece and Rome. In the imagination of such a task Milton's ambitions take the form of a loftier enthusiasm than the desire to rival an Ovid or even a Spenser, and though he is still questioning "what king or knight before the conquest might be chosen in whom to lay the pattern" of a Christian hero, it is easy to see that such a theme will fail to satisfy his present more comprehensive purposes. From the standpoint of the present discussion we may affirm that the emotions of love and friendship have given way to that of patriotism as the dominant motive of Milton's expressive power. His passion for individual perfection henceforth clothes itself in zeal for public righteousness and his vision is more often directed toward outward objects and events.

There is no real break, however, in the continuity of his inner life. Whenever Milton is attacked, as he was by Bishop Hall, he becomes acutely introspective. Affliction also has the natural effect of turning his imagination upon the world of his own moral and religious consciousness. Such utterances as the autobiographical statements in the *Second Defense,* the lyric parts of *Paradise Lost,* and the sonnets are the result. In these expressions we have the full fruit of Milton's mature lyric emotion, so far as it is generated by conscious superiority of personality and moral ideals. The mood is that of the *Sonnet on His Being Arrived to the Age of Twenty-three,* intensified by a sharper sense of the opposition of circumstance and enriched by a profounder religious feeling.

The development of his thought of sex is more complicated. To follow it we must return again to the end of the Horton period when Milton was beginning to regard the chapter of his youth as closed. The change is marked by a turning of his thoughts toward the philosophy of marriage, a direction clearly indicated by certain entries in the *Commonplace Book* which belong to the later Horton period. These entries cite the testimony of various authors regarding the practice of marriage among the apostles and the clergy of the early church. Milton is evidently satisfying himself that marriage is no defilement even for a priest, and, inferentially, that his own not inferior priesthood of poetry does not demand a state of celibacy. One sentence from Justin Martyr is to the effect that the Jews countenanced polygamy "propter varia mysteria sub ea latentia," a curious bit of evidence of Milton's early interest in the vagaries of radical Protestantism. In the *De Doctrina Christiana,* written a whole generation later, he is at pains to show that polygamy is countenanced by Scripture and is not abhorrent to reason. I am not disposed to take this strain in Milton's thought too seriously. It is for him a kind of *a fortiori* directed against the lingering tendency of men like Laud to return to an attitude regarding marriage which did violence at once to Milton's instinct and to his reason, and which he felt to be unscriptural and unprotestant. For him the married state was divinely instituted and without the shadow of a stain. His militant enthusiasm on the subject is recorded poetically in the famous passage in *Paradise Lost:* [51]

> Nor turn'd, I ween,
> Adam from his fair spouse, nor Eve the rites
> Mysterious of connubial love refused:
> Whatever hypocrites austerely talk
> Of purity, and place, and innocence,
> Defaming as impure what God declares
> Pure, and commands to some, leaves free to all.
> Our Maker bids increase; who bids abstain
> But our destroyer, foe to God and Man?
> Hail, wedded Love, mysterious law, true source
> Of human offspring, sole propriety
> In Paradise of all things common else! . . .
> Far be it that I should write thee sin or blame,
> Or think thee unbefitting holiest place.

In Milton's matured philosophy there was, of course, no inconsistency between the praise of purity and the praise of married love. Yet it is apparent that his mood has changed since the publication of *Comus.* His moral sense no longer throws him into opposition with nature; his idealism takes the form of a glorification of the true and humane conception of love as a spiritual and religious companionship, where the satisfaction of the senses has merely an instrumental though a necessary function. Milton thus makes his personal convictions an element in his public message of reform. Such is the motive of the

[51] Book IV, lines 741–759.

divorce pamphlets, and such is the theme of a considerable portion of *Paradise Lost*. In the passage cited Milton not only defends marriage against asceticism and exalts it in both its physical and its spiritual aspects as a divine mystery, but inveighs against mere sensuality, the domination of passion, the subjection of reason to desire. His direct antagonism to the romantic ideal of love here reaches its culmination and he repudiates as false the whole chivalric conception:

> Here Love his golden shafts employs, here lights
> His constant lamp, and waves his purple wings,
> Reigns here and revels: not in the bought smile
> Of harlots, loveless, joyless, unendear'd,
> Casual fruition; nor in court-amours,
> Mix'd dance, or wanton mask, or midnight ball,
> Or serenate, which the starved lover sings
> To his proud fair, best quitted with disdain.[52]

This motive underlies his insistence on the subordination of Eve. The expression "He for God only, she for God in him" exactly reverses the attitude of the medieval and the Petrarchan lover, whose deification of woman, when it is not actually the mask of sensuality, does violence to the facts and is in all cases full of danger. It is this attitude in Adam to which Eve appeals when she has sinned, and in his momentary adoption of it Adam falls. The doctrine is that of *Comus* in its ethical rather than its ascetic aspect. We recognize in Eve the enchantress Circe and the enchanter Comus, but we perceive that what is exacted of Adam is the control of his instinct, not its denial. What survives of the Platonic view of love, now domesticated and happily wedded to the Christian teaching of St. Paul, is to be found in Raphael's words to Adam in Book VIII:

> What higher in her society thou find'st
> Attractive, human, rational, love still;
> In loving thou dost well; in passion not,
> Wherein true love consists not. Love refines
> The thoughts, and heart enlarges; hath his seat
> In Reason, and is judicious; is the scale
> By which to heavenly love thou may'st ascend,
> Not sunk in carnal pleasure; for which cause
> Among the beasts no mate for thee was found.[53]

[52] Book IV, lines 763–770. [53] Lines 586–594.

Even here, however, Milton feels it necessary to modify the ascetic implications in the angel's too uncompromising statement. He does so in Adam's half-abashed reply:

> Neither her outside form'd so fair, nor aught
> In procreation common to all kinds
> (Though higher of the genial bed by far,
> And with mysterious reverence, I deem)
> So much delights me as those graceful acts,
> Those thousand decencies, that daily flow
> From all her words and actions, mix'd with love
> And sweet compliance, which declare unfeign'd
> Union of mind, or in us both one soul; [54]

and in the interested inquiry whether angels love and in what fashion. This opens the way for a final statement of the doctrine of paradisiac love. The passage, which ranks as one of the prime curiosities of Milton's angelology, is as follows:

> To whom the Angel, with a smile that glow'd
> Celestial rosy red, love's proper hue,
> Answer'd: " Let it suffice thee that thou know'st
> Us happy, and without love no happiness.
> Whatever pure thou in the body enjoy'st
> (And pure thou were created) we enjoy
> In eminence, and obstacle find none
> Of membrane, joint, or limb, exclusive bars;
> Easier than air with air, if Spirits embrace,
> Total they mix, union of pure with pure
> Desiring; nor restrained conveyance need
> As flesh to mix with flesh, or soul with soul." [55]

The idea here is obviously the same that we have met at the close of *Comus, Lycidas* and the *Epitaphium.* But it now presents itself in different terms. The heavenly marriage, instead of being the " bliss to die with dim descried " of the human Psyche which has preserved herself free from earthly stain, is rather the celestial counterpart of an experience already known on earth, and the rapture which had attached itself to the contemplation of the mystic garden of Adonis is transferred to the lower but more comprehensible mysteries of the Garden of Eden.

[54] Lines 596–604. [55] Lines 618–629.

With this final integration of his sensuous and ideal experience Milton's poetic evolution may be said to be complete. The sequence of his development, while it could hardly have been predicted with assurance, represents a normal and logical unfolding of his unique and powerful personality from youth to maturity under the influence of literary and philosophic culture. It was not, of course, unaffected by his personal circumstances and the outward events of his career. But these incidents and circumstances, even such intimate and moving ones as his marriage with Mary Powell, his blindness, the death of his second wife, while they were of immense importance in quickening his emotions and in furnishing him with occasions for the exercise of his philosophy and faith, were in no case the factors which determined the main direction of his creative effort. The same may be said of his years of public service. The struggles of the Commonwealth and Milton's share in them are clearly enough reflected in *Paradise Lost,* but there is no sound basis for the supposition that the poem differs in its general intention from what it would have been if Milton had written it in 1642. If, then, we continue to look to the conditions and events of Milton's later life for much of the substance and fiber of his major works, it is in the records of his youth that we must seek the essential bent of his genius and the primary moulding forces of his imagination. The great initial impulses of his nature, as these impulses were stimulated and guided by a succession of ideal influences, remain the all-important motives of his poetic art.

NOTE. — It is pointed out to me by Mr. Harris Fletcher of the University of Michigan that the verse epistle to Thomas Young (*Elegy IV*), dated by Milton "anno aetatis 18" and discussed on page 114 of the present study as presumably belonging to the year 1627, was actually written in March, 1625 (*cf.* Stern, *Milton und seine Zeit,* I. 29–30, and note). It therefore antedates *Elegy I* and suggests that the first stages of the process of self-realization which I have described go back to a period earlier than the beginnings of his University career.

SAMSON AGONISTES AND MILTON IN OLD AGE

SAMSON AGONISTES AND MILTON IN OLD AGE

JAMES HOLLY HANFORD

PARADISE LOST, the "monumentum aere perennius" which Milton had planned in youth but whose execution he perilously delayed till beyond his fiftieth year, stood complete and glorious by the summer of 1665. Before its publication in 1667 its author had probably finished the second masterpiece of his maturity, *Paradise Regained.* The composition of *Samson Agonistes* presumably fell within the immediately succeeding years. The two poems appeared together in 1671. Were these later works really afterthoughts, as Thomas Ellwood's well-known anecdote regarding the first of them suggests? Despite the gentle Quaker's unquestionable candor I cannot think so. At his comment, "Thou hast said much here of Paradise lost, but what hast thou to say of Paradise found?", the poet sat in silence and seemed to meditate. We are under no compulsion to believe that he was struck dumb by the novelty of the idea! There is, to be sure, the later very explicit statement, quoted by Ellwood as made when Milton showed him in London the manuscript of *Paradise Regained:* "This is owing to you, for you put it in my head at Chalfont which before I had not thought of," but is it not quite possible that Ellwood is here innocently twisting some merely polite or even ironical remark of Milton's into conformity with his own self-flattering opinion that he was the "fons et origo" of an epic poem?

However this may be, there is a kind of inevitability in these last two works which makes it difficult to accept the idea that a chance suggestion in any very important way determined either of them. In form and general character, at least, we may regard them as predestinate. The evidence goes back to a passage in the *Reason of Church Government,* written in 1641, where Milton takes the reader into his confidence regarding his literary ambitions. He is in doubt, he tells us, whether to adopt the form of an extended epic like the *Aeneid,* or of the brief epic which he says is illustrated by the Book of Job, or of drama, " in which Sophocles and Euripides reign." Since life and energy endured he did all three, taking thereby a triple bond of fame. *Paradise Lost* is the new *Aeneid,* exhibiting all the recognized technique of the full and perfect epic; *Paradise Regained* is something more unusual, a heroic poem composed entirely of dialogue, save for a narrative introduction and conclusion and a few links. Its formal precedent is obviously the Book of Job, regarded not as a drama but, more strictly, as a modification of the epic type. *Samson Agonistes,* finally, is Hellenic tragedy restored.

With his plan of life endeavor thus beyond expectation fulfilled, it seems unlikely that Milton would ever have considered a further addition to his poetical works. The lengthy list of dramatic subjects in the Cambridge manuscript (which includes a " Samson Agonistes " under the title " Dagonalia " and a kind of " Paradise Regained " under that of " Christus Patiens ") together with the corresponding one of epic themes which Professor Gilbert supposes him to have drawn up at the same time [1] — these lists were not in any sense a program. Milton was not given, like the dreamer Coleridge, to projecting vaguely a host of works which he could never write. The manuscript materials are notes taken in the process of canvassing the whole range of available materials before making a final choice. Had Milton enjoyed twenty more years of life and had there been twenty Ellwoods to urge him on, we should never have had at his hands the suggested epic on the deeds of Alfred, or the drama of " Sodom Burning " or the new Macbeth. To write any one of them would have been to mar the antique symmetry of his achievement.

It is not, however, from the standpoint of outward form alone

[1] *The Cambridge Manuscript and Milton's Plans for Epic, Studies in Philology,* 16 (1919). 172–176.

that Milton had reason to regard his contemplated work as done. The three poems are complementary in theme and in ethical idea. Taken together they constitute a complete and unified embodiment of Milton's Christian humanism, the full working out of the didactic purpose which he had accepted as a responsibility implied in his abandonment of the office of preacher for the more congenial one of poet. Let us, as an approach to the present object of giving sharper definition to the significance of *Samson Agonistes* as a work of the poet's last years, consider first the relation of the two companion epics. This relation is clearly not the mechanical one which their contrasting titles might at first suggest, and which, had *Paradise Regained* been named but never written, we should naturally have inferred from Milton's initial statement of his theme:

> Of man's first disobedience and the fruit
> Of that forbidden tree whose mortal taste
> Brought death into the world and all our woe,
> With loss of Eden till one greater man
> Restore us, and regain the blissful seat.

These lines appear to promise a scheme of salvation, according to the ideas of traditional Christianity, and for such a scheme we do not have to await a second work. It is already amply given in the first. But the truth is that Milton pays little more than lip honor to the theological system which his work bears in its superscription. His deeper interest is to be sought elsewhere. At the close of *Paradise Lost* the Archangel Michael, after revealing to Adam at somewhat wearisome length the history of redemption, instructs him in quiet but thrilling words how he may regain what he has lost and build for himself "a paradise within thee happier far."[2] The program is that of all humanity, for Adam is the representative of man. Mere repentance and the sacrifice of Christ are but the form of salvation. The thing itself involves the coöperating will as manifested in the successful meeting of future trial. It is the work of no vicarious and of no single act, but of patient moral discipline in a world of evil, according to a pattern from above. The

[2] Book XII, lines 574 ff.

actual exhibition of the process is not included in *Paradise Lost.* The unique situation of Adam made it impossible for him to serve as an illustration of the struggles and triumphs which raise man from his degraded state. His story is of a fall. It remained for Milton to embody in another work its counterpart, to set forth in detail the successful encounter of humanity with the manifold forms of evil which present themselves in the complexities of a developed civilization. In this view *Paradise Regained* becomes a necessary sequel of *Paradise Lost.* Its theme, in its ethical as distinct from its theological aspect, is, indeed, already foreshadowed in the earlier poem, where the Christian virtues of faith, hope, love, humility, patience are indicated by the angel for Adam's attainment.[3] Their exemplification is in Christ, who becomes for Milton the second Adam, protagonist of a humanity confronted with choices which the first Adam in the freshness of the world could not have known. This is the key to the development of the temptation scenes in *Paradise Regained.*[4] The first and third temptations are special, having to do with the peculiar character and mission of Christ. The second — the kingdoms of the world and the glory of them — is universal, implying all human moral issues. Milton accordingly elaborates it into a "survey of vice with all its baits and seeming pleasures," for which Christ's calm answers afford the antidote of reason. The critical objection that the temptations, given the nature of Christ, are not tempting, is beside the point. They are such temptations as experience shows to be the characteristic ones of men at large — luxury, wealth, power, fame, the pride of knowledge. By his indifference to these allurements and by his Socratic exposition of their emptiness Christ instructs all men how they may despise them. It is no mere piece of biblical commentary that Milton is composing, nor is it an attempt at portraiture of the historic Christ (though this

[3] *Loc. cit.*

[4] This view of the theme of *Paradise Regained* and the corresponding interpretation of the conflict in *Samson Agonistes* are set forth in a different connection in my article *The Temptation Motive in Milton, Studies in Philology,* XV (1918). 176–194.

motive from time to time appears). It is rather a pictorial map of the moral universe, a representation of the happier inner Paradise of life according to right reason, an image of redemption in the only sense in which Milton in his maturer years could even pretend to understand redemption.

The theme was one which commanded the full resources of a life of meditative study, not in the dubious realms of demonology and Christian myth, but in the sun-clear walks of moral and religious wisdom, in history and political philosophy, in the biography of good men and great, in the exalted teachings of poet and seer, most of all in the gospels taken in their plain historical and moral sense, and such a theme gave Milton the opportunity to be altogether his humanistic self. In *Paradise Lost* he had been committed to a more or less inflexible story and to a traditional system of ideas which his best endeavor could not wholly rationalize or adopt to his own more individual thought, with the result that though his imagination was stimulated to unexampled activity, the work is but an imperfect and distorted image of his philosophical point of view. In *Paradise Regained* he was largely free. It is no wonder that he resented the suggestion that the second work was inferior to the first. Though lacking in color and vivid outward incident, it had even its points of superority. Its drama was of an inward intensity like that of the Book of Job. Its truth was unmixed with the accessory element of fiction. To Milton, in the severity of his age, this was argument of excellence. He knew, moreover, that the poem was more harmonious than *Paradise Lost,* simpler if less sensuous, and woven more close in "matter, form, and style."

It is now possible to consider the less obvious position of *Samson Agonistes* in Milton's poetic scheme. Formally and theologically the poem has no relation at all to its predecessors. For Milton does not, in his interpretation of the Old Testament material, adopt the point of view of the medieval religious drama, which built everything it treated into a single structure, regarding the events and characters of Hebrew history as episodes in an action which proceeded logically from the creation of the angels to the day of judgment. The story of Samson has for him an independent human value, neither implying nor prefiguring the life of Christ. For this very reason it adapts itself more naturally to his purposes, and affords the means of completing his representation of the state of man. The function of Christ we have already seen. He is, besides being the redeemer, the second Adam and the model man. But unlike Adam, Christ is without sin. Hence while he is the pattern and guide of human life, his victory is not, as ours must be, a recovery of something lost. The full account of man in his relation to the forces of good and evil demands another picture — the representation of frail humanity, burdened with the memory of former sin, but now repentant, restored to strength, and wrestling successfully with further trial. To what extent can *Samson Agonistes* be shown to fit this ideal prescription? The question raises some points of interpretation which appear to have been neglected by the numerous critics who, since Samuel Johnson, have discussed the merits of the work as drama.

When Milton, in 1641, first considered the life of the great but erring Hebrew champion as possible literary material and set down five subjects from it in the Cambridge manuscript, he was doubtless prompted chiefly by the coincidence of the story with characteristic themes of ancient drama. Samson was blind through his own guilt like Oedipus. In all other respects he was a Hebraic Herakles — the performer of incredible labors, enthralled by woman, sealing his baffled strength by a final destructive act. Such circumstances meant much in Milton's predisposition to a literary theme. More influential, however, in his final decision in favor of the subject was his perception of the parallel between Samson's sin and that of Adam. The point had already impressed itself upon him when he wrote of Adam's fall in the Ninth Book of *Paradise Lost,*

> So rose the Danite strong,
> Herculean Samson from the harlot lap
> Of Philistean Dalilah, and waked
> Shorn of his strength, they desolate and bare
> Of all their virtue.[5]

[5] Lines 1059–1062.

In the tragedy itself he is concerned with the fallen Samson's recovery of God's lost favor. The process involves his punishment and repentance, and the facing of new trials with a firmness won of experience and faith. It involves also a reward in the consciousness of God's having again accepted him as a worthy instrument of his purposes.

The trial itself is, I believe, the real center of the inward action, providing the play with such vital dramatic conflict as it exhibits. The Chorus and Manoa continually suggest distrust and compromise. They imply, in their attempted consolation, that Samson has been deceived in his belief that he once enjoyed God's special favor and was his chosen vessel. His marriages were not, as he had supposed, of a divine suggestion. God's dealings in sending the angel of his birth and apparently electing him as the champion of Israel, only to desert and leave him impotent, are unintelligible, if not unjust, for all has been turned to the glory of the Philistines. Against this Samson opposes, on the whole, the attitude of faith. He resists the suggestion that God was not really with him in the past. He reiterates the cry that nothing of all his evils has befallen him but justly. He meets the challenge of Manoa's

> Yet Israel still serves with all his tribes,

with the rejoinder that it is they themselves who through their own weakness have neglected God's proposed deliverance. For himself he knows that he has forfeited all hope, but he remains unshaken in the belief that God will not

> Connive, or linger, thus provoked,
> But will arise, and his great name assert.

Throughout the dialogue there are marked similarities to the Book of Job. Manoa and the Chorus have a function analogous to that of the friends who sharpen Job's agony by their mistaken comfort. Samson's resistance of the attempt to shake the convictions of his innermost experience has its counterpart in Job's passionate denial of the imputation of unrighteousness. There is, of course, a formal contrast between the two, in that Samson, unlike Job, is afflicted by a sense of sin, but both are loyal to truth and both maintain their positions against the apparent facts. Both, finally, are rewarded for their consistency by a manifestation of God's approval. With Job it is the voice out of a whirlwind, with Samson the renewal of "rousing motions" of innermost impulse, which have stirred and guided him to great deeds before his fall.

Of these motives there is in the Scriptural account of Samson not the slightest hint. The hero of the Hebrew chronicle is a naïve and semi-humorous märchen figure, whose sluggish intellect is far removed from any capability of spiritual conflict. Milton preserves the traits of his impulsiveness of temper and his original simplicity of spirit, but endows him, after his disillusionment, with extraordinary force of mind and with penetrating insight. The infusion into this mighty champion of old, of the complex emotions of the maturest and most profound creation of Hebrew thought, is the last masterful stroke of Milton's genius. For it, he had, to my knowledge, no precedent in literary tradition.

But if Milton is indebted to Job for the most essential elements in his conception of Samson's character, it is to his own constructive imagination, working within the artistic forms provided by occidental drama, that he owes the development of his theme. In the Book of Job there is little outward action and no clear progression. In *Samson* there are both. The framework of the plot is that of a Greek play. It is simple even to meagerness. Samson is consoled by the Chorus, worried by Dalilah, insulted by Harapha, summoned before the Philistines by an officer. Old Manoa is busy meanwhile with misguided plans for his release, the moment of his success ironically coinciding with that of Samson's death. A messenger relates the catastrophe. The Chorus sings of Samson's fate and triumph.

Within this formal action the spiritual movement is richer than one at first observes. At the opening Samson is a spectacle of tragic misery and debasement. Out of his intense depression there rises higher and higher the note of active pain. At first his utterance concerns chiefly his physical and outward state:

O loss of sight, of thee I most complain!
Blind among enemies! O worse than chains,
Dungeon or beggery, or decrepit age!

The first chorus, unheard by the protagonist, echoes and interprets his lament, with emphasis on the contrast between what once he was, is now. In the ensuing dialogue Samson's attention is diverted from his present wretchedness to its causes and significance. The memory of his fault is more bitter than the punishment wherewith it has been visited.

Ye see, O friends,
How many evils have enclosed me round;
Yet that which once was the worst now least afflicts me,
Blindness, for had I sight, confused with shame,
How could I once look up, or heave the head,
Who, like a foolish pilot, have shipwracked
My vessel trusted to me from above.

The sight of Manoa wakes "another inward grief," and his words are as a goad to Samson's bitter remembrance. His proposal to treat with the Philistine lords serves only to reveal his son's indifference to his outward fate. The scene culminates in a spiritual outburst, expressive no longer of the hero's physical misery and obvious disgrace,

Ensnared, assaulted, overcome, led bound,
Thy foes' derision, captive, poor, and blind,

but of the inner agony of soul which springs from full contemplation of his sins, "and sense of Heaven's desertion." The opening words of the passage clearly indicate the forward movement:

Oh, that torment should not be confined
To the body's wounds and sores,
With maladies innumerable
In heart, head, breast, and reins,
But must secret passage find
To the inmost mind,
There exercise all his fierce accidents,
And on her purest spirits prey,
As on entrails, joints, and limbs,
With answerable pains, but more intense,
Though void of corporal sense! [6]

[6] Lines 606–616.

The conclusion is one of unrelieved despair and marks the darkest moment of Samson's suffering, corresponding precisely to Adam's remorseful misery as he meditates upon his sin:

> Hopeless are all my evils, all remediless.
> This one prayer yet remains, might I be heard,
> No long petition — speedy death,
> The close of all my miseries and the balm.

Henceforth we have recovery. By confronting his own guilt without evasion, and by resisting the temptation to doubt God's ways are just, or to fear for the ultimate triumph of his cause, Samson has won the right to be put to proof a second time. His firmness is subjected first to the insidious approaches of Dalilah, whose visit, however doubtfully motivated in itself, is essential to the idea of the drama. Her plea is specious, but Samson remains unmoved, the significance of his victory being pointed out in the choric comment,

> Yet beauty, though injurious, hath strange power,
> After offence returning, to regain
> Love once possessed, nor can be easily
> Repulsed, without much inward passion felt
> And secret sting of amorous remorse.

He next confronts physical force in the person of Harapha, who collapses, like all brute menace, before the champion's indifference to fear, and the chorus, participating for the moment in Samson's strength, sings the great ode,

> O how comely it is, and how reviving,
> When God into the hands of their deliverer
> Puts invincible might,
> To quell the mighty of the earth, the oppressor,
> The brute and boistrous force of violent men.[7]

They are, of course, like Samson himself, still blind to what is to come, and they go on to sing of patience as the final crown of saints.

The coming of the officer creates a problem. Samson's refusal, at first, to do his bidding illustrates his uncompromising alle-

[7] Lines 1267 ff.

giance to the God of his fathers and his contempt of personal safety. The Chorus suggests the easier way of yielding, pointing out the fact that he has already served the Philistines (with the old implication that he cannot regard himself as a being set apart). Their reasoning is met with a clear distinction between compromise in things indifferent and the surrender of a point of conscience. Then, as if in answer to this final proof of Samson's single devotedness to God's service, comes again the inner prompting, " disposing to something extraordinary my thoughts." He obeys it unhesitatingly and goes forth under divine guidance as of old. He has, in a sense, regained his own lost Paradise, and in his story Milton, by vindicating the power of a free but erring will to maintain itself in obedience and be restored to grace, has again asserted eternal Providence and justified the ways of God to man.

The fact that Samson is an Old Testament figure and achieves his triumph before the time of the Redeemer shows the true place of Christ in Milton's system. The blood of his sacrifice is plainly no necessary instrument of salvation; even his example may be dispensed with by those who enjoy a direct and special relation with the Divine. Yet the Hebrews did have Christ in prophecy, and for the men of later time he is the way. By his present example the path is open, not for chosen heroes alone, but for all, to

> love with fear the only God, to walk
> As in his presence, ever to observe
> His providence, and on him sole depend,
> Merciful over all his works, with good
> Still overcoming evil, and by small
> Accomplishing great things — by things deemed weak
> Subverting worldly-strong, and worldly-wise
> By simply meek; [8]

Such is Milton's final teaching and the ethical goal of his poetic art. The desire expressed in the introduction to Book IX of *Paradise Lost* to sing " the better fortitude of patience and heroic martyrdom," is fulfilled by the portrayal of a divine pattern in *Paradise Regained*. *Samson Agonistes* is its nearest

[8] *P. L.*, XII. 562–569.

possible fulfillment in the life of mortal man. To embody it more completely by representing the humbler trials and victories of daily life would have been incompatible with the tradition of Milton's literary allegiance — incompatible, too, with the memory of the heroic struggle in which he himself had been engaged.

Of this experience and this struggle I have as yet said nothing. How deeply it enters into the bone and sinew of *Samson Agonistes* no one can doubt. That Milton felt the parallel between his own situation and that of Samson and that he in some way identified himself with his hero is obvious and has been emphasized by the biographers. I have myself elsewhere pointed out that in making Samson wrestle with despair Milton was championing his own faith assaulted by inward murmuring and challenged by the apparent failure of his cause.[9] It remains to enquire as to the extent and nature of this personal identification and to analyze more exactly the psychological reactions, conscious and unconscious, which are implied in the composition of the play.

Let us recognize at once that *Samson Agonistes* is a work of art and not a disguised autobiography. To a reader unacquainted with Milton's life the poem would seem as monumentally independent as *Prometheus Bound.* It deserves to be so judged and would, perhaps, stand higher as a masterpiece of art if it had been less often used as an illustration of Milton's personal life and temper. It should not, however, suffer from interpretation in the light of the poet's characteristic moods and thoughts, if we clearly recognize the conditions of their operation in his creative work. His most intimate emotions are invariably sublimated by the imagination and so far depersonalized. The process enables him to project himself with sympathy into characters and situations which have only a partial analogy with his own. So it is with his representations of Comus, or of Satan and Adam in *Paradise Lost.* In other cases, as in those of Dalilah, Eve, or Mammon he is capable, within a limited range, of being as objective as any artist of essentially romantic temper.

In the representation of Samson, Milton has undoubtedly put

[9] *Studies in Philology,* XV. 176–194.

more of himself than in any other of his imaginative creations. The sense of power and dignity, the "plain heroic magnitude of mind," the will toward championship are Milton. So too is the noble self-pity, expressed in the consciousness of deprivation in the loss of sight ("The sun to me is dark, and silent as the moon"), and the feeling of physical helplessness ("In power of others, never in my own"). But all this is heightened and idealized for purposes of art. The tragic gloom and flat despair of Samson, the wretchedness of pain, the distaste of life, are the embodiments of an aesthetic mood which owes quite as much to literature as to personal experience. As a matter of fact the impression left by such direct biographical records as we have of Milton in old age is quite the reverse of this, suggesting the persistence in him to the end of a temper unspoiled by tribulation. The "cheerful godliness" of Wordsworth's sonnet appears to be an entirely appropriate description of the poet's habitual outward mood in the last years of his life.

With regard to his blindness it is worth noting that the most poignant allusions to it were written longest after the event itself. At the actual moment of the catastrophe Milton was silent. His poetical occupation in the immediately succeeding years was the translation of Psalms, a literary and religious discipline. In 1654 he gives expression in prose, not to his sense of irrecoverable loss, but to the consciousness of spiritual compensation in "an interior illumination more precious and more pure." [10] In 1655, on the third anniversary of his loss of sight, he allows himself to consider how his "light is spent ere half his days," and to give voice to the pathos of his condition, only, however, as a preparation for the expression of acquiescence and of the consolations which come from the sense of having sacrificed himself in a noble cause. The utterances in *Paradise Lost* are touched with a deeper pathos, but it is first in *Samson,* where they are no longer directly personal, that they become a tragic cry:

> Dark, dark, dark, amid the blaze of moon,
> Irrecoverably dark, total eclipse,
> Without all hope of day.

[10] *Defensio Secunda, Prose Works* (Bohn), I. 239.

A similar account might be given of the poet's antifeminism. It is entirely absent from the sonnets which belong to the days of his estrangement from Mary Powell. Indeed the two poems written at that time, *To a Virtuous Young Lady* and *To the Lady Margaret Ley,* are sincere though sober tributes to female virtue. The general indictment of the sex begins with Adam's words to Eve in Book X of *Paradise Lost* and reaches a strain of unrelieved bitterness in *Samson Agonistes.*

Such are the facts, as we read them in the chronological consideration of Milton's works. One cannot fail to be struck by the analogy which exists between the processes of the poet's expression of certain phases of his inmost experience in this last epoch of his literary life and the youthful development which we have studied in the preceding essay. The position of *Samson Agonistes* in its relation to the complex of emotions and ideas which centered in the poet's blindness is singularly like that of *Comus* with reference to the conflict of sensuous and ideal impulses in his adolescence. Each represents the culmination of a train of introspective thoughts which may easily be conceived to have been disturbing to Milton's mental equilibrium. In each work he appears to achieve for the first time a full expression of these emotions, and in achieving it to obtain a spiritual mastery of them. The result is one which is always, perhaps, in some degree present in the intenser activity of the creative imagination, and it has received general recognition from the critics and philosophers of literature. The most luminous statement is the following by Croce in his *Aesthetic.*[11] "By elaborating his impressions man frees himself from them. By objectifying them, he removes them from him and makes himself their superior. The liberating and purifying function of art is another aspect and another formula of its character as activity. Activity is the deliverer, just because it drives away passivity. This also explains why it is usual to attribute to artists both the maximum of sensibility and the maximum of insensibility or Olympian serenity. The two characters are compatible, for they do not refer to the same object. The sensibility or passion re-

[11] Chapter 2. Douglas Ainsley's translation, 1922.

lates to the rich material which the artist absorbs into his psychic organism, the insensibility or serenity to the form with which he subdues and dominates the tumult of sensations and passions."

It is scarcely possible to determine the degree to which Milton, in recreating and transforming emotions which in their rawer form made inroads upon his carefully cherished serenity, experienced a similar deliverance. Some light may be gained, however, by a consideration of certain neglected aspects of the play itself, the indications, namely, which the poet has given of what he himself thought of its function as a work of art. These indications refer mainly, to be sure, to what he looked for in its effect upon the reader or spectator, but they are not without application to the artist as well and it seems to me quite clear that Milton must have been guided in his interpretation of the power of tragedy to effect spiritual benefits upon others by what he had himself experienced in creating it.

The question centers in his understanding of the formula for tragedy and its purgative effect as given in the famous Aristotelian definition. The importance of this formula in Milton's thought and the degree to which he must have been conscious of it in constructing his drama are suggested by the fact that he quotes it in Latin on his title page and devotes the first part of his prose preface to its elaboration. His opening statement is as follows: "Tragedy as it was anciently composed hath been ever held the gravest, moralest, and most profitable of all other poems; therefore said by Aristotle to be of power by raising pity and fear, or terror, to purge the mind of those and such like passions, that is to temper and reduce them to just measure with a kind of delight, stirred up by seeing those passions well imitated."

In considering the application of this principle to *Samson Agonistes* we must observe, first of all, that, by representing a clearly marked triumph of the human will over its own weakness, and by the substitution of Providence for blind fate as the power which overrules the action, the play provides material for a different understanding of catharsis from that contemplated by Aristotle, an understanding which falls in with the first part of Milton's description — that tragedy is the gravest, moralest, and most profitable of poetic forms — rather than with the last — that it transforms painful emotions into pleasurable. On a superficial view we might, indeed, be tempted to regard the purgation, as Milton actually worked it out, as a purely ethical and religious process, the result of a consciously didactic purpose by which our faith is strengthened and our sympathy with Samson's pain swallowed up in our exultation in his triumph. It is the function of Manoa's last speech and of the final chorus to emphasize this motive:

> Come, come, no time for lamentation now,
> Nor much more cause; Samson hath quit himself
> Like Samson, and heroicly hath finished
> A life Heroic. . . .
> With God not parted from him as was feared,
> But favouring and assisting to the end.
>
> . . . .
>
> All is best, though we oft doubt,
> What the unsearchable dispose
> Of highest wisdom brings about
> And ever best found in the close.

To some critics[12] these quotations have seemed an adequate formula for the poem as a whole, and a mark of the failure of *Samson Agonistes* to embody the genuinely tragic motive of the unsuccessful struggle of man with fate. Such a judgment is obvious and in part correct. It fails, however, to take account of the actuality of the tragic impression which the drama must leave upon every reader who comes to it unhampered by definitions and comparisons. The pain of the earlier scenes is something which cannot be so easily displaced. Sealed as it is with the hero's death, it outlives all consolation, as the tragic suffering of Hamlet outlives the accomplishment of his purpose, the choric benediction of Horatio, and the restoration of a wholesome commonwealth by Fortinbras. The pronouncement "All is best" is of scarcely more avail than the identical formulae which bring Greek plays to their conclusion and from which this

[12] See Paull F. Baum, *Samson Agonistes Again, Publications of the Modern Language Association,* XXXVI (1921). 365 ff.

one is derived. The consolation which is offered of "what can quiet us in a death so noble" is not enough. Samson should have gone on from one glad triumph to another and emerged unscathed. Outward circumstance, the treacheries of others, and his own conspiring fault have brought him low, and have constrained him to wear, however gloriously, the crown of martyrdom. Here surely is tragedy enough. Though Providence is proclaimed, its ways are dark and its face, at times, is hardly to be distinguished from the countenance of Fate herself. The secret is that there remains an irreducible element in the midst of Milton's faith — a sense as keen as Shakespeare's of the reality of suffering which neither the assurance of God's special favors to himself nor his resolute insistence on the final triumph of his righteousness can blot out. The antique strain in Milton's experience and thought stands side by side with the Christian. and the two alternate or combine in their domination of his artistic moods. It is in vain that he repudiates stoicism as a futile refuge and a false philosophy; he is betrayed by the vehemence of his declarations against it, and he instinctively adopts its weapons.

These considerations prepare us to examine the operation in *Samson Agonistes* of catharsis in its strict Aristotelian sense. Milton's effort to demonstrate in his drama the truth of Aristotle's pronouncement is part and parcel of a thoroughgoing conscious classicism, which extends far beyond such matters as the ordering of the incidents and the employment of ancient devices like the messenger. It is shown in a more philosophic and intrinsic way in the subtle turns which the poet gives to the interpretation of his theme in order to bring it more nearly into conformity with the spirit of ancient tragedy. Professor Baum [13] counts it a major defect of *Samson Agonistes* that the hero's tragic fault is undignified and sub-heroic. But observe the means which Milton takes to dignify it. He associates it with the most dignified of all tragic faults — rebellious pride. Intoxicated by success Samson forgets to refer his victories to their source, and so becomes, in Milton's interpretation, an instance of

[13] *Loc. cit.*

classical hybris. Like Shakespeare's Mark Anthony he "struts to his destruction."

> Fearless of danger, like a petty God,
> I walked about, admired of all, and dreaded
> On hostile ground, none daring my assault.
> Then swollen with pride, into the snare I fell
> Of fair fallacious looks, venerial trains.[14]

This is somewhat forced, one must confess, and Milton appears to be aware of it. Witness the shading he is compelled to give to the idea in the following:

> But I
> God's counsel have not kept, his holy secret
> Presumptiously have published, impiously,
> *Weakly at least and shamefully* — a sin
> That Gentiles in their parables condemn
> To their Abyss and horrid pains confined.[15]

The cloak of Prometheus and Tantalus evidently refuses to fit the less majestic Hebrew Titan. The conception of hybris and Ate applies more perfectly to the Philistines and is accordingly invoked in the triumphant semi-chorus beginning in line 1669:

> While their hearts were jocund and sublime,
> Drunk with idolatry, drunk with wine
> And fat regorged of bulls and goats,
> Chaunting their idol, and preferring
> Before our Living Dread, who dwells
> In Silo, his bright sanctuary,
> Among them he a spirit of phrenzy sent,
> Who hurt their minds,
> And urged them on with mad desire
> To call in haste for their destroyer.
> They, only set on sport and play,
> Unweetingly importuned
> Their own destruction to come speedy upon them.
> So fond are mortal men,
> Fallen into wrath divine,
> As their own ruin on themselves to invite,
> Insensate left, or to sense reprobate,
> And with blindness internal struck.

Both passages, however, are illustrative of the degree to which Milton had grasped the central motive of Greek tragedy and

[14] Lines 529–533. [15] Lines 496–501.

the pains he was at to bring his own material under the ethical, religious, and artistic formulae afforded by it.

A more vital result of his assimilation of the point of view of his ancient models is to be found in the great chorus which follows Samson's deeper expression of despair, in lines 608–650. If anything in Milton or indeed in all modern literature deserves to be called a reproduction of antiquity it is this passage. It is as perfectly representative as Milton could have wished of "Aeschylus, Sophocles, Euripides, the three tragic poets unequalled yet by any, and the best rule to all who endeavor to write Tragedy," and it comes little short of their noblest choral odes in the grandeur and intensity of its tragic feeling. In the majestic rhythms of the opening the Chorus sings of the vanity of consolation in the ears of the afflicted and expostulates with Providence in its uneven course with men. Thoroughly Greek and as thoroughly Miltonic is the centering of attention on the woes, not of the common rout of men who grow up and perish like the summer fly, but on those of heroic mould, "with gifts and graces eminently adorned." The ensuing lines embody the idea of the excess of evil which rains down on the head of the tragic hero according to Aristotle's description in the *Poetics:*

> Nor only dost degrade them, or remit
> To life obscured, which were a fair dismission,
> But throw'st them lower than thou didst exalt them high —
> Unseemly falls in human eye,
> Too grievous for the trespass or omission;
> Oft leav'st them to the hostile sword
> Of heathen and profane, their carcasses
> To dogs and fowls a prey, or else captived,
> Or to the unjust tribunals, under change of times,
> And condemnation of the ungrateful multitude.
> If these they escape, perhaps in poverty
> With sickness and disease thou bow'st them down,
> Painful diseases and deformed,
> In crude old age;
> Though not disordinate, yet causeless suffering
> The punishment of dissolute days. In fine,
> Just or unjust alike seem miserable,
> For oft alike both come to evil end.

The personal note here is too distinct to be mistaken. "Unjust tribunals under change of times," "their carcasses to dogs and fowls a prey" are certainly echoes of the Restoration, with its brutal trials of men like Henry Vane, and the indignities to which the bodies of Cromwell and Ireton were subjected. The parallel and not less wretched fate of poverty and disease is Milton's own. He goes so far as almost to specify the rheumatic ills from which we know him to have suffered — "painful diseases and deformed" — with the bitter reflection that these afflictions, justly the fruit of dissipation, may come also to those who, like himself, have lived in temperance. Nowhere else in his works, not even in the laments of Adam, does Milton permit himself to indulge in so unrelieved an expression of pagan sentiment. He does so under the shield of dramatic objectivity, yet none of his words spring from deeper sources in his consciousness. Here momentarily he faces the world with no other arms than those of pure humanity, giving utterance to a view of life directly opposed to that to which he had subdued his thinking as a whole.

It is in such a mood as this and in such an utterance that Milton must, if ever, have felt, in his own emotional experience, the reality of the Aristotelian catharsis, and the need of it. The question of the means whereby affliction may be soothed is one which had always interested him, and his works contain numerous suggestive utterances on the subject. It is prominent in the discussion of the case of Samson. Thus, contemplating, at this point, his hero's misery, he makes the Chorus tell how useless for the sufferer in his pangs are those wise consolations of philosophy, "writ with studied argument, lenient of grief and anxious thought." It is only, they affirm, by "secret refreshings from above" that the afflicted wretch can be restored. But such refreshings are obviously not always to be commanded. To prepare for their benign influence the mind must first be emptied of its pent-up bitterness, and for such a process tragedy, in the Aristotelian conception, supplies the means. So, one would suppose, might Milton have thought and felt. And if such was his experience it is not surprising that he should have dwelt with such insistence on the rationale of the process in his prose preface.

His initial statement I have already quoted. Pity, fear, and like passions, it implies, are, in their raw state, dangerous and painful. Objectively represented, they are tempered and reduced to just measure by a kind of delight. "Nor is Nature," adds Milton, "wanting in her own effects to make good his assertion; for so, in Physic, things of melancholic hue and quality are used against melancholy, sour against sour, salt to remove salt humours." This passage has often been cited with approval by classical scholars as expressing the soundest modern interpretation of the dark oracle of Aristotle's pronouncement, and there has been discussion of Milton's priority in employing the medical analogy. No one, I think, has called attention to his application of this conception to the analysis of Samson's spiritual ills in an outstanding passage in the play itself. The hero has just expressed his indifference to the efforts proposed in his behalf and his expectation of an early death. Manoa replies:

> Believe not these suggestions, which proceed
> From anguish of the mind, and humours black
> That mingle with thy fancy.[16]

There follows the great lyric outburst of Samson's spiritual woe, which must now be given at greater length.

> O that torment should not be confined
> To the body's wounds and sores,
> With maladies innumerable
> In heart, head, breast, and reins;
> But must secret passage find
> To the inmost mind,
> There exercise all his fierce accidents,
> And on her purest spirits prey,
> As on entrails, joints and limbs,
> With answerable pains, but more intense,
> Though void of corporal sense!
> My griefs not only pain me
> As a lingering disease,
> But, finding no redress, ferment and rage;
> Nor less than wounds immedicable
> Rankle, and fester, and gangrene,
> To black mortification.
> Thoughts, my tormentors, armed with deadly stings,
> Mangle my apprehensive tenderest parts,

[16] Lines 599–601.

> Exasperate, exulcerate, and raise
> Dire inflammation, which no cooling herb
> Or medicinal liquor can assuage,
> Nor breath of vernal air from snowy Alp.
> Sleep hath forsook and given me o'er
> To death's benumbing opium as my only cure;
> Thence faintings, swoonings of despair,
> And sense of Heaven's desertion.

The idea which Milton here develops with somewhat shocking explicitness is obviously the same as that which underlies his conception of catharsis—the idea, namely, that the passions operate in precisely the manner of bodily poisons, which, when they find no outlet, rage destructively within. Samson is given over to pity and fear, and there is no apparent prospect of relief, no cooling herb or medicinal liquor to purify the "black mortification" of his thoughts. It is quite clear, then, that Milton intends to suggest a kind of Aristotelian diagnosis of Samson's tragic state, parallel to the more obvious religious interpretation which I have previously expounded. But if he partly identified himself with his hero, then such a diagnosis would serve also to that extent to describe his own. As, however, he draws a sharp distinction on the religious side between Samson's spiritual darkness and his own illumination by an inner light, so here he must have been conscious of a difference in the manner of their deliverance from the morbid introspection to which they are equally subject. The intensity of Samson's pain lasts only so long as he remains inactive. His lyric elaboration of his inward woe is immediately followed by the unexpected visits of his foes. His attention is thus distracted from his suffering to a series of situations which confront him and he finally loses himself in glorious though disastrous action.

For Milton, in the impotence of his situation after the Restoration, there can be no such deliverance. He is enrolled perforce among those "whom patience finally must crown." But he has in his possession a recourse without which the way of patience is at times too hard. The purgation which the untutored champion of Israel must find in deeds is available to the man of culture through the activity of the mind and spirit. It offers itself to Milton in a dual form, corresponding to his twofold inheritance from the Reformation and the Renaissance. As the play draws to an end the two motives are subtly balanced and as nearly reconciled as, perhaps, it is within the power of human skill to reconcile them. The champion's final deed and the triumph of God's uncontrollable intent promote in us a sense of exultation and confirm our faith, but the greatness of his suffering and the pathos of his death produce a different effect, making possible the serene dismission of the close:

> His servants he, with new acquist
> Of true experience from this great event,
> With peace and consolation hath dismissed
> And calm of mind, all passion spent.

It is characteristic of the critical self-consciousness which Milton carries with him even in his moments of highest creative inspiration and suggestive also of the vital uses to which he turned aesthetic as well as religious doctrine that the last word of all should be an almost explicit reference to the tragic formula which he had derived from the authority of "the master of those who know."

THE RELIGIOUS THOUGHT OF DONNE IN RELATION TO MEDIEVAL AND LATER TRADITIONS

THE RELIGIOUS THOUGHT OF DONNE IN RELATION TO MEDIEVAL AND LATER TRADITIONS

LOUIS I. BREDVOLD

THE term "metaphysical poetry," consecrated by use since the time of Dryden, has been a fruitful source of misunderstanding of Donne and his followers. It originated at a time when the metaphysical style was regarded as a literary fad or affection, an intellectual gymnastic. Donne, said Dryden, "affects the metaphysics, not only in his satires, but in his amorous verses, where nature should reign; and perplexes the minds of the fair sex with nice speculations of philosophy, when he should engage their hearts, and entertain them with the softnesses of love." Dr. Johnson, in a famous passage, spoke of the *discordia concors* of the metaphysical style as of a mere exhibition of ingenuity. The reader, "though he sometimes admires, is seldom pleased;" and the desire of these poets, Johnson thought, "was only to say what they hoped had never been said before." Dryden and Johnson provided the fundamental ideas and set the tone for succeeding scholarship and criticism down to comparatively recent times. Even so different a critic as Hazlitt praised fervently Johnson's denunciation of the "conceitists."[1] Hallam thought that in the poetry of Donne "it would perhaps be difficult to select three passages that we should care to read again."[2] Masson, indeed, ventured the surmise that "the admiration of his contemporaries was not a mere pretence," but he could nevertheless see in Donne's verses only mental acrobatics.[3] "Metaphysical poetry" suggested only a meaningless preoccupation with the forms of a decayed scholasticism.

1 Hazlitt, *The Comic Writers,* Lecture III.
2 Hallam, *Literature of Europe* (2d ed.; London, 1843), II. 31–33.
3 Masson, *Life of Milton* (Boston, 1859), I. 377.

Since Masson criticism of Donne and his followers has become much more enlightened and sympathetic, and the studies of them are too numerous to be discussed here. But the most important recent contributions, by Courthope, Palmer, and Grierson, have in common, very significantly, that they attempt to explain the metaphysical style as the result of the manner in which these poets understood and experienced life. They all relate the school of Donne to the general movement of the Renaissance, in its modern conception since Burckhardt,[4] that is, as a disintegration of Medievalism and a liberation of the individual. Palmer thought that Donne belonged to the second phase of the development of this new individualism.

> " A second period of the Renaissance began," he says, " a period of introspection, where each man was prone to insist on the importance of whatever was his own. At the coming of the Stuarts this great change was prepared, and was steadily fostered by their inability to comprehend it. In science, Bacon had already questioned established authority and sent men to nature to observe for themselves. In government, the king's prerogative was speedily questioned, and Parliament became so rebellious that they were often dismissed. A revolution in poetic taste was under way. Spenser's lulling rhythms and bloodless heroes were being displaced by the jolting and passionate realism of Donne. . . . The soul of man took the place of the outer world, while the old delight in daring and difficult tasks appeared in this new sphere as a kind of intellectual audacity and an ardent exploration of mental enigmas. To how many strange theories did this England of the first half of the seventeenth century give rise! To exploit a new doctrine became more exciting than a voyage to the Spanish main." [5]

Courthope insisted that the school of " wit " which developed simultaneously in all the literatures of Europe must be " the result of the operation of similar forces, religious, social and political, and of the influence of some wide-spread literary tradition." [6] Its essential characteristics, paradox, hyperbole, and

[4] On the importance of Burckhardt's work in laying the foundations of modern study of the Renaissance, see Walter Goetz, *Mittelalter und Renaissance, Historische Zeitschrift*, 98 (1907). 30–54, and Émile Gebhart, *La Renaissance Italienne et la Philosophie de l'Histoire, Revue des Deux Mondes*, 72 (1885). 342–379.

[5] *The English Works of George Herbert* (ed. G. H. Palmer; Boston, 1905), I. 98–99, 155–156.

[6] *Pope's Works* (ed. Elwell and Courthope; London, 1889), V. 52–61.

excess of metaphor, he traced to the survival of Medievalism; but they were only the fragments of a decayed age. Many poets of the Renaissance, characterized by " a new kind of Pyrrhonism " represented by Montaigne, " seized upon the rich materials of the old and ruined philosophy to decorate the structures which they built out of their lawless fancy. On such foundations rose the school of metaphysical wit, of which the earliest and most remarkable example is furnished in the poetry of John Donne."[7] Grierson, likewise, explains the metaphysical style as a blending of the " dialectic of the Schools " with the " new temper of the Renaissance."[8]

These three students therefore agree, though with varying emphasis and interpretation, on the fundamental principle that the metaphysical style is an expression of the disintegration of medieval thought under the influence of the new individualism and scepticism of the Renaissance.

Rather surprisingly, a still more recent study seeks to minimize the Renaissance element in Donne.[9] The author, Mary Paton Ramsay, is a disciple of Professor Picavet of Paris, whose special contribution to the history of medieval philosophy has been an emphasis on the strong Plotinian element in it. And it is in the most complete discipleship to M. Picavet that Miss Ramsay has written her study of Donne; she sought to explain by the persistence of this medieval Plotinian tradition " la mentalité du poète lui-même, et celle de sa génération."[10] She therefore ignores the Pyrrhonism, not only in Donne, but in the English Renaissance as a whole. " Nos remarques," she says, " sont limitées à la littérature, mais nous croyons pouvoir affirmer qu'il ne faut pas parler de l'esprit sceptique dans la première partie du [dixseptième] siècle. L'esprit de critique sceptique ne fit vraiment son apparition en Angleterre qu'avec

[7] Courthope, *History of English Poetry* (London, 1911), III. 103–117, 147–148.

[8] *The Poems of John Donne* (Oxford, 1912), II, *Introduction.*

[9] *Les Doctrines Médiévales chez Donne, Le Poète Métaphysicien de l'Angleterre* (Oxford, 1917). I have discussed the methods and results of this study in a review in *The Journal of English and Germanic Philology,* XXI (1922). 347–353.

[10] *Op. cit.,* p. 2.

Hobbes." [11] John Donne was, she believes, a thorough Plotinian, untouched by metaphysical doubts.

> " Chez lui," she says of the poet, " on découvre, en étudiant à fond ses écrits en prose et en vers, un penseur profondément religieux en même temps que fermement convaincu de la valeur de la raison humaine. . . . Dans les hautes régions de la spéculation métaphysique dont les docteurs du moyen âge lui montraient le chemin, il n'y avait pas de place pour les doutes. Des doutes pouvaient tourmenter Donne devant des questions ecclésiastiques mêlées à des conceptions politiques, ou devant son propre coeur conscient de faiblesse et de péché. Mais non quand son esprit s'élève à ces hauteurs. Alors l'idée crée l'expression qui lui convient et nous voyons ce que Donne est capable de produire comme poète." [12]

In other words, the mind of Donne, both as poet and preacher, was seriously and consistently medieval, and untouched by the storm and stress of the Renaissance.

We may object at once that this conception of Donne as an exponent of Plotinianism simplifies beyond recognition his complex and enigmatic personality and removes from the story of his inner life that element of dramatic uncertainty and suspense which makes his biography so fascinating. For Donne cannot be explained by any mere systematization of his ideas. His riddle must be read by a sympathetic appreciation of his personality, his greed for knowledge and experience, his difficulties, disappointments and dissatisfactions, and the increasing depth and intensity of his religious feeling; the final study of Donne must be biographical. And yet Donne was obviously a learned man, whose mind had been enriched by many cultural traditions, whose personal feeling and literary expression were conditioned by medieval and Renaissance modes of thought. In another place I have discussed the traditional aspect of Donne's early verse.[13] In this paper I propose to study in a similar way certain aspects of his intellectual and religious experience, his mingled scepticism and mysticism, with the double purpose of tracing his religious development and of re-stating, with special emphasis on some hitherto neglected phases, his relation to

[11] *Ibid.*, pp. 11–12. [12] *Ibid.*, p. 18.

[13] *The Naturalism of Donne in Relation to Some Renaissance Traditions,* in *The Journal of English and Germanic Philology,* Vol. XXII (1923).

medieval thought. The various influences that contributed to his religious experience I shall therefore try to present in their proper biographical, as well as historical, setting.

I

We must, to begin with an effort of the imagination, endeavor to see life as it appeared to the youthful Donne, the law student and courtier in London. He would have been greatly astonished had he heard predicted his future failure at court and his subsequent greatness as a saintly divine. The young man was ambitious for a secular career, and with reason felt himself the master of his fate. He was conscious from the first of very distinguished powers. Educated a Catholic, and anxious to make his way at a Protestant court, he decided to settle for himself the truth about the ecclesiastical question with which he was faced. In his own words, he avoided "any violent and sudden determination till I had, to the measure of my power and judgment, surveyed and digested the whole body of divinity, controverted between our and the Roman Church."[14] This extended study, however, did not lead him to any definite decision, it seems, for some years, although his outward allegiance must have been Protestant. For he soon rose in his profession, saw military service in 1596 with the Earl of Essex, and by 1601 was well on the way to a career. A sensitive, proud, high-bred young man, of great intellectual and personal distinction, he was winning the friendship and confidence of men of prominence in state affairs. After such brilliant prospects, Donne found his career ruined by his secret marriage in 1601.

But Donne had been up to this time something more than an ambitious lawyer and courtier and student of "controverted divinity." Like Bacon, he had taken all knowledge for his province. In a letter, written probably in 1608, he complains that his early study of law was interfered with "by that worst voluptuousness, which is an hydroptic, immoderate desire of

[14] Quoted from *Pseudo-Martyr* (1610), by Gosse, *Life and Letters of John Donne,* I. 25.

human learning and languages — beautiful ornaments to great fortunes; but mine needed an occupation." [15] His restless curiosity in those years led him also into some rather questionable regions of experience and thought, which Walton thought fit to pass over rather lightly in his biography, and which have been largely neglected even by modern scholars. The libertine verse of Donne is no doubt unfit in places for general reading, but as a whole it has a philosophical aspect of such importance that it cannot be ignored in studying the development of the man.[16] In the first place, it is clear from his early verse that Donne was interested in philosophical scepticism, the philosophy of Sextus Empiricus, which had previously so profoundly influenced Montaigne. Whether he studied this recently revived Greek philosophy in Montaigne, or directly in the writings of Sextus Empiricus, or perhaps in both,[17] is not material. Its fascination for him is everywhere evident in his early poems. The cynical *Progresse of the Soule,* written in 1601, closes with an allusion to this mode of thought:

> There's nothing simply good, nor ill alone,
> Of every quality comparison,
> The onely measure is, and judge, opinion.[18]

[15] Gosse, *op. cit.,* I. 191.

[16] I am forced here to use some of the results of my own paper already referred to.

[17] Donne had read Montaigne some time before 1603 or 1604, as appears from a letter in Gosse, *op. cit.,* I. 122. The *Hypotyposes* of Sextus Empiricus had been printed in Greek with a Latin translation, by Henri Estienne, in 1562. This little known publication was in fact, through its influence on Montaigne and others, one of the momentous events in the history of modern thought. It was soon known in England. In 1591 Nashe refers to an English translation, now lost. See Nashe's *Works* (ed. McKerrow), III. 32, and compare also the reference to the "Pironicks," II. 116, and McKerrow's discussion of other borrowings from Sextus, IV. 428 ff. Raleigh's posthumous essay, *Sceptick,* is a fragmentary account of some of the tropes of the Greek sceptics, based directly on Sextus Empiricus, not, as Upham, in his *French Influence in English Literature,* says, on Montaigne. Donne knew the *Hypotyposes* of Sextus as well as the account of Pyrrho in Diogenes Laertius, both of which he quotes in his *Essays in Divinity;* see Jessopp's edition (London, 1855), pp. 67 and 70–71. Compare also a reference to the "sceptic philosophers" in a sermon preached at Whitehall in 1618, in *Works of Donne* (ed. Alford), V. 562.

[18] *Donne's Poetical Works* (ed. H. J. C. Grierson; Oxford, 1912), I. 316.

That this was not merely a passing whim of the young man, must be apparent to the careful reader. For instance, in a letter written in 1613 he remarks: "Except demonstrations," that is, mathematical proofs, "(and perchance there are very few of them) I find nothing without perplexities. I am grown more sensible of it by busying myself a little in the search of the eastern tongues, where a perpetual perplexity in the words cannot choose but cast a perplexity upon the things." [19] The criticism implied is perhaps more one of language than of reason itself, but it indicates a mind disposed to sceptical considerations. And passages will be quoted later from his sermons in which he reflects some of that dissatisfaction with the results of reason which marks philosophical sceptics. To return to the youthful poet, we find him fascinated also by the theory that infinite variety is the law of life, that the universe is in a continual flux. It is illuminating here to compare him in this respect with his contemporary Spenser, who in his last fragments of the *Faerie Queene* has expressed the humanist's sad longing for surcease of change:

> Then gin I thinke on that which Nature sayd,
> Of that same time when no more *Change* shall be,
> But stedfast rest of all things firmely stayd
> Upon the pillours of Eternity,
> That is contrayr to *Mutabilitie:*
> For, all that moueth, doth in *Change* delight:
> But thence-forth all shall rest eternally
> With Him that is the God of Sabbaoth hight:
> O that great Sabbaoth God, graunt me that Sabaoths sight.

But Donne contemplated this mutability without sadness, rather with joy, with eagerness to find therein his own full expression:

> "Change," he said, "is the nursery
> Of musick, joy, life and eternity." [20]

Furthermore, in his early poems he applies this relativist philosophy to the social code which required constancy in love, and especially to the basic doctrine of the *Jus Naturale et Gentium* — the Law of Nature and of Nations. This conception

[19] Gosse, II. 16.

[20] Grierson, I. 83.

of the Law of Nature, ultimately derived from the Stoics, had grown in importance with its constant reiteration through the Middle Ages, until in the Renaissance it was regularly appealed to as the fundamental principle in law, in ethics, in natural theology, — in short, it was the one indisputable philosophical defense of the worthiest and most ideal elements in civilization. The conception of the Law of Nature had thus become the conservative and stabilizing doctrine of Renaissance thought, a bulwark against excessive individualism. It was this ancient and revered doctrine that Donne set himself gaily to disintegrate by means of his corrosive wit, and deride by his extravagant paradox and hyperbole. Still another element in his early poetry is its outspoken and shameless Naturalism — not merely a literary trick, but a code of ethics. He substituted for the Stoic Nature a different nature with its own goddess — Aphrodite Pandemos. All these elements of his thought, namely scepticism, revolt against the Stoic Law of Nature, and libertine Naturalism, are to be found earlier than Donne in Montaigne, and may have been inspired in Donne by a reading of the *Essays*. How seriously he adhered to these professed doctrines is a problem, perhaps insoluble. But they unquestionably fascinated him and left a permanent impress upon his mind. Nevertheless, these sceptical and naturalistic ideas served him not as an abiding place, but as a point of departure in his development. In a very interesting passage of *The Calme*, a passage which need not be taken too literally as autobiography, he suggests three reasons for his joining the Cadiz expedition of 1596:

> Whether a rotten state, and hope of gaine,
> Or to disuse mee from the queasie paine
> Of being belov'd, and loving, or the thirst
> Of honour, or faire death, out pusht mee first,

he will not say, allowing the reader to suppose, if he wishes, that all three motives may have contributed to his decision.[21] This allusion to love as a "queasie paine," in a poem written as early as 1597, is significant in the light of Donne's interest at the same time in the libertine naturalism of the Renaissance. It is a note

[21] Grierson, I. 179.

of restlessness. Avid of experience and knowledge, filled with the Renaissance spirit of sounding the depths of life and truth, Donne was not finding peace in that philosophy of life which gave such contentment to Montaigne. His intellectual and spiritual life — and in this respect he resembles Pascal — began at the point where Montaigne's was concluded. In passing through this stage of naturalistic ethics, Donne attained to a deeper knowledge of himself and his limitations, to an awareness of the need of some transcendental power to save humanity from itself.

> Be more than man, or thou'rt lesse than an Ant,[22]

he wrote in *The First Anniversary* (1611). His experience of the inadequacy of naturalism could not but contribute to the inwardness, the passionate humility, the deep feeling of dependence on some source of spiritual power outside of himself, which marked the saintly divine of later years.

His youthful phases were thus transformed with his more mature experience. Biographers have no doubt been right in crediting much of this transformation to his reversal of fortune and his happy marriage. But it seems probable also that his study of the new astronomy produced something like a crisis in his intellectual and religious development. Donne certainly experienced to a greater degree than most Englishmen of his time the disquieting effect of "Copernicism." Barclay, in his *Icon Animorum* (1614), implies indeed that the followers of Copernicus were numerous in England: "But in Philosophy and the Mathematicks," wrote the satirist, "in Geography and Astronomy, there is no opinion so prodigious and strange, but in that Island was either inuented, or has found many followers, and subtile maintainers, but such as through tedious disputations cannot plainly state the question which they would seeme to vphold: That the Earth is moued round, and not the Heauens: that the Sunne, with the Planets, and all the other Stars are not moued in their globes caelestiall," and the like.[23] Whether or

[22] Grierson, I. 237. The reader may be reminded by this line of the last pages of Montaigne's *Apology of Raymond Sebond*.

[23] Barclay, *The Mirror of Minds* (trans. by Tho. May; London, 1633), pp. 84–85.

not there were many who accepted the new science so early as 1614, there are few traces of it in English writings of the period. Bacon, as is well known, did not understand the mathematical efforts of the Copernicans. Fulke Greville, who took a despondent view of most things in the world, expressed a doubt as to whether the new system could be proved.[24] Donne therefore appears exceptional, both in his eagerness to read the new scientific books and in his readiness to accept their conclusions. In his *Biathanatos,* written probably in 1608, he refers to Kepler's *De Stella Nova in Pede Serpentarii,* published in 1606.[25] Again in 1611, in his *Conclave Ignatii,* he reveals an enthusiastic study of Copernicus and Tycho Brahe and a knowledge of the publications of Galileo and Kepler as recent as that year and the preceding.[26] Donne was following closely the latest research. In the same year, in *The First Anniversary,* he expressed the dejection produced by this new science. Describing the melancholy state of the world, he says that the

> new Philosophy calls all in doubt,
> The Element of fire is quite put out;
> The Sun is lost, and th'Earth, and no mans wit
> Can well direct him where to looke for it.
> And freely men confesse that this world's spent,
> When in the Planets, and the Firmament
> They seeke so many new; they see that this
> Is crumbled out againe to his Atomies.
> 'Tis all in pieces, all cohaerence gone;
> All just supply, and all Relation.[27]

"Copernicism in the mathematics," he writes in a letter in 1615, "hath carried earth farther up, from the stupid centre; and yet not honoured it, nor advantaged it, because for the necessity of appearances, it hath carried heaven so much higher from it." [28] Even towards the end of his life, in a sermon preached in 1626,

[24] In *A Treatise of Human Learning. Works* (ed. Grosart), II. 17.

[25] *Biathanatos* (London, 1644), p. 146. It is interesting to note in this connection that there is in the British Museum a presentation copy of this book given by Kepler to James I.

[26] Gosse, I. 257.

[27] Grierson, I. 237. Cf. letter to Countess of Bedford, I. 196.

[28] Gosse, II. 78–79.

he reproaches his age for the slowness with which the new science is accepted.

> "What one thing," he asks, "do we know perfectly? Whether we consider arts, or sciences, the servant knows but according to the proportion of his master's knowledge in that art, and the scholar knows but according to the proportion of his master's knowledge in that science; young men mend not their sight by using old men's spectacles; and yet we look upon nature, but with Aristotle's spectacles, and upon the body of man, but with Galen's, and upon the frame of the world, but with Ptolemy's spectacles." [29]

He makes two pointed uses of this reference to science. In the first place, he manifests the full force of his scepticism regarding traditional philosophical and scientific knowledge.

> "Almost all knowledge," he says, "is rather like a child that is embalmed to make mummy, than that is nursed to make a man; rather conserved in the stature of the first age, than grown to be greater; and if there be any addition to knowledge, it is rather a new knowledge, than a greater knowledge; rather a singularity in a desire of proposing something that was not known at all before, than an improving, an advancing, a multiplying of former inceptions; and by that means, no knowledge comes to be perfect. One philosopher thinks he has dived to the bottom, when he says, he knows nothing but this, that he knows nothing; and yet another thinks, that he hath expressed more knowledge than he, in saying, that he knows not so much as that, that he knows nothing." [30]

In the second place, Donne uses the new science here, as in *The First Anniversary,* to illustrate the transitoriness and imperfection of this earth and all it contains:

> I need not call in new philosophy, that denies a settledness, an acquiescence in the very body of the earth, but makes the earth to move in that place, where we thought the sun had moved; I need not that help, that the earth itself is in motion, to prove this, that nothing upon earth is permanent; the assertion will stand of itself, till some man assign me some instance, something that a man rely upon and find permanent.[31]

The gaiety of the young philosopher of flux and change has now departed; that mutability is a perplexing spiritual problem was a discovery of the mature Donne, and when he at last acquired a sense of the sadness of this transitoriness, it was the more acute because of the new scientific knowledge which had never troubled Spenser.

[29] Alford, III. 472. [30] *Ibid.,* III. 472. [31] *Ibid.,* III. 483.

II

Having seen in these adventures in the Naturalism, Scepticism and new astronomy of his own day, what freedom of movement and independence of judgment was characteristic of Donne, we may ask what his relation was to some of the central philosophical conceptions of the Middle Ages. In this discussion I shall follow those historians who regard Realism as the typically medieval philosophy, and Nominalism as the first sceptical or liberating reaction of the modern spirit against medievalism.[32] For in medieval thought the possibility of knowledge was regarded as axiomatic; the human mind must be fitted to know reality, and reality must be such that it can be known. "Knowledge," says Dante, at the beginning of the *Convivio*," is the distinguishing perfection of our soul, wherein consists our distinguishing blessedness." And the chief impediment within the soul to this perfection appears "when vice hath such supremacy in her that she giveth herself to pursuing vicious delights, wherein she is deluded to such a point that for their sake she holds all things cheap." Only a debased character, it was thought, could be tormented by doubt, and therefore those who were suspected of questioning the orthodox plan of salvation were significantly called "Epicureans," a term which remained current in that sense from the thirteenth century to the seventeenth.

To appreciate the power which such rigid and intolerant orthodoxy exercised over the medieval mind, we must remember the work medievalism had to do after the barbarian invasions and the Dark Ages, namely to organize anew and institutionalize

[32] See especially Hauréau, a fervent champion of the French Revolution, in his *Histoire de la philosophie scolastique* (1850; revised, 1872–1880); a similar position is taken by Andrew Seth Pringle-Pattison, in his article on Scholasticism in the *Encyclopedia Britannica,* 11th edition. English students of the great Nominalist Occam have not failed to find significance in the fact that he was a countryman of Francis Bacon and Hobbes, a "thinker mentally akin to them," full of sturdy English independence. See T. M. Lindsay, in *British Quarterly Review,* Vol. LVI (July, 1872), and George Croom Robertson, *Philosophical Remains* (London, 1894), p. 37.

civilization. In the intellectual as well as political and ecclesiastical spheres, it had to restore order and authority. On the political side, this contructive effort aimed at a universal empire; on the ecclesiastical side, at a universal church. On the intellectual side it aimed at a counterpart and support of these: a Summa Philosophiae and Summa Theologiae. The Middle Ages required a thorough and dogmatic intellectualism, which Aquinas, the representative medieval philosopher, thought he had achieved. "The prime author and mover of the universe is intelligence," he says in his *Summa contra Gentiles*.[33] "Therefore the last end of the universe must be the good of the intelligence, and that is truth. Truth then must be the final end of the whole universe" (Book I, chap. i). However, for various practical reasons few people are qualified to pursue knowledge and thus achieve their blessedness (Book I, chap. vii); therefore they have to accept on faith as much of it as is necessary to salvation. But to say that the natural dictates of reason are *contrary* to faith, is to accuse God of having given us two contradictory principles, an obviously absurd proposition (Book I, chap. vii). Reason is dependable so far as it can go. We cannot know the essence of God, because "the human understanding cannot go so far of its natural power to grasp His substance, since under the conditions of the present life the knowledge of our understanding commences with sense; and therefore objects beyond sense cannot be grasped by human understanding except so far as knowledge is gathered of them through the senses" (Book I, chap. iii). But although what we now accept on faith cannot give us perfect blessedness, when we shall see God we shall have knowledge itself; for happiness consists in the perfect activity of the human intellect and the end of all "Subsistent intelligences" is to know God (Book III, chaps. i-lxiii). According to the philosophy of Realism, God must be conceived of as the highest universal, *Ens*, Being. The intellectual approach to God was therefore a disciplining and enlightenment of the mind as it ascended the pyramid of universals,

[33] Translation by Joseph Rickaby, S. J., *Of God and His Creatures* (London, 1905).

until at the apex it achieved a mystic comprehension of the Mosaic "I am that I am."[34]

But, as the Nominalists questioned the whole rationalistic philosophy of the Realists, so they also attacked this idea of the identity, in their absolute aspects, of reason and faith. John Duns Scotus, the first great critic of Aquinas, maintained that God is not absolute intelligence, but absolute will. The good is good merely because God wills it. As there is no science which can explain the inexplicable, the world is thus reduced to an indeterminism with no rational principle. Though the full sceptical conclusion of such a philosophy was not clear to the Scotists, it is easy to see in retrospect the development of a cleavage between reason and faith as we recede farther and farther from Aquinas. In the Nominalism of Occam the distinction between reason and faith is made absolute. For Occam, by denying the philosophical value of universals, denied that God could be known, and thoroughly rejected the basis of Natural Theology; all knowledge of God, even of His existence, and all the truths of religion and ethics, had to be accepted on faith.[35] Thus arose the notion of a double truth, a separation of philosophy and theology, in the interests of a less rationalistic religious experience. Such influential followers of Occam as Peter D'Ailly (1350–1425) and John Gerson (1363–1429), both Chancellors of the University of Paris, went beyond Occam both in their scepticism and in their emphasis on faith. Gerson, especially, is known as a mystic. It has frequently been observed that mysticism flourishes best outside of the bounds of dogma; the spirit of rationalism tends to dispel the ecstatic vision. And this lesson of religious wisdom the seventeenth century could learn from the late Middle Ages. It was this tradition of the antagonism

[34] Dante, likewise, found the intellect in this life inadequate to comprehend God, not because of its own weakness, but because it is condemned to use the imagination and thus see through a glass darkly. *Paradiso,* XXXIII. 142: "All' alta fantasia qui mancò possa." The same idea is expressed in other passages of the *Paradiso:* IV. 37–42; X. 46–48; XXIV. 24. See also Edmund G. Gardner, *Dante and the Mystics* (London, 1913), pp. 175–177.

[35] See the summary of his *Centilogium theologicum,* in Erdmann, *History of Philosophy* (London, 1898), I. 511–512.

between faith and reason that made the poet Cowley, even though not a mystic, identify the tree in the garden of Eden, whose forbidden fruit brought all our woe, with the *Arbor Porphyrii,* the medieval "tree of universals" which bore the fruit of Realism:

> That right *Porphyrian Tree* which did true *Logick* shew,
> Each *Leaf* did learned *Notions* give,
> And th' *Apples* were *Demonstrative*. . . .
> The onely *Science* Man by this did get,
> Was but to *know* he nothing *Knew*. . . .[36]

In this railing "against the dogmatists" Cowley shows not a trace of Sextus Empiricus and classical philosophy; the seventeenth century poet is expressing the spirit of medieval Nominalism.

The historical rôle of Nominalism was to emancipate the European mind from medieval rationalism. But a similar service was also performed by some heretical rationalists who, finding the theory of the "double truth" a useful defense when in trouble with the authorities, urged this separation of the jurisdictions of faith and reason. The most notorious case was that of Pomponatius (1462–1525), professor of philosophy at Bologna, whose writings implied a doubt as to the immortality of the soul and the freedom of the will. When accused of heresy, he defended himself on the principle, "I believe as a Christian what I cannot believe as a philosopher."[37] The church of course never accepted officially the theory of the double truth, and the Lateran Council in 1512 condemned the proposition of Pomponatius: "as what is true," it was decreed, "can never contradict what is true, we determine that every proposition which is contrary to the truth of the revealed faith is entirely false."[38]

The Thomistic identity of reason and faith was thus attacked

[36] Abraham Cowley, *The Tree of Knowledge,* in *Poems* (ed. Waller; Cambridge, 1905), p. 45.

[37] In his *Biathanatos,* ed. cit., p. 216, Donne referred to Pomponatius as an "excellent philosopher." But he maintained in a sermon in 1617 that truth in philosophy must be truth in divinity. Alford, V. 470.

[38] Pünjer, *History of the Christian Philosophy of Religion* (Edinburgh, 1887), pp. 50–52.

on various sides, but the Catholic Church, which had already accepted Aquinas as the unique Christian philosopher, established his intellectual tradition as orthodoxy and continued it amid the philosophical turmoil of the late Middle Ages and the Renaissance. Its consistency with this tradition was perhaps most decisively indicated in its rejection of the revived Augustinianism of the sixteenth and seventeenth centuries, especially of the Jansenists.

This brief sketch of some of the main developments of scholastic thought regarding the nature of religious truth should at least serve to emphasize the complexity of the medieval heritage of the Renaissance; when we say that Donne was a student of Scholastic philosophy, we must remember that he read, besides Aquinas, such men as Occam, Gerson, Pomponatius and Raymond of Sebonde. Donne was immensely curious and receptive, and in him we can find the whole ferment of his age in all its variety. On the other hand, it would be an error to suppose, although he frequently refers with scorn to the "doctrines of the schools,"[39] that Donne brushed away with one gesture all medieval philosophy as if it were cobwebs. The intellectual doctrine of Aquinas attracted him profoundly. In his *Essays in Divinity,* written in 1614–15, as he was preparing to enter orders, he places Aquinas beside Augustine, his favorite theologian, calling him, as he addresses himself to God in prayer and contemplation, "another instrument and engine of Thine, whom Thou hadst so enabled that nothing was too mineral nor centric for the search and reach of his wit."[40] Donne studied Aquinas as he studied everything, with ardor, but with critical independence, and with reference to his own experience. We can therefore best estimate his allegiance to Aquinas and other medieval influences by examining the nature of his religious experience. Three aspects of it are especially important in this connection: his indecision as to which was the true church, his conception of the relation between faith and reason, and his Augustinianism.

[39] See, for illustrations, Alford, I. 508; V. 517; V. 588–589.
[40] *Essays in Divinity,* ed. cit., p. 37.

III

The medieval church, relying on and taking full advantage of the principle of intellectual certainty expressed in the philosophy of Aquinas, was in spirit and ideal statesmanlike. It dealt with intellectual vagrancy by administrative methods. So in the seventeenth century the growing variety among Protestant sects seemed to Bossuet, that statesman of the church, a self-evident proof of the error of all Protestantism. A heretic he defined as a man who has formed an opinion. Many Protestants, it is to be feared, would at that time and even this, have subscribed to Bossuet's definition; nevertheless, the tendency of Protestantism was to place emphasis less and less on the enforcement of established truth, and more and more on the search after truth. The differences and debates of the Protestant theologians contributed largely to the establishment of the new principle of toleration — a principle not without some sceptical implications. "Where there is much desire to learn," Milton said in his *Areopagitica*, "there of necessity will be much arguing, much writing, many opinions; for opinion in good men is but knowledge in the making."

Into the wilderness of opinion Donne had, as we have seen, courageously set out, with a fine youthful — not to say medieval — assurance that he could find the true religion. In his satire, *Kinde pitty chokes my spleene*,[41] written in his youth, he speaks with scorn of those feeble, hesitating spirits who adhere to any sect without studying and thinking the problem through for themselves. Mirreus the Catholic, Crantz the Calvinist, Graius the Anglican, are sketched with a few strong, uncomplimentary strokes. Then there are others:

> Carelesse Phrygius doth abhorre
> All, because all cannot be good, as one
> Knowing some women whores, dares marry none.
> Graccus loves all as one, and thinkes that so
> As women do in divers countries goe
> In divers habits, yet are still one kinde,
> So doth, so is Religion; and this blind-
> nesse too much light breeds.

[41] Grierson, I. 154–158.

He expresses confidence that truth can be found by earnest effort, provided one goes back far enough to the original sources and cultivates an open mind. And one cannot escape the obligation of making a choice:

> unmoved thou
> Of force must one, and forc'd but one allow;
> And the right; aske thy father which is shee,
> Let him aske his; though truth and falsehood bee
> Neare twins, yet truth a little elder is; [42]
> Be busie to seeke her, beleeve mee this,
> Hee's not of none, nor worst, that seekes the best.
> To adore, or scorne an image, or protest,
> May all be bad; doubt wisely; in strange way
> To stand inquiring right, is not to stray;
> To sleepe, or runne wrong, is.

But unceasing labor is necessary.

> On a huge hill,
> Cragged, and steep, Truth stands, and hee that will
> Reach her, about must, and about must goe;
> And what the hills suddenness resists, winne so;
> Yet strive so, that before age, deaths twilight,
> Thy Soule rest, for none can worke in that night.

But Donne himself discovered that this truth was even more difficult to reach than he had imagined. All sects, he says in a letter dated by Gosse 1607, need to be purged of false doctrines:

> I begin to think that as litigious men tired with suits admit any arbitrament, and princes travailed with long and wasteful wars descend to such conditions of peace as they are soon after ashamed to have embraced; so philosophers, and so all sects of Christians, after long disputations and controversies, have allowed many things for positive and dogmatical truths which are not worthy of that dignity; and so many doctrines have grown to be ordinary diet and food of our spirits, and have place in the pap of catechisms, which were admitted but as physic in that present distemper, or accepted in a lazy weariness, when men so they might have something to rely upon, and to excuse themselves from more painful inquisition, never examined what that was.[43]

[42] In a sermon in 1618 Donne says "that is best in matter of religion that was first."—Alford, V. 583; cf. III. 292. The paradox that the newest philosophy is soundest, and the oldest divinity, seems to have been proverbial. See De Mornay, *De la Verité de la Religion Chrestienne* (Leyden, 1651), p. 88; Overbury, *Works* (London, 1890), p. 179; and Francis Osborne, *Works* (8th ed.; London, 1682), p. 92.

[43] Gosse, I. 174.

In a letter impossible to date exactly, Donne expresses a broad tolerance towards all sects as containing some truth:

"You know," he says, "I never fettered nor imprisoned Religion, not straightening it friarly, *ad Religiones factitias* (as the Romans call well their orders of Religion), nor immuring it in a Rome, or a Wittenberg, or a Geneva; they are all virtual beams of one Sun, and wheresoever they find clay hearts, they harden them and moulder them into dust; and they entender and mollify waxen. They are not so contrary as the North and South Poles, and that (?) they are co-natural pieces of one circle. Religion is Christianity, which being too spiritual to be seen by us, doth therefore take an apparent body of good life and works, so salvation requires an honest Christian."[44]

In his toleration, his comprehensive sympathy with opposed sects, and his willingness to simplify and therefore to discard non-essential doctrines, Donne thus anticipated such latitudinarians as Falkland, Hales, Chillingworth and Sir Thomas Browne.[45] In a letter written in 1615, as he stood on the threshold of his career in the church, he suggested that the merits of the various religions or sects within Christianity may not be absolute, and that violent conversions from one to another may be dangerous, irrespective of the relative degrees of ascertainable truth in each:

As some bodies are as wholesomely nourished as ours with acorns, and endure nakedness, both which would be dangerous to us, if we for them should leave our former habits, though theirs were the primitive diet and custom; so are many souls well fed with such forms and dressings of religion, as would distemper and misbecome us, and make us corrupt towards God, if any human circumstance moved it, and in the opinion of men, though none. You shall seldom see a coin, upon which the stamp were removed, though to imprint it better, but it looks awry and squint. And so, for the most part, do minds which have received divers impressions.[46]

In the same letter, referring to Protestantism and Catholicism, he says: "I will not, nor need to you, compare the religions. The channels of God's mercies run through both fields; and they

[44] Gosse, I. 226.

[45] The untrustworthy gossip, John Aubrey, has recorded that Falkland and Hales were the first Socinians in England, and that Chillingworth in his youth much delighted in Sextus Empiricus. *Brief Lives* (Oxford, 1898), I. 150, 173, 279. Whether authentic or not, the remark concerning Chillingworth indicates that the sceptical trend of latitudinarianism was evident at that time.

[46] Gosse, II. 78.

are sister teats of His graces, yet both diseased and infected, but not both alike."

Evidently Donne could at best make a compromise in deciding upon allegiance to any one church. He insisted nevertheless upon the necessity of the visible church and of the ecclesiastical element in religion. He was in no sense a dissenter. He realized the religious value of rituals and symbols, as making a deeper appeal than merely to the understanding.[47] "He that undervalues outward things," he said in a sermon in 1621, "in the religious service of God, though he begin at ceremonial and ritual things, will quickly come to call sacraments but outward things, and sermons, and public prayers, but outward things, in contempt."[48] Donne was opposed to extreme individualism in religious experience; the individual must find his religion in the church. "I see not this mystery," he said in another sermon, "by the eye of nature, of learning, of state, of mine own private sense; but I see it by the eye of the church, by the light of faith, that is true; but yet organically, instrumentally, by the eye of the church."[49] Since an ecclesiastical organization, even though at its best it is so imperfect, is so essential, it is wise and right to be loyal to that church which has served us. "It is an irreverent unthankfulness, to think worse of that church, which hath bred us, and fed us, and led us thus far towards God, than of a foreign church, though reformed too, and in a good degree."[50] And yet, these imperfect churches could not satisfy Donne; he longed for *the* true church, the truly Catholic and universal church. "The church loves the name of Catholic," he said in a sermon at the Hague, "and it is a glorious, and an harmonious name; love thou those things wherein she is Catholic, and wherein she is harmonious, that is . . . those universal, and fundamental doctrines, which in all Christian ages, and in all Christian churches, have been agreed by all to be necessary to salvation; and then thou art a true Catholic."[51]

[47] Alford, VI. 19 ff. and 42–43; V. 66 ff.
[48] *Ibid.*, V. 67.
[49] *Ibid.*, V. 419. Cf. III. 344.
[50] *Ibid.*, IV. 485.
[51] *Ibid.*, III. 273. Cf. *Essays in Divinity*, ed. cit., pp. 130–132.

It seems clear therefore that Donne's allegiance to the Church of England was of a compromising and pragmatic nature; as Grierson has said, it "never made the appeal to Donne's heart and imagination it did to George Herbert." [52] He never found the one true church he had been seeking for. Even in the *Holy Sonnets,* written after 1617, when he was eminent as an Anglican divine, he was still searching, now no longer in "controverted theology," but in prayer, for a church to which he could give undivided, uncritical allegiance:

> Show me deare Christ, thy Spouse, so bright and cleare.[53]

Thus this man of unusual intellectual passion and power, whose desire for truth was deep and imperative, saw it always eluding his grasp; always a seeker after truth, but pursuing it in vain, he suffered painful dejection and disillusionment. He lived always intellectually tormented. Doubt was not to him, as it had been to Montaigne, a soft pillow on which to rest his head, but pain and restlessness, search and endless labor.

IV

Donne had, however, in the meantime found a new source of spiritual insight and comfort. It seems probable, as Courthope says,[54] that his happy marriage had a redeeming influence upon him and inspired his nobler love poems. But he had a religious awakening also. In one of his love poems, *A Valediction,* occurs a striking statement that "all Divinity is love and wonder," [55] an idea which Donne repeated years later in *The First Anniversary:*

> The world containes
> Princes for armes, and Counsellors for braines,
> Lawyers for tongues, Divines for hearts, and more,
> The Rich for stomackes, and for backes, the Poore;

[52] Grierson, II. 236.

[53] *Ibid.,* I. 330. This sonnet was omitted, for obvious reasons, in seventeenth century editions, and was first printed by Gosse, II. 371.

[54] *History of English Poetry,* III. 156.

[55] Grierson, I. 30. Compare Carlyle's sentence in *The Hero as Divinity:* "Worship is transcendent wonder; wonder for which there is now no limit or measure; that is worship."

> The Officers for hands, Merchants for feet,
> By which, remote and distant Countries meet.
> But those fine spirits which do tune, and set
> This Organ, are those peeces which beget
> Wonder and love; and these were shee.[56]

The thought had been impressed upon his mind that the soul of the world is not knowable to reason, that the true theology appeals in some other way; in some personal experience or crisis he had acquired an insight into a mystery not explained by "controverted divinity" and become a mystic. From that time reason began to lose its preëminence, his spiritual life gained in power and intensity, and his prayer became

> Looke to mee faith, and looke to my faith, God.

The relation between reason and faith, we have seen, was one of the crucial problems in medieval thought. Aquinas had given it an intellectualistic solution, affirming that reason and faith are identical in their absolute aspects, and that faith is therefore provisional. In the seventeenth century Malebranche, in his fusion of Cartesianism with the Catholic tradition, went even farther than Aquinas and declared an emphatic preference for reason: "La raison doit toujours être la maîtresse; Dieu même le suit. L'Intelligence est préférable à la Foi: car la Foi passera, mais l'Intelligence subsistera éternellement." [57] Such a conclusion is natural if one premises that the universe is knowable and the blessedness of man consists in the perfect knowledge of it. Donne, on the contrary, always gives reason the subordinate place. He begins a verse letter to the Countess of Bedford, some time between 1608 and 1614, with the statement:

> Reason is our Soules left hand, Faith her right,
> By these we reach divinity.

But he would,

> not to encrease, but to expresse
> My faith, as I beleeve, so understand.[58]

[56] Grierson, I. 246. Cf. "All love is wonder," in *The Anagram,* I. 81.
[57] Malebranche, *Traité de Morale.*
[58] Grierson, I. 189. Cf. *Essays in Divinity,* ed. cit., p. 142.

He labored always to understand. "No one may doubt," he wrote in a letter in 1612, "but that that religion is certainly best which is reasonablest." [59] And in his *Elegy on Prince Henry* (1613), he almost identifies the spheres of reason and faith:

> Looke to mee faith, and looke to my faith, God;
> For both my centers feele this period.
> Of waight one center, one of greatnesse is;
> And Reason is that center, Faith is this;
> For into'our reason flow, and there do end
> All, that this naturall world doth comprehend:
> Quotidian things, and equidistant hence,
> Shut in, for man, in one circumference.
> But for th'enormous greatnesses, which are
> So disproportion'd, and so angulare,
> As is Gods essence, place and providence,
> Where, how, when, what soules do, departed hence,
> These things (eccentrique else) on faith do strike;
> Yet neither all, nor upon all, alike.
> For reason, put to'her best extension,
> Almost meetes faith, and makes both centers one.[60]

The reason, too, is a valuable defender of the faith against rationalistic attacks. "It is not enough for you," Donne said in a sermon in 1623, "to rest in imaginary faith, and easiness in believing, except you know also what, and why, and how you come to that belief. Implicit believers, ignorant believers, the adversary may swallow; but the understanding believer, he must chaw, and pick bones, before he come to assimilate him, and make him like himself." [61]

Reason, Donne gladly admitted, has its place in religion, but subordinate to faith. Faith goes beyond it both in power and authority. "Rectified reason," he said in a sermon, "is religion." [62] Again, "Mysteries of religion are not the less believed and embraced by faith, because they are presented, and induced, and apprehended by reason." [63] Natural theology, too, has its place, but is inadequate. "The invisible God was presented in visible things, and thou mightest, and wouldest not see him: but this is only such a knowledge of God as philosophers, moral

59 Gosse, II. 8.
60 Grierson, I. 267.
61 Alford, I. 314. Cf. V. 571, 576, 582 ff., and VI. 24.
62 *Ibid.*, III. 286.
63 *Ibid.*, V. 453.

and natural men may have, and yet be very far from making this knowledge any means of salvation."[64] Religion is therefore of a distinctly supra-rational origin. "Grace does not grow out of nature; for nature in the highest exaltation and rectifying thereof cannot produce grace. . . . Nature, and natural reason do not produce grace, but yet grace can take root in no other thing but in the nature and reason of man."[65] Natural reason can at best point in the direction of faith. "The light of faith, in the highest exaltation that can be had, in the elect, here, is not that very beatifical vision, which we shall have in heaven, but it bears witness of that light. The light of nature, in the highest exaltation is not faith, but it bears witness of it."[66]

Not only did Donne regard reason as inadequate, but he was also troubled by a consciousness of a contradiction between reason and faith. In his *Litany,* written about 1609 or 1610, he had already formulated for himself the prayer:

> Let not my minde be blinder by more light
> Nor Faith, by Reason added, lose her sight.[67]

"The Scriptures," he said in the sermon preached at the Hague, "will be out of thy reach, and out of thy use, if thou cast and scatter them upon reason, upon philosophy, upon morality, to try how the Scriptures will fit them, and believe them but so far as they agree with thy reason; but draw the Scripture to thine own heart, and to thine own actions, and thou shalt find it made for that."[68] The unreasonableness of Christianity he could celebrate as its glory, the seal of its divine character. Was it easy to believe, he asks,

> that from that man, that worm, and no man, ingloriously traduced as a conjurer, ingloriously apprehended as a thief, ingloriously executed as a traitor; they should look for glory, and all glory, and everlasting glory? And from that melancholic man, who was never seen to laugh in all his

[64] *Ibid.,* VI. 36. Cf. I. 297; V. 517–518, 574, and 582 ff.
[65] *Ibid.,* VI. 44.
[66] *Ibid.,* V. 66.
[67] Grierson, I. 340. Cf. Alford, III. 261.
[68] Alford, III. 302. Compare V. 64, where Donne defines the light of faith as "not only a knowing, but an applying, an appropriating of all to thy benefit."

life, and *whose soul was heavy unto death;* they should look for joy, and all joy, and everlasting joy: and for salvation, and everlasting salvation from him, who could not save himself from ignominy, from the torment, from the death of the cross? If any state, if any convocation, if any wise man had been to make a religion, a gospel; would he not have proposed a more probable, a more credible gospel, to man's reason, than this? [69]

Among the numerous passages on this subject, perhaps the most emphatic occurs in a sermon preached on Christmas Day, 1621, on the text, " He was not that Light, but was sent to bear witness of that Light" (John, i. 8.).

" In all philosophy," he said, " there is not so dark a thing as light; as the sun, which is *fons lucis naturalis,* the beginning of natural light, is the most evident thing to be seen, and yet the hardest to be looked upon, so is natural light to our reason and understanding. Nothing clearer, for it is clearness itself, nothing darker, it is enwrapped in so many scruples. Nothing nearer, for it is around about us, nothing more remote, for we know neither entrance, nor limits of it. Nothing more easy, for a child discerns it, nothing more hard, for no man understands it. It is apprehensible by sense, and not comprehensible by reason. If we wink, we cannot choose but see it, if we stare, we know it never the better. No man is yet got so near to the knowledge of the qualities of light, as to know whether light itself be a quality, or a substance. If then this natural light be so dark to our natural reason, if we shall offer to pierce so far into the light of this text, the essential light Christ Jesus, (in his nature, or but in his offices) or the supernatural light of faith and grace, . . . if we search farther into these points, than the Scripture hath opened us a way, how shall we hope to unentangle, or extricate themselves? They had a precious composition for lamps, amongst the ancients, reserved especially for tombs, which kept light for many hundreds of years; we have had in our age experience, in some casual openings of ancient vaults, of finding such lights, as were kindled, (as appeared by their inscriptions) fifteen or sixteen hundred years before; but, as soon as that light comes to our light, it vanishes. So this eternal, and this supernatural light, Christ and faith, enlightens, warms, purges, and does all the profitable offices of fire, and light, if we keep it in the right sphere, in the proper place, (that is, if we consist in points necessary to salvation, and revealed in the Scriptures) but when we bring this light to the common light of reason, to our inferences, and consequences, it may be in danger to vanish itself, and perchance extinguish our reason too; we may search so far, and reason so long of faith and grace, as that we may lose not only them, but even our reason too, and sooner become mad than good." [70]

These illustrations of Donne's wrestling with the problem of reason and faith afford an insight into some of those contradic-

[69] *Ibid.,* V. 430–431. [70] *Ibid.,* V. 55.

tory impulses which make his life and character seem so paradoxical. He began with an almost Thomistic confidence in reason; he labored to *know*. But though he rightly felt himself more successful in this effort than most men about him, he was forced to confess that knowledge is difficult and uncertain even to the best minds, and that much philosophizing is often a vanity of the spirit. This defeat of the reason was, however, a spiritual gain. Unconvinced by " controverted divinity," Donne discovered in his own experience another divinity of " love and wonder." Not indeed by any sudden revelation of his spiritual powers, but through years of privation, disappointment, doubt, years of the " agony and exercise of sense and spirit," [71] did the student, lawyer and courtier yield his life and soul fully to the guidance of faith. One need only compare Donne with his contemporaries, Sir John Davies and Lord Herbert of Cherbury, to realize how largely he had been liberated from the inhibitions of rationalism. The darkening of the understanding, Donne has said himself, is one of those afflictions by which God turns the soul to himself. " Those helps," he said in a sermon, " which are

> deduced from philosophy and natural reason, are strong enough against afflictions of this world, as long as we can use them, as long as these helps of reason and learning are alive, and awake, and actuated in us, they are able to sustain us from sinking under the afflictions of this world, for, they have sustained many a Plato, and a Socrates, and Seneca in such cases. But when part of the affliction shall be, that God worketh upon the spirit itself, and damps that, that he casts a sooty cloud upon the understanding, and darkens that, that he doth *exuere hominem,* divest, strip the man of the man, *eximere hominem,* take the man out of the man, and withdraw and frustrate his natural understanding so, as that, to this purpose, he is no man, yet even in this case, God may mend thee, in marring thee, he may build thee up in dejecting thee, he may infuse another, *ego vir,* another manhood into thee, and though thou canst not say *ego vir, I am that moral man,* safe in my natural reason and philosophy, that is spent, yet *Ego vir,* I am that Christian man, who have seen this affliction in the cause thereof, so far off, as in my sin in Adam, and the remedy of this affliction, so far off, as in the death of Christ Jesus, I am the man, that cannot repine, nor murmur, since I am the cause; I am the man that cannot despair, since Christ is the remedy.[72]

[71] Donne's own words; see Gosse, I. 190.

[72] Alford, V. 320.

V

The relation of the religious experience of Donne, in its essential nature and not merely its incidental aspects, to the main currents of religious thought in his age and to the main traditions within Christianity, involves necessarily a discussion of his Augustinianism. For not only was he peculiarly the disciple of Augustine,[73] but the influence of the Bishop of Hippo was highly important in the development of thought in the sixteenth and seventeenth centuries. The nature and extent of this influence must here be indicated as briefly as possible.

Even externally, the career of Augustine has striking resemblances to that of Donne. His personal distinction, his secular ambition, his extensive experience with the argumentative aspect of religion, his mature conversion, can all be paralleled in the life of Donne. But more striking, and certainly more important, is the similarity in the religious experience of the two men, in their assimilation and rejection of philosophical thought, in the fundamental needs of their personalities and in the direction in which these guided their religious development. Augustine, it is true, passed more definitely through his first two stages, his study of scepticism in the New Academics, and his adherence to Platonism. The influence of the first was sufficient to make him a keen and profound critic of the theory of knowledge, and to force his attention back upon his own nature as the only source of certainty. "Noli foras ire, in teipsum redi; in interiore homine habitat veritas."[74] In searching within himself he discovered, long before Descartes, the basic fact of his own self-consciousness and its significance in the search for certain knowledge.[75]

[73] Miss Ramsay has frequently noted this fact, although she missed its significance. *Op. cit.*, pp. 179, 181–182, 220, 225, 252–253, 257, etc.

[74] *De Vera Religione,* 72. Quoted by W. Cunningham, *S. Austin and his Place in the History of Christian Thought* (London, 1886), p. 22, n. 1.

[75] Augustine's anticipation of Descartes has often been pointed out. Already Bossuet, in a letter to Bishop Huet, declared that the "choses utiles" said by Descartes were already familiar to him in Plato, Augustine, Anselm and Aquinas. See quotation by Brunetière, *Études Critiques* (Paris, 1896), 5. 48–49.

Spiritual realities are within us, but they are the manifestations of Eternal Being. The knowledge of oneself leads to a knowledge of God. For a time an ardent student of Platonism, Augustine acquired a belief in a rational and intelligible order in the universe through an apprehension of which we might ascend to its source in God. This Platonic phase of Augustine explains the statement so often made that he was "the father of scholasticism in virtue of his dialectic mind."[76] "Here are the ideas," says one authority, "which were developed in the splendid structure of the scholastic philosophy and which in another form reappeared in the *Théodicée* of Leibnitz, and the *Analogy* of Butler."[77]

But Augustine developed beyond Platonism and its rational Logos, and became also the father of mysticism. In his introspection he discovered desires that Platonism could not satisfy, and inclinations that it could not correct. "Thou didst set me face to face with myself," he says in a meditative passage, "that I might behold how foul I was, and how crooked and sordid, bespotted and ulcerous."[78] The weakness of his own will, his sense of sin, and a perception of his own personality, these discoveries in his own nature showed him the necessity of a redemption beyond the power of Platonic ideas. The doctrine of grace, which became in later centuries known as the distinctive doctrine of Augustinianism, is an expression of Augustine's feeling of the utter helplessness of human nature to accomplish its own salvation. In humility of spirit he felt a supreme need for a personal God, not merely a Plotinian Universal Reason. He read in the Platonists, he says in a well-known passage in his *Confessions*, the doctrine of the Logos: In the beginning was the Word, and the Word was with God, and the Word was God. But that "the Word was made flesh, and dwelt among us," he did not read there.[79] The Word become flesh and living

[76] Schaff, Philip, *History of the Christian Church* (5th ed.; New York, 1899), III. 1018.

[77] Cunningham, *op. cit.*, p. 35.

[78] *Confessions*, VIII. vii. 16. I quote from the translation by Marcus Dods (Edinburgh, 1876).

[79] *Ibid.*, VII. ix. 13–14.

among us, bearing for us our miseries and frailties and sins, giving us the inexpressible consolation and comfort of a personal love and sacrifice for us, such was the religion of Augustine. He desired, not primarily to *know* God, but to rest his soul in the bosom of God, in the bosom of Christ, who was God become humanity and therefore full of the sympathy he craved. "I know not," he says, "how any rational demonstration of God could satisfy me; for I do not believe that I know anything as I desire to know God." [80] Though not a philosophical sceptic, Augustine was nevertheless ready to discard not only Platonism, but all philosophy and knowledge if it hindered in any way his devotion to the Christian religion. "For unhappy is the man who knoweth all those things, but knoweth Thee not; but happy is he who knoweth Thee, though these he may not know." [81]

The complex personality of Augustine thus stimulated down through the ages two divergent types of religious thought, the intellectualistic and the mystic. Although revered as the founder of the idealistic philosophy of the Catholic church, Augustine also attracted certain disciples in the Middle Ages and the Reformation primarily by his mysticism and piety. He was widely read among the Nominalists and the medieval mystics, who had in common at least an aversion to the intellectualism of Thomas Aquinas. He stimulated their tendency towards a spiritual mode of thought, based on a very distinct dualism of mind and body; he confirmed their belief that the moral life depends more on the will of man than on his intellect; and he taught them the art of observing the processes of the inner life, on which especially the mystics concentrated their attention.[82] In medieval England, Thomas Bradwardine felt his inspiration.[83] Such early reformers on the Continent as Huss and Wessel cultivated Augustine more than any other religious

[80] Quoted by R. L. Ottley, *Studies in the Confessions of St. Augustine* (London, 1919), p. 89.

[81] *Confessions,* V. iv.

[82] Siebeck, *Die Anfänge der neueren Psychologie in der Scholastik,* in *Zeitschrift für Philosophie und phil. Kritik,* 93 (1888). 188–191.

[83] Cunningham, *op. cit.,* pp. 153–154 and 178.

writer except Paul. "It may very well be said," declares Harnack, "that there never would have been a Reformation had there not been first a revival of Augustinianism." [84] Luther and Melancthon, Zwingli and Calvin were moulded by Augustine more than by any other church teacher. Thus, although Augustine was one of the saints and accepted authorities in the Catholic church, the Augustinianism of the sixteenth and seventeenth centuries became anti-Catholic in spirit, continuing and intensifying the medieval opposition to Thomism. Nourisson, himself a Catholic, admitted this antinomy and tried to resolve it: 'On ne saurait le méconnaître, de l'Augustinianisme corrompu, mais enfin de l'Augustinianisme procède le Protestantisme. Car, sans parler de Wiclif et de Huss. . . . Luther et Calvin ne font guère autre chose, dans leurs principaux ouvrages, que cultiver des semences d'Augustinianisme." [85] Within the Catholic church there were only two important Augustinian developments of a pietistic or anti-intellectual kind, and both were declared heretical; the first was led by Michael Bajus, at Louvain, whose Augustinian doctrines were condemned by Pius V in 1567; the second was of course Jansenism, whose greatest representative was Pascal.

To this tradition Donne belongs as a religious teacher and mystic; true to this tradition, he was dissatisfied with the impersonal and intellectual conception of God, desiring a personal God in which his heart, not his mind, might find rest. He repeats Augustine's criticism of Platonism: to think, he says, "that we can come to this by our own strength, without God's inward working a belief, or to think that we can believe out of Plato, where we may find a God, but without a Christ, or come to be good men out of Plutarch or Seneca, without a church or sacraments, to pursue the truth itself by any other way than he hath laid open to us, this is pride, and the pride of the angels." [86] The consciousness of his sin and weakness and misery he fostered and desired as essential to religious insight and religious longing.

[84] Harnack, *History of Dogma* (London, 1899), VII. 17.

[85] Nourisson, *La philosophie de saint Augustin* (2me ed.; Paris, 1866), II. 176.

[86] Alford, III. 47. Cf. V. 424–425.

"Man's infirmity requires spectacles; and affliction does that office."[87] Humility is the beginning of wisdom; it is "the seed, and kernel, and soul of all virtues."[88] "We are not worthy as to profess our unworthiness; it is a degree of spiritual exaltation, to be sensible of our lowness; . . . even humility itself is a pride, if we think it to be our own."[89] Donne is of the Augustinian tradition also in his insistence on the helplessness of man and the necessity of grace. "Miserable man!" he says. "A toad is a bag of poison, and a spider is a blister of poison, and yet a toad and a spider cannot poison themselves; man hath a drachm of poison, original sin, in an invisible corner, we know not where, and he cannot choose but poison himself and all his actions with that; we are so far from being able to begin without grace, as then when we have first grace, we cannot proceed to the use of that, without more."[90] Therefore Donne did not look to philosophy to illuminate the path of life with such confidence as, for instance, Spenser; the pure in heart, he said, get by their purity "this main purchase, that which all the books of all the philosophers could never teach them so much as what it was, that is true blessedness."[91] Donne learned in the school of affliction and anguish, which he so often refers to as the best school for the soul, that he needed another blessedness than truth and knowledge. And therefore the humiliation of the intellect, too, was necessary, lest the feeble light of the reason make us blind to the greater light of faith. In a sermon preached in 1624, on the conversion of St. Paul, he speaks of the light which struck Paul blind:

"This blindness of which we speak," he says, "which is a sober and temperate abstinence from the immoderate study, and curious knowledges of this world, this holy simplicity of the soul, is not a darkness, a dimness, a stupidity of the understanding, contracted by living in a corner, it is not an idle retiring into a monastery, or into a village, or a country solitude, it is not a lazy affectation of ignorance; not darkness, but a greater light,

[87] *Ibid.*, IV. 565.
[88] *Ibid.*, V. 571. Cf. 600 ff.
[89] *Ibid.*, V. 555.
[90] *Ibid.*, V. 577. Cf. VI. 108–109. For a criticism of Catholic doctrine, see VI. 48.
[91] *Ibid.*, I. 191.

must make us blind. . . . There are birds, that when their eyes are sealed, still soar up, and up, till they have spent all their strength. Men blinded with the lights of this world, soar still into higher places, or higher knowledges, or higher opinions; but the light of heaven humbles us, and lays flat that soul, which the leaven of this world had puffed and swelled up." [92]

Donne's religious experience, then, was a mystical one, and though he sought always to make it reasonable and even comprehensible, he had to recognize that his spiritual life was beyond the power of reason and weakened by a rationalistic mode of thought. He belonged to the anti-intellectual tradition of Augustine. And it is perhaps partly due to Donne's influence on the religious and poetical development of Herbert and Vaughan, that we find in them also, a recognition of this dualism of faith and reason. Herbert was hardly a mystic; but in a poem called *Divinitie* he says:

> As men, for fear the starres should sleep and nod,
> And trip at night, have spheres suppli'd;
> As if a starre were duller then a clod,
> Which knows his way without a guide:
>
> Just so the other heav'n they also serve,
> Divinities transcendent skie:
> Which with the edge of wit they cut and carve.
> Reason triumphs, and faith lies by. . . .
>
> Then burn thy Epicycles, foolish man;
> Break all thy spheres, and save thy head.
> Faith needs no staffe of flesh, but stoutly can
> To heav'n alone both go and leade.[93]

And Vaughan, in a poem with the sceptical title *Vanity of Spirit,* has explained how his repeated attempts to know the secrets of the world and of himself had failed, one after another, until, his intellect exhausted, he gave himself up to the mystical experience which can be complete only in another world.

> Quite spent with thoughts, I left my cell, and lay
> Where a shrill spring tun'd to the early day.
> I begg'd here long, and groan'd to know
> Who gave the clouds so brave a bow,

[92] *Ibid.,* II. 307–308.
[93] *The English Works of George Herbert* (ed. Palmer), III. 97.

Who bent the spheres, and circled in
Corruption with this glorious ring;
What is His name, and how I might
Descry some part of His great light.
I summon'd Nature; pierc'd through all her store;
Broke up some seals, which none had touch'd before
Her womb, her bosom, and her head,
Where all her secrets lay abed,
I rifled quite; and having past
Through all the creatures, came at last
To search myself, where I did find
Traces, and sounds of a strange kind.
Here of this mighty spring I found some drills,
With echoes beaten from th' eternal hills.
Weak beams and fires flash'd to my sight,
Like a young East, or moonshine night,
Which show'd me in a nook cast by
A piece of much antiquity,
And hieroglyphics quite dismember'd
And broken letters scarce remember'd.
I took them up, and — much joy'd — went about
T' unite those pieces, hoping to find out
The mystery; but this ne'er done,
That little light I had was gone.
It griev'd me much. At last, said I,
"Since in these veils my eclips'd eye
May not approach Thee — for at night
Who can have commerce with the light? —
I'll disapparel, and to buy
But one half-glance, most gladly die." [94]

As has been said earlier, Donne resembles Pascal in that his development began at the place where Montaigne's ended. Such a comparison between Donne and Pascal must be made with reservations, but it is helpful in indicating the position of Donne in relation to the seventeenth century. Profoundly influenced by the philosophical scepticism which had been popularized by Montaigne, Pascal built upon this philosophical scepticism an apologia for the Christian religion. This development was not so singular as it is generally thought to have been.[95] It has not

[94] Vaughan, Henry, *Poems* (ed. Chambers), I. 57. Passages from Augustine's *Confessions,* especially Book X, would furnish an excellent commentary on this poem.

[95] Edouard Droz has discussed the similarity, in this respect, of Pascal to Lactantius and Augustine. *Le Scepticisme de Pascal* (Paris, 1886), pp. 282–296.

been sufficiently noticed that a parallel development appeared in England at the same time and even earlier. Sir Thomas Browne, in his *Religio Medici* (1642), anticipated Pascal. Glanville appeared as an apologist for Christianity as well as for science in his *Vanity of Dogmatizing* (1661) and *Scepsis Scientifica* (1665). In Dryden's poems on religion we find the same paradox of moderate Pyrrhonism as the basis of submission to faith. Donne was the earliest of these seventeenth century religious Pyrrhonists in England, and because he came early his scepticism is less obvious and daring. But all his experience, his youthful interest in the relativist thought typified by Montaigne, his search for the true church, his wrestling with scholastic divinity, his gradually deepening religious insight, had all directed him towards the conclusion of Pascal, that philosophical dogmatism is a danger to the religious life, that the heart has its reasons of which the reason knows nothing. Pascal's thought is a fusion of the scepticism of Montaigne and the Augustinianism of the Jansenists. Donne had studied the same scepticism, in Sextus Empiricus and probably in Montaigne, and cultivated Augustine as his favorite religious teacher. He thus knew intimately the two traditions which converged also in Pascal.

VI

Unlike Pascal, however, Donne wrote in the "metaphysical style." Since this phrase, so well established, is yet so conducive to misinterpretations of Donne, it is necessary in a survey of the relation of Donne to medieval and modern traditions of thought, to discuss the significance of his style. I do not intend here to give any complete account, from either the historical or the esthetic point of view, of the "conceit" in Renaissance poetry and prose; its origins were too remote and the explanation of its popularity is too complex. My one purpose is to glance briefly at Donne's use of it, to see in what way the "conceit" was made expressive of his idiosyncracies, and thus not only to appreciate better the sincerity of his mode of expression, but also to formulate a definite conception of what is medieval and what is modern in his style, both in prose and poetry.

The "conceit," everyone knows, was common in English poetry before Donne. He appropriated it and gave it that peculiar quality and power which was his own, but which influenced his admiring successors to the extent of forming a poetical school. Professor Alden has given a definition of the "conceit," based on an analysis of it in Sidney and Shakespeare: "A conceit is the elaboration of a verbal or an imaginative figure, or the substitution of a logical for an imaginative figure, with so considerable a use of an intellectual process as to take precedence, at least for the moment, of the normal poetic process." [96] This definition expresses admirably also that dualism of Donne's nature which heightened the disharmony between his intellect and that poetic and mystical experience out of which his poetry and prose were made. His constant return upon himself, his study of his own feelings and emotions, and his attempts to state them in intellectual terms, all this introspection and analysis is as apparent in his sermons as in his verse. It is especially marked in Donne because of the imperfect harmony between the intellectual and poetic sides of his nature. Schelling coined an illuminating phrase when he said that "no one, excepting Shakespeare . . . has done so much to develop intellectualized emotion in the Elizabethan lyric as John Donne." [97]

This intellectuality, or "wit," as it was then called, of Donne's poetry and prose appears also in other forms than the "conceit"; it is sometimes paradox, sometimes hyperbole, sometimes a plain and straightforward reasoning about his subject. But in its most characteristic form it is a symbolism, a rendering of spiritual or emotional experience in terms apprehensible, not to sense or imagination primarily, but to the intellect. We may quote one of his most daring, yet successful, conceits in his early verse, the familiar one of the compass. It expresses a transcendental conception of the unity of two souls in love:

[96] Alden, Raymon Macdonald, *The Lyrical Conceit of the Elizabethans*, in *Studies in Philology*, XIV (1917). 137.

[97] Schelling, *A Book of Elizabethan Lyrics* (Boston, 1895), *Introduction*, xxiii.

> But we by a love, so much refin'd,
> That our selves know not what it is,
> Inter-assured of the mind,
> Care lesse, eyes, lips, and hands to misse.
>
> Our two soules therefore, which are one,
> Though I must goe, endure not yet
> A breach, but an expansion,
> Like gold to ayery thinnesse beate.
>
> If they be two, they are two so,
> As stiffe twin compasses are two,
> Thy soule the fixt foot, makes no show
> To move, but doth, if th'other doe.
>
> And though it in the center sit,
> Yet when the other far doth rome,
> It leanes, and hearkens after it,
> And growes erect, as that comes home.
>
> Such wilt thou be to mee, who must
> Like th'other foot, obliquely runne;
> Thy firmnes makes my circle just,
> And makes me end, where I begunne.[98]

By using the " conceit," an intellectual and impersonal mode of expression, to communicate his most intensely personal, inward and mystical feelings, Donne gave it imaginative and poetic power. The concepts of the intellect became the symbols of inexpressible spiritual experience. The recent editor of Donne's prose, Mr. Logan Pearsall Smith, after reading and re-reading his volumes of sermons, speaks of this mysticism, this " something baffling which still eludes our last analysis. Reading these old hortatory and dogmatic pages, the thought suggests itself that Donne is often saying something else, something poignant and personal, and yet, in the end, incommunicable to us." [99] Only long reading, perhaps, can give us the full sense of this incommunicable feeling beneath some of the apparently arid discussions in the sermons. In his labor to express it he draws upon all life and all knowledge, upon the most homely matters of daily experience as well as upon the distinctions of the Scholastic

[98] Grierson, I. 50.

[99] Smith, Logan Pearsall, *Donne's Sermons* (Oxford, 1920), *Introd.*, p. xxxv.

philosophy. It is a great error to represent Donne's mind as always preoccupied with the subtleties of medieval thought. He was really preoccupied with the subtleties of his own soul. Donne preached out of his own experience, as he startled his contemporaries, and all his understanding readers since, by the sincerity of his poetry written out of his own experience. No one has looked more directly upon the realities of life, no one has had his vision of reality less impeded by tradition, than Donne. But in the expression of even the most subtle, evanescent or mystical phases of his experience, he puts it into intellectual terms, into " conceits." There is a truth, in spite of its perverse and unsympathetic statement, in the comment of Macdonald: " The central thought of Dr. Donne is nearly sure to be just: the subordinate thoughts by means of which he unfolds it are often grotesque, and so wildly associated as to remind one of the lawlessness of a dream, wherein mere suggestion without choice or fitness rules the sequence." [100]

To illustrate this symbolical value of the " conceit " in Donne's sermons I shall quote first a passage in which the " conceits " are called " images," and in which there is no borrowing from medieval philosophy; the real subject is transcendental, but is evoked by a succession of not unfamilar metaphors and symbols:

> No image, but the image of God, can fit our soul; every other seal is too narrow, too shallow for it. The magistrate is sealed with the *Lion;* the *Wolf* will not fit that seal: the magistrate hath a *power* in his hand, but not *oppression.* Princes are sealed with the *Crown:* the *Mitre* will not fit that seal. Powerfully, and graciously they protect the Church, and are supreme heads of the Church; but they minister not the Sacraments of the Church: they give preferments; but they give not the capacitie of preferments: they give order who shall have, but they have not Orders by which they are enabled to have that they have. Men of inferior and laborious callings in the world are sealed with the *Crosse;* a *Rose,* or a *bunch of Grapes* will not answer that seal: ease and plentie in age must not be looked for without crosses, and labour, and industrie in youth. All men, Prince, and people; Clergie, and Magistrate, are sealed with the image of God, with a conformitie to him; and worldly seals will not answer that, nor fill up that seal. We should wonder to see a mother in the midst of many sweet children, passing her time in making babies and puppets for her own delight. We should wonder to see a man, whose chambers and galleries were full of curious masterpieces, thrust in a village fayre, to look

[100] Macdonald, George, *England's Antiphon* (N.Y., n.d.), p. 114.

upon sixpenie pictures, & three-farthing prints. We have all the image of God at home; and we all make babies, fancies of honour in our ambitions. The masterpiece is our own, in our own bosome; and we thrust in countrey fayres, that is, we endure the distempers of any unseasonable weather, in night-journeys and watchings; we endure the oppositions, and scorns, and triumphs of a rivall, and competitour, that seeks with us, and shares with us. We endure the guiltinesse and reproach of having deceived the trust which a confident friend reposes in us, and solicit his wife or daughter. We endure the decay of fortune of bodie, of soul, of honour, to possesse lovers pictures, pictures that are not originals, not made by that hand of God, Nature; but artificiall beauties: and for that bodie we give a soul; and for that drug, which might have been bought where they bought it, for a shilling, we give an estate. The image of God is more worth then all substances; and we give it for colours, for dreams, for shadows.[101]

We may compare the method of this passage, which seems to the modern reader comparatively simple and natural, with another, in which Donne uses in a similar manner symbols which are antiquated to us; the image is based on the medieval belief that the circle is a symbol of God, because it is the most perfect geometrical figure:

One of the most convenient Hieroglyphicks of God, is a Circle; and a Circle is endlesse; whom God loves, hee loves to the end: and not onely to their own end, to their death, but to his end, and his end is, that he might love them still. His hailestones, and his thunderbolts, and his showres of bloud (emblemes and instruments of his Judgements) fall downe in a direct line, and affect and strike some one person, or place: His Sun, and Moone, and Starres, (Emblemes and Instruments of his Blessings) move circularly, and communicate themselves to all. His Church is his chariot; in that, he moves more gloriously, then in the Sun; as much more, as his begotten Son exceeds his created Sun, and his Son of glory, and of his right hand, the Sun of the firmament; and this Church, his chariot, moves in that communicable motion, circularly; It began in the East, it came to us, and is passing now, shining out now, in the farthest West.[102]

Donne's experience in the second passage is as comprehensible to us as that in the first, but the imagery gives it a medieval flavor. Even so, however, Donne uses the image of the circle here exclusively as an image, and not as a philosophical concept.[103]

[101] *Donne's Sermons* (ed. Smith), p. 153.

[102] *Ibid.*, p. 134. For parallel uses of the circle see Donne's *Devotions upon Emergent Occasions* (ed. Sparrow; Cambridge, 1923), note, page 152.

[103] The medieval respect for the circle had Aristotle for authority. In

In conclusion I shall quote two characteristic passages from his *Divine Poems,* both illustrating his feeling of dependence on God for forgiveness, strength and blessedness. We know how deep that feeling was in Donne, and we cannot doubt the sincerity of even such "conceited" verse as the beginning of *The Litanie:*

> Father of Heaven, and him, by whom
> It, and us for it, and all else, for us
> Thou madest, and govern'st ever, come
> And re-create mee, now growne ruinous:
> My heart is by dejection, clay,
> And by selfe-murder, red.
> From this red earth, O Father, purge away
> All vicious tinctures, that new fashioned
> I may rise up from death, before I'am dead.[104]

In the concluding stanzas of his *Hymne to God, my God, in my sicknesse,* the "conceit" is raised almost to the sublime by its intensity:

> We thinke that *Paradise* and *Calvarie,*
> *Christs* Crosse, and *Adams* tree, stood in one place;
> Looke Lord, and finde both *Adams* met in me;
> As the first *Adams* sweat surrounds my face,
> May the last *Adams* blood my soule embrace.
>
> So, in his purple wrapp'd receive mee Lord,
> By these his thornes give me his other Crowne;
> And as to others soules I preach'd thy word,
> Be this my Text, my Sermon to mine owne,
> Therfore that he may raise the Lord throws down.[105]

---

his *Metaphysics,* Book XII, Chap. viii, he had said that the stars and planets must be eternal essences, for they move in perfect circles, and a body which moves in a perfect circle must be eternal and unresting. The medieval mind, believing that the world is to be explained by forms and essences, had a profound faith in a priori reasoning, not only in philosophy, but in science. Kepler, as he worked over his calculations on the paths of the planets, was forced, though reluctantly, to abandon these perfect circles for ellipses. The circle lost its mysterious significance, and the world its beautiful order. As Donne said, in the poem quoted above:

> 'Tis all in pieces, all cohaerence gone;
> All just supply, and all Relation.

[104] Grierson, I. 338.
[105] *Ibid.,* I. 368.

The style of Donne, then, was an expression of his mind. If the term "metaphysical" be understood to signify a poet expounding medieval philosophy, or indeed any philosophy, it is not applicable to Donne; he expounded no system, he was not a philosophical poet in the sense that Lucretius was, or Sir John Davies, his contemporary. If by the epithet we mean only that Donne used, in his "conceits," some of the terms and distinctions of medieval thought, it may be admitted to be partially applicable, though misleading in its emphasis. Donne took his imagery wherever he found it — from Renaissance science, from daily life, or from the Church Fathers or the disquisitions of the Schools. He used the imagery understood by the educated men of his time. But his purpose was to express his inner self, his moods, whims, emotions, aspirations, in their infinite complexity and subtlety. He was a "psychological" poet in the sense that he found his poetical material in his own experience; his poetry, like his preaching, is introspective. The genuineness of his poetic and religious nature shines through the crabbed verse and the tortured "conceits." It is true that Donne was one of the most intellectual of writers. His mind was made of the toughest fibre, and there is the same toughness in his style. But he is a great writer because he expresses with such intensity, thoughts and experiences that are poetical and human.